CHELSEA HOUSE PUBLISHERS
Modern Critical Views

Further titles in preparation.

Modern Critical Views

VIRGIL

Modern Critical Views

VIRGIL

Edited with an introduction by

Harold Bloom

Sterling Professor of the Humanities
Yale University

1986
CHELSEA HOUSE PUBLISHERS
New York
New Haven   Philadelphia

PROJECT EDITORS: Emily Bestler, James Uebbing
ASSOCIATE EDITOR: Maria Behan
EDITORIAL COORDINATOR: Karyn Gullen Browne
EDITORIAL STAFF: Perry King, Bert Yaeger
DESIGN: Susan Lusk

Cover illustration by James Forman

Printed and bound in the United States of America

Library of Congress Cataloging in Publication Data

Virgil.
        (Modern critical views)
        Bibliography: p.
        Includes index.
        Summary: Thirteen critical essays on Virgil and his works.
        1. Virgil—Criticism and interpretation—Addresses,
essays, lectures. [1. Virgil—Criticism and interpreta-
tion—Addresses, essays, lectures.   2. Latin literature
—History and criticism—Addresses, essays, lectures]
I. Bloom, Harold.   II. Series.
PA6825.A3   1986   871'.01   85-25493
ISBN 0-87754-728-9

Chelsea House Publishers
Harold Steinberg, Chairman and Publisher
Susan Lusk, Vice President
A Division of Chelsea House Educational Communications, Inc.
133 Christopher Street, New York, NY 10014

Contents

Editor's Note

This volume gathers together a representative selection of the best criticism available in English upon the poetry of Virgil, arranged in the chronological order of its publication. It begins with the editor's "Introduction," which is a meditation upon Virgil's peculiar gift of negative imagination, which can be said to constitute his originality. The editor wishes to acknowledge the assistance of Wendell Piez, without whose erudition several of these essays would not have been included.

E. R. Curtius, the great scholarly critic of the entire tradition that moves between Homer and Goethe, opens this collection with his unrivaled remarks upon Virgil's presence in our literature; remarks which are supplemented by Bruno Snell's beautifully humane observations upon Virgil's spiritual Arcadianism.

Criticism of the *Aeneid* begins here with Adam Parry's incisive distinction between the poem's two voices, Augustan and elegiac; a distinction relevant to Thomas Greene's subsequent study of "the moral ambivalences which personality entails" throughout Virgil's epic. These ambivalences inform Kenneth Quinn's essay, with its dark conclusion that every revisionary gesture by Virgil in the poem that made it "more the expression of a mature, civilized sensibility" also made it more impossible for Virgil to get the poem right, as it were.

A second essay by Adam Parry, on the concept of art in the *Georgics*, deepens Parry's previous suggestions as to Virgil's ambiguous distrust of the moral possibilities of art. We return to the *Aeneid* in six of the seven remaining analyses, but with an increasing sense of how problematical the belated epic truly is. Douglas J. Stewart, addressing himself to "Aeneas the Politician," insists that Virgil's portrait of the moral limitations necessarily imposed by his role of leadership upon the pious Aeneas is the most honest vision of any and every politician's dilemma that we have in literature. Parallel to this is J. William Hunt's exegesis of Virgil's "labyrinthine ways" of such intermixing glory and despair that we scarcely can trace the differences between the two.

A selection from W. R. Johnson's remarkable *Darkness Visible* severely qualifies our usual sense of "the worlds Virgil lived in"; Augustan ostensibly, yet darkening into the shadows of an age of anxiety and a time of darkened speculations upon the ends of human existence. Michael C. J. Putnam, reviewing the intimacy between Roman piety and Roman power, gives us a memorable image for the failure of Aeneas to learn consistently to place piety before power. A second essay by W. R. Johnson on the *Georgics*, details the difference between the vision of Augustus and the Roman world in that work, and the rather more shaded images of both Augustus and Rome that are given us in the *Aeneid*.

Something of this same ambivalence is analyzed rather differently by Gordon Williams, who suggests that Virgil never expresses beliefs directly, but rather conveys a sense of profound pessimism at achieving any ideals whatsoever in a hostile cosmos. The final essay, K. W. Gransden's study of the funeral of Pallas, reads the *Aeneid* as an intertextual subsuming of the *Iliad*, with the prime purpose of writing an ending forever to the tale of Troy. Virgil, with his characteristic conversion of victory into defeat, subtly shows us that the triumph of Aeneas is also the yielding up by Aeneas and his people of their separate identity. Such an image of man's discomfort with culture is a fitting coda to the critical quest for the enigmatic secrets of Virgil's troubled radiance as a poet.

Introduction

When Aeneas is sent by Virgil to the shades, he meets Dido the Queen of Carthage, whom his perfidy had hurried to the grave; he accosts her with tenderness and excuses; but the lady turns away like Ajax in mute disdain. She turns away like Ajax, but she resembles him in none of those qualities which give either dignity or propriety to silence. She might, without any departure from the tenour of her conduct, have burst out like other injured women into clamour, reproach, and denunciation; but Virgil had his imagination full of Ajax, and therefore could not prevail on himself to teach Dido any other mode of resentment.

—DR. SAMUEL JOHNSON, *The Rambler*, no. 121

To be employed as the key instance of "the dangers of imitation" by the greatest Western literary critic, is the saddest of all Virgil's melancholy-ridden posthumous vicissitudes. It is unhappy enough that the excessively noble Aeneas should be considered by many readers to be a prig, a Trojan version of George Eliot's Daniel Deronda, as it were. But to read Virgil while keeping Homer too steadily in mind is clearly to impose upon the strongest Latin poet a burden that only a few Western writers could sustain. Virgil is not Dante or Shakespeare, Tolstoy or Joyce. He has his affinities with Tennyson, and with other poets in the elegiac mode, down to Matthew Arnold and T. S. Eliot, both of whom celebrated Virgil as a beautiful "inadequacy" (Arnold) and a mature "poet of unique destiny" (Eliot), two apparently antithetical judgments that actually say much the same thing, which is not much. Like Arnold and Eliot, poor Virgil has become the poet of professors, many of whom praise Virgil as a splendid revisionist of Homer, a very different view from Dr. Johnson's.

Other classicists have given us a more Tennysonian Virgil, a knowing latecomer infatuated "with twilight moods, with blurred images, with haunted, half-enacted interviews and confrontations that disintegrate before our eyes just as we begin to perceive them." I quote from *Darkness Visible* by W. R. Johnson, the best study of Virgil that I have read, and hasten to add that Johnson is eloquently summing up the judgment of other critics, rather than stating his own, which seems to me more persuasive. W. R. Johnson's Virgil is marked by a "vast Epicurean sensitivity to pain and suffering," and is not concerned so much "about winning battles but about losing them and learning how to lose them." This Virgil has the "imagination of darkness" and has "discovered and revealed the perennial shape of what truly destroys us."

In some sense, W. R. Johnson moves the fantastic and menacing figure of Virgil's Juno to the center of the epic, which is certainly a useful corrective to many previous readings of Virgil. Juno is Virgil's most ambiguous achievement, and doubtless is one of the major Western representations of what contemporary feminist critics like to call the projection of male hysteria. I would prefer to name Virgil's Juno as the male dread that origin and end will turn out to be one. We do not judge Nietzsche to be hysterical when he warns us, in his *Geneology of Morals,* that origin and end, for the sake of life, must be kept apart. Despite his all-too-frequently deconstructed dislike of women (so amiable, compared to his master Schopenhauer's), Nietzsche is hardly to be dismissed as what feminists like to call a "patriarchal critic" (are there any? could there be?). What Nietzsche suggests, as Freud does after him, is that all Western images are either origin or end, except for the trope of the father.

It is frightening that the only Western image that is neither origin nor end is, in Virgil, reduced to the pathetic figure of Anchises, who has to be carried out of burning Troy upon the shoulders of his pious son, the drearily heroic Aeneas. The image of the mother in the poem is somehow not that of the merely actual mother, Venus, but rather the hardly maternal Juno, who is truly one of the great nightmare images in Western literary tradition. Virgil is rightly wary of her, and if we read closely, so are we:

> O hateful race, and fate of the Phrygians
> Pitted against my own. Could they be killed
> On the Sigean battlefield? When beaten,
> Could they be beaten? Troy on fire, did Troy
> Consume her men? Amid the spears, amid
> The flames, they found a way. I must, for my part,
> Think my powers by this time tired out,
> Supine, or sleeping, surfeited on hate?
> Well, when they were ejected from their country
> I had the temerity as their enemy
> To dog them, fight them, over the whole sea,
> These refugees. The strength of sea and sky
> Has been poured out against these Teucrians.
> What were the Syretës worth to me, or Scylla,

What was huge Charybdis worth? By Tiber's
Longed-for bed they now lay out their town,
Unworried by deep water or by me.
Mars had the power to kill the giant race
Of Lapiths, and the Father of Gods himself
Gave up old Cálydon to Diana's wrath:
And what great sin brought Cálydon or Lapiths
Justice so rough? How differently with me,
The great consort of Jove, who nerved myself
To leave no risk unventured, lent myself
To every indignity. I am defeated
And by Aeneas. Well, if my powers fall short,
I need not falter over asking help
Wherever help may lie. If I can sway
No heavenly hearts I'll rouse the world below.
It will not be permitted me—so be it—
To keep the man from rule in Italy;
By changeless fate Lavinia waits, his bride.
And yet to drag it out, to pile delay
Upon delay in these great matters—that
I can do: to destroy both countries' people,
That I can do. Let father and son-in-law
Unite at that cost to their own! In blood,
Trojan and Latin, comes your dowry, girl;
Bridesmaid Bellona waits now to attend you.
Hecuba's not the only one who carried
A burning brand within her and bore a son
Whose marriage fired a city. So it is
With Venus' child, a Paris once again,
A funeral torch again for Troy reborn!
                    (VII. 295–326, Fitzgerald translation)

There is certainly a dark sense in which Juno is Virgil's pragmatic
Muse, as it were, the driving force of his poem. She represents, in this
passage, Virgil's authentic if repressed agressivity towards his daunting
father, Homer. As the inspiration of an agonistic intensity, she necessarily
speaks for Virgil himself when he confronts the *Iliad* and the *Odyssey*:

Well, if my powers fall short,
I need not falter over asking help
Wherever help may lie. If I can sway
No heavenly hearts I'll rouse the world below.

Is not that Virgil's actual achievement as compared to Homer's?
Juno, though she is a nightmare, is Virgil's own nightmare, his dark creation, a "darkness visible" in the great Miltonic phrase that W. R. Johnson

chose as title for his study of the *Aeneid*. What Virgil most powerfully and originally gives us might be called the creatures of Juno: Allecto and the Dira (though technically the Dira is sent by Jupiter). Virgilian invention, though deprecated by Dr. Samuel Johnson, is marked by a negative exuberance that cannot have pleased the author of *Rasselas*, who rightly had his positive imagination full of Homer, and necessarily feared his own dark side.

II

It is no fresh oddity for a poet to become the official representative of the sensibility and ideology of an age, while actually producing work of morbid splendor and equivocal pathology. Virgil's double fate is precisely prophetic of Tennyson's and T. S. Eliot's. Walt Whitman, belatedly accepted as our national bard, would be a parallel figure if his poetry had received wide contemporary acceptance in post-Civil War America, as would Hart Crane, had he been acclaimed in the days of the Depression.

This phenomenon is now over, since our era is overtly paranoid in its sensibility. The best writers in contemporary America—John Ashbery, Thomas Pynchon, James Merrill—are truly representative of the dumbfoundering abyss between the private, aesthetic sensibility and the public sphere of Ronald Reagan. The abyss was as great between Virgil and the Emperor Augustus, but both chose to believe and act otherwise. A vision of President Reagan placing Thomas Pynchon under his patronage is not without its charm.

Virgil, as Dante's precursor, became for Western literary tradition a kind of proto-Christian poet. He can hardly be blamed for this, though perhaps Aeneas can, since Aeneas unfortunately *is* sometimes prophetic of that civic ideal, the Victorian Christian gentleman, Gladstone say, rather than the exotic Christian Jew, Disraeli. However, Aeneas (though replete with noble sentiments) actually behaves like a cad towards Dido, and finally like a brute towards Turnus. Though no Achilles, Aeneas pragmatically is quite frightening, and really about as benign as the Emperor Augustus, his contemporary model. Machiavelli is more in the line of Aeneas than of Virgil. Perhaps the greatest strength and lasting puzzle of the poem is Virgil's relation to his own hero. Does Virgil, like most of us, prefer Turnus to Aeneas? He was not writing the *Turneid*, but would he have been happier doing so?

The violent nature of Turnus, at once neurotic and attractive, has about it the aura of a Latin Hotspur, though Turnus lacks Hotspur's antic wit. But then Hotspur exists in a cosmos ultimately centered, not upon Bolingbroke the usurper and Prince Hal, but upon Falstaff, legitimate monarch of wit. Virgil is not exactly a humorous writer, and I suspect that, if he *was* in love with any of his own characters in the poem, it was with Turnus, rather than Dido, let alone Aeneas. The dreadful death of Turnus, which causes the poem to break off, in some sense is also the death of Virgil, or at least of Virgil's poetry:

The man brought down, brought low, lifted his eyes
And held his right hand out to make his plea:

"Clearly I have earned this, and I ask no quarter.
Make the most of your good fortune here.
If you can feel a father's grief—and you, too,
I Iad such a father in Anchises—then
Let me bespeak your mercy for old age
In Daunus, and return me, or my body,
Stripped, if you will, of life, to my own kin.
You have defeated me. The Ausonians
Have seen me in defeat, spreading my hands.
Lavinia is your bride. But go no further
Out of hatred."
　　　　　Fierce under arms, Aeneas
Looked to and fro, and towered, and stayed his hand
Upon the sword-hilt. Moment by moment now
What Turnus said began to bring him round
From indecision. Then to his glance appeared
The accurst swordbelt surmounting Turnus' shoulder,
Shining with its familiar studs—the strap
Young Pallas wore when Turnus wounded him
And left him dead upon the field; now Turnus
Bore that enemy token on his shoulder—
Enemy still. For when the sight came home to him,
Aeneas raged at the relic of his anguish
Worn by this man as trophy. Blazing up
And terrible in his anger, he called out:

"You in your plunder, torn from one of mine,
Shall I be robbed of you? This wound will come
From Pallas: Pallas makes this offering
And from your criminal blood exacts his due."

He sank his blade in fury in Turnus' chest.
Then all the body slackened in death's chill,
And with a groan for that indignity
His spirit fled into the gloom below.
　　　　　(XII. 930–952, Fitzgerald translation)

The death of Turnus indeed is a terrible indignity, heroic neither for him nor for Aeneas. Turnus is truly slaughtered by Jove, who has been able to impose his will upon Juno, and then takes on something of her spirit when she yields. The Dira, manifesting as a gruesome carrion bird, sickens poor Turnus, numbing his giant force until he does not know himself. In a waking nightmare, unable to speak, standing defenseless, Turnus becomes merely an object into which Aeneas hurls a spear. Aeneas furiously stabbing to death a man already ruined by the Dira is hardly an Achilles or a Roland, and it is very good that the poem abruptly ends there. Could we forgive an Aeneas who exulted in such a triumph? Why does Virgil end his poem with so gratuitous a slaughter? Can he have intended to give us a Jupiter so contaminated by Juno? Such a Jupiter is more like a Gnostic Archon than in any way an Epicurean vision of the divine.

All we can be certain of is that Virgil deliberately wounds himself even as he wounds us. All of Book XII is an effective horror, an epiphany of lacerations and self-destroyings. I do not pretend to understand the scene in which Jupiter and Juno are reconciled to one another, and she agrees to give up her vendetta against the Trojans. Perhaps Virgil did not understand it either. If he was a convinced Epicurean, then he must have turned against his own rationality in his final vision of Jove, who is certainly not indifferent but positively malevolent, and pragmatically as sadistic as Juno. A passionately intense Valentinian Gnostic could have ended on no darker vision of the demonic, masquerading as the fury of God.

Against Book XII, every reader rightly sets the poignance of Book VI, and yet Book VI does not culminate the poem. It is well to remember that Book V ends with the elegiac words of Aeneas to the memory of the lost helmsman, Palinurus:

> For counting
> Overmuch on a calm world, Palinurus,
> You must lie naked on some unknown shore.

Book VI concludes with the passage of Aeneas and the Sibyl out of the world below by the Ivory Gate, and yet Book VII is Juno's book, and Allecto's, "with her lust for war,/For angers, ambushes, and crippling crimes." W. R. Johnson finds the poem's center, for him, in Book XII, lines 665–669, where Turnus makes a great recovery:

> Stunned and confused
> By one and another image of disaster,
> Turnus held stock-still with a silent stare.
> In that one heart great shame boiled up, and madness

Mixed with grief, and love goaded by fury,
Courage inwardly known. When by and by
The darkness shadowing him broke and light
Came to his mind again, wildly he turned
His burning eyes townward and from his car
Gazed at the city.

That is magnificent, but each reader of the *Aeneid* chooses his or her own center. Mine is Book VI, lines 303–314, always admired by readers through the generations:

Here a whole crowd came streaming to the banks,
Mothers and men, the forms of life all spent
Of heroes great in valor, boys and girls
Unmarried, and young sons laid on the pyre
Before their parents' eyes—as many souls
As leaves that yield their hold on boughs and fall
Through forests in the early frost of autumn,
Or as migrating birds from the open sea
That darken heaven when the cold season comes
And drives them overseas to sunlit lands.
There all stood begging to be first across
And reached out longing hands to the far shore.

Homer's fiction of the leaves as the human generations is transumed here with an inventiveness that has inspired poets from Dante to Spenser, Milton and Shelley, and on to Whitman and Wallace Stevens. What is, to me, peculiarly Virgilian and surpassingly beautiful is the movement from the tropes of the autumnal leaves and the migrating birds to the terrible pathos of the "pauper souls, the souls of the unburied," who must flutter and roam the wrong side of the black waters for a century. To stretch out one's longing hands to the farther shore, when that shore is oblivion, is a purely Virgilian figure, not Homeric, and has about it the uniquely Virgilian plangency. The *Aeneid* is a poem that attempts to compel itself to the grandeur of Augustan vistas, but its genius has little to do with Augustus, and at last little to do even with Aeneas. Of all the greater Western poems, it reaches out most longingly to the farther shore.

E. R. CURTIUS

Virgil in European Literature

The tomb of Virgil and that of the first emperor lie buried beneath the bricks and mortar of populous Italian cities, surrounded by the bustle of our modern life. Virgil is known to us through historical records even to the date of his birth. To be able to celebrate its two-thousandth recurrence must inspire every lover of Rome with a shudder of pious joy. This is no scholarly reminiscence; it is a day of living remembrance, a reverent solemnization.

It would often seem as if our present, hurried generation had lost time through tempo, the past through lust for contemporaneity. We divagate into the far reaches of space—only to pay for our truancies with an undignified, ignoble contraction or a chimerical, flimsy expansion of our sense of time. It is well, therefore, that anniversaries that move to the rhythm of millennia should exhort us to reflection: the six hundred years since the death of Dante, the fifteen hundred years since the death of Augustine, the two thousand years since the death of Virgil. The one hundred years since Goethe only make plainer the meaning and value of millennial dates.

Virgil's anniversary is not popular, and for that reason doubly significant. Rightly understood it could be a landmark in the great mysterious movement of Western self-consciousness: in the dim unfolding of a process that would be memorable even if its struggle to be born occurred only as the dream of our highest, as the ineffable word of our best spirits—a process of integration and restoration of the Occident such as was envisaged by the profound and intuitive mind of a Hofmannsthal, whose meditations spanned centuries.

That the Virgil Festival impinges upon such connections, that it evokes or can evoke such reverberations should be enough to declare the uniqueness of the name in whose honor it is being held. And how inexhaustible is that uniqueness! We shall never be able to fathom what the Fourth Eclogue meant to its author. It enjoys the mystic privilege of inexpressibility of substance as does that Eastern book of erotic mysticism which has entered our Holy Scriptures as the Song of Songs. And nevertheless it may be permitted us to confirm the mediaeval legend in our own sense; to believe that in the synchronicity of the divinely human revelation and the poet of the Roman Empire a European mystery lies concealed and waiting to be rediscovered. For this belief we possess the time-honored testimony of Dante. And we may account it one of the happy auguries of our history that an indissoluble bond unites Virgil with Dante, the great Roman *paganus*, the singer of flocks and fields, and the great Roman Christian, the pilgrim of the next world and the institutor of order in this one.

No one who clings, consciously or unconsciously, to the outmoded aesthetics of original genius will ever understand Virgil. Virgil's greatness and importance, his irreplaceable and unreplaced mission through all our ages, does not, or does not solely, derive from what he was personally. It can only be grasped if we are aware of what the *kairos* is able to impart to the individual.

That Virgil could be taken up and enhanced, after thirteen hundred years, by a Dante, that his message could find a response in the Florentine of the Trecento as it found a sanction in [Phocas (c. A.D. 500)], the last poet of the collapsing temporal Empire—that is part of the very element and definition of Virgil's greatness. To appreciate this one has to break with all modern criteria and practice counting in long intervals of time. It is a way to which we are not accustomed. But might it not be wholesome and necessary for that very reason? What has lasted two thousand years will last another two thousand. That much at least we can know precisely—and should we really refuse to correct our current perspective in the light of this knowledge?

For previous ages the *exempla maiorum* were a confirmation; for us they are a confrontation, and tradition is reversed into a corrective. We are so far removed from tradition that it appears new to us. Periods like these are perhaps the dawn of all renaissances. Thus our present German estrangement from Virgil might be reinterpreted as a preparation and a guarantee. A deeper understanding of *Romanitas* seems to be awakening among us—and can it have a representative more valid and more binding, mightier and milder, sweeter and more sonorous, than Virgil?

He is the most official of poets, for it was his poetic task to trace the eternity of Rome from its primitive origins even as Augustus, with the founding of the Principate, elevated it to the highest realization of its power. Here, on the plane of world-history, is demonstrated that realism, that irrefutable solidity rooted in and bound to the soil, that is part of the Roman Genius, like the Travertine marble, hardened by time, of which the tomb of Cecilia Metella and the dome of St. Peter's alike are constructed.

There is scarcely a building material so resistant to the erosion of time as this stone of the golden patina. It has its intellectual equivalent in the material of which Virgil's work is constructed: in that Latin speech the source of which is the swamps of Mantua and whose stone flags support a universal poem and a universal empire. The passionate self-abnegating will to permanence has hardened this substance. It is deeply significant that an early poem of Virgil's contains a renunciation of rhetoric. Cicero's Atticist prose could still appeal to our forefathers; today its formal ostentation pales beside the cadences of the patient craftsman, who began with jesting, satirical poems and, in unparalleled fashion, worked his way free to ever stricter, ever greater tasks. However controversial the *Appendix Virgiliana* may be, one thing is certain: Virgil's poetic and emotional beginnings approach a frivolity of soul and sense that combines, in a fashion we can scarcely conceive, the faunic with the sentimental. We shall never know what event in his life raised the imitator of Catullus and Priapic poet to the vates of Orphism, to the laureled servant of the will of the State and prophetic annunciator of the turning-point in history. Was it resignation? Was it initiation? Was it both at once as well as an early, pre-Christian form of sanctification? It must be left in that twilight, which the poet himself desired and loved.

It is the strange twilight that gleams so often in Virgil, and that Victor Hugo, in a spirit of emulation and artistic fellowship, graciously acknowledges:

. . . dans Virgile parfois
Le vers porte à sa cime une lueur étrange,

. . . sometimes in Virgil the verse at its summit bears a strange gleam,

a reflection as it were of that numinous radiance which, full of future promise, shone in Troy's darkest night upon the head of Ascanius.

So through all the ages of Rome and the Romania, through all those historical realms still touched by the Roman will to order, Virgil's silent flame shines as a guarantee and a promise. For fundamental to Virgil is the strength and the will to preserve the permanent through all change. Repetition as restoration, invention as rediscovery, renovation as confirmation and sublimation of what is already possessed—this was Virgil's most cherished concern.

So Dido (iv, 327 ff.) seeks for herself a childish copy of Aeneas:

. . . si quis mihi parvulus aula
Luderet Aeneas, qui te tamen ore referret.

. . . if in my hall a little Aeneas were playing, whose face would recall yours.

So for Virgil's herdsmen, heroes, and rulers, the law of life is identity (the *flumina nota* of the First Eclogue) and stability, or, lacking these (for exile as sociological necessity and constraint is the *fatum* of both Meliboeus and Aeneas), renewal and palingenesis, repristination and instauration in one. To take the lost and past and rebuild it out of new substance on foreign soil, this is the will and the way of Virgilian wisdom.

The individual character of Virgil's art, which it is so difficult for our vulgar aesthetics to grasp—the much discussed *imitatio*—perhaps also has its roots in this emotional disposition, which we are probably correct in perceiving as an essential trait of Virgil's personality: a need for security, born of elegiac sorrow and longing, that has been ennobled by piety and transmuted by lofty historical relations into constructive will. This personal quality is linked to one that lies beyond the personal: to the Roman function of continuity, and perhaps, indeed, to the fundamental law of life that applied throughout Antiquity; the law, according to which the sanction for all new creations was in the traditional works from which they derived and to which they had to refer: as the colony to the mother city, the statute to the founder, the song to the Muses, the copy to the original, and the work of art to the model.

We can have no idea what Virgil would have become had he not met Augustus, but he would certainly not have become the poet of the *Aeneid.* His personal contact with the Emperor made him into the poet of Rome:

Scilicet et rerum facta est pulcherrima Roma.

Indeed Rome became the most beautiful city in the world.

And yet we shall fail to understand Virgil if we see in him only or primarily the poet of the State. Underneath, at a deeper level, lives a contemplative, artistic person who is not moved by affairs of state. He is aware of his detachment from the sphere of mere politics and history which, being essentially impure and infelicitous, is subject to the vicissitudes and the inscrutable wrath of the Gods:

> Ferus omnia Juppiter Argos transtulit . . .
> Excessere omnes adytis arisque relictis
> Di quibus imperium hoc steterat . . .

Savage Jupiter transferred all our possessions to Argos. . . . All the gods have left their sanctuaries and abandoned the altars, the gods on whom this empire had depended.

The authentic ancient and Romanic philosophy of history as *vicissitudines* speaks in these lines. Dante and Vico hold it too. It contains an element of resignation, but only dialectically, as a moment of transition. Far from enjoining a negation of history, it leads rather to a cyclical conception of it. The prophecy of the Fourth Eclogue, the soteriological hope of both Virgil and Dante, the pious expectation of a "restitution to wholeness", of a return of the Golden Age, is possible and makes sense only if the "collapse into the worse" is also accepted as true. It goes without saying that to our historical realism, our poverty-stricken sense of historical reality, this dimension of experience is as lost as eschatology to our religion. But it is the only dimension capable of resolving the contradiction between Virgil's two statements about Rome: "a rule that shall pass away" and "empire without limit." The ethos of the Roman Odes gives us a palpable sense of how completely different could be the moral and political experience awakened by the Augustan age in two of its representative poets. The comparison with Horace brings out Virgil's uniqueness all the more clearly.

Virgil's most secret longing is quite simply the Golden Age and its sensuous representation in rustic surroundings. Its content is blessed idleness, conferred by divine favor. *Otium* is one of the key words of Virgil's poetry.

The God Augustus bestows this happiness:

> O Meliboee, deus nobis haec otia fecit.

> Meliboeus, a god gives us this leisure.

The God of the shepherds approves too:

> . . . amat bonus otia Daphnis.

> . . . the good Daphnis loves leisure.

It is the felicity of rural life:

> . . . secura quies et nescia fallere vita
> Dives opum variarum, et latis otia fundis.

. . . tranquil quiet and a life which knows not how to deceive, rich in various resources, and leisure amidst broad estates.

And this image of earthly leisure also serves Virgil as the model for the bliss of Elysium. Of course we agree with Fénelon when he measures this description against the glories of the Christian Paradise:

> This poet promises no other reward in the next life to the purest and most heroic virtue than the pleasure of playing on the grass, or fighting on the sand, or dancing, or singing verses, or having horses, or driving chariots and possessing arms. Such is the greatest consolation that antiquity proposed to the human race.

Of course Dante was the first who was able to create out of the plenitude of the grace of Revelation the vision of the hereafter to which not even the most pious paganism could attain. But as grace is said not to supersede but to fulfill nature, so in the region of Virgil's soul to which *otium* is the password it is possible to discern a bit of eternal human nature, with its eligibility for grace. I am certain that much of the deathless charm that continues to attach new generations to Virgil comes from this region. For despite the wretched efficiency-ethic of our modern age, does there not live in all of us something of that elemental longing for a pastoral world, for the earthly paradise, for the divinely-blessed gardens of Eden and Elysium?

The bucolic idyll cannot be explained away as simply the wish-projection of Hellenistic urban culture. It is an innate archetypal image of our species that moves us with a melancholy joy, like a song we had long thought to be forgotten. It is the *dulce refrigerium* of Christian-Asiatic mythology, the refreshing coolness of brook and meadow, "muscosi fontes et somno mollior herba" ("mossy springs and grass softer than sleep"). *Otium* is only the time-honored name for a type of idleness rooted in the social conditions of Antiquity, but belonging to the images of a golden life, and reminding us that we can fully realize our human destiny only where the compulsion of labor has been lifted from us. Our ethic of work lacks the balance of an ideal of leisure. It could, of course, be derived from Goethe's *Westöstlicher Divan* (*West-Eastern Divan*), were we ever to liberate ourselves from the pedagogical scheme that grants the German nation its greatest poet only on condition that he admonishes it to tireless effort.

Actually, the "cultural poet" Virgil is a singer who has the most original and immediate tones for all the fundamental moods of human nature. What has been said about *otium* is only one example. All the elements of man's nature, insofar as they coincide with his humanity, have been represented by Virgil in exemplary fashion. His rich, autocthonous, yet delicate soul created a canon of affects that was as authoritative as the one created in a later period by the cartoons of Raphael. He had the power to sound the natural notes of the soul. This naturalness is classical and ancient. But such is the emotional intensity of Virgil's language that it is understood by modern ages too. This combination of simple nature and feeling intensified by passion is the distinguishing mark of Virgil's finest verses. They carry their own conviction as surely as that "sunt lacrimae rerum," which eludes grammatical analysis; as that "per amica silentia lunae" or "nunc scio quid sit amor": each an example of the highest concentration, in which the conciseness of the Latin seems bathed in an aura of infinity. Virgil is not only the herald of the State, of the Penates, of *pietas*, of the meadows and fields. He has also been the poet of love for nearly two thousand years, and neither Laura nor Juliet has kindled the hearts of so many young men as Dido, "cette figure d'immortelle ardeur qui, de son bois de myrthes vírgilíens, enchante à travers les âges l'élite des adolescents:

> Hic quos durus amor crudeli tabe peredit. . . ."

And Anatole France continues: "Heureux qui frissonne aux miracles de cette poésie! Il y a au monde un millier, peut-être, de vers comme ceux-là; s'ils perissaient, la terre en deviendrait moins belle."

> that figure of immortal ardor who, from her wood of Virgilian myrtles, enchants throughout the ages an élite among adolescents: Here, those whom harsh love has consumed with cruel wasting. . . . Happy are they who thrill to the miracles of this poetry! There are perhaps a thousand lines like that in the world; if they should perish, the earth would become less fair.

It cannot be denied, of course, that Dido is the very character who does not share in the author's inner sympathy. Like Virgil's other female figures she leads a shadowy and pallid existence, even though one decked out with the trappings of ideal dignity. She has not been nourished with the blood of a living love, and it may be surmised that Virgil's life was lacking in the flame from which Catullus' odes to Lesbia and Propertius' to Cynthia took their fire. Does not Suetonius relate: "He was barely touched by male desire, and he remained unmarried. Such purity lay over his mouth and heart that in Naples he was popularly known as Parthenias (the Virginal)?" Aeneas may be the son of Venus, but he inherited few of her gifts. Furthermore the Venus of Virgil is less Aphrodite than Artemis: the virgin huntress whenever she is not the strong-willed disposer. Creusa too appears shadowy, and is soon removed to the shades. She is only allowed to follow her husband at a distance: "pone subit coniunx." The poet indicates the nuptials of Dido and Aeneas only by their attendant cosmic meteorological phenomena; and when the forsaken woman reproaches him, the hero replies rather sheepishly. Only in her tragic fall does Dido rise to impassioned life. So she lives on in poetry and memory as a romantic heroine: "she who killed herself for love," (*Inferno*, v, 61). The substance that Virgil had to deny her is compensated by the dignity of her function within his universal poem. Not the Aphrodisian female is the highest embodiment of womanhood for the "maidenly" poet, but the consecrated virgin: the Sybil, the Astraea, the Muse.

A breath of adolescent shyness and innocence plays round the figure of Virgil. This area of his sensibility, so palpably evident in all his works, is the source of his bucolic and heroic young men. They constitute one of the most significant and personal elements in his poetry. Eduard Fraenkel writes: "The Roman character is not only unyouthful, it is alien to youth, almost hostile to it," and he cites the pejorative meaning of the term *puerilis*. The conclusion of this learned specialist is incontrovertible, and it is especially gratifying as it sets off the originality of our poet all the more distinctly. Engraved in the heart of every reader of the *Aeneid* are the flower-like youths—"purpereus veluti flos"—Nisus and Euryalus, Lausus and Pallas, and, above all the rest, Ascanius. The very word *puer* acquires, in Virgil's usage, a tender, almost sacred tinge. Nisus addresses his companion as "venerande puer," and with the same solemnity ("iuvenis memorande") the poet raises his own voice to the honored memory of Lausus. In the "incipe, parve puer" of the Fourth Eclogue and the offering of lilies upon the early grave of Marcellus ("miserande puer") this sympathy of Virgil's extends to what is highest and holiest. Virgil's young male figures, the "warrior and history-making *pueri*," "one of the poet's most significant inventions," according to Wili, undoubtedly vibrate with the recollection of his own youth and that of Octavian. But beyond that they live by virtue of an inner affiliation with Virgil's cyclical view of the universe, and with his prophecy of a new golden age. They stand as the poetic guarantee and spiritual anticipation of Virgil's belief in the rejuvenation of the world. They cast upon the grave dignity of the *Aeneid* a luminous shimmer of youthful beauty that is still capable of mysteriously touching receptive young people today.

In the autobiography of a great English critic anyone who has not felt it himself will find proof of how the first contact with Virgil can bind a young reader with a sudden and magical spell. The stimulus to the imagination provided by novel or idyll can explain this effect only in part. The Virgilian magic, in the last and deepest analysis, emanates from the beauty of the sound and the vibrations of the rhythm. Here we touch upon a new aspect of the inexhaustible phenomenon of Virgil's uniqueness. The *Odyssey* can be enjoyed in translation; the *Aeneid* cannot; not even in the Romance tongues. Virgil is as essentially untranslatable as Dante (while Shakespeare would be an example of the contrary). In the two great Italic poets form and content are fused in a different and as it were more intimate manner than in Homer. Only this unsatisfactory way of putting it enables us at least to intimate a fact of experience which is no less self-evident for defying all analysis. The most that can still be said is that an adequate understanding of the Virgilian hexameter (like that of the Dantean terza rima) also comprises an aesthetic initiation—the sudden radiant "having" of "art." I say comprises, and am thereby arguing against a misleading dichotomy of form and content. The sense of satisfaction provided by "formal beauty" always yields much more than and, consequently, something essentially different from, "form." Without getting lost in subtleties one can still distinguish various grades within the possibilities of linguistic pleasure, and only poverty of language prevents us from doing more in this respect than feeling our way. That Virgil's beauty cannot be transferred is partly due to the properties of the Latin language; but only partly, for of Horace and Ovid less is lost in translation. It can most readily be explained by reference to our experience of great statuary. Sculpture defies reproduction in a very different sense from music or painting. Of all the plastic arts none fails so miserably in reproduction as the plaster cast beside the marble original. None affords so little room for the workings of caprice or chance, be it on the side of technical execution or of appreciative reception. Sculpture subdues the greatest fullness to the hardest matter, the greatest lifelikeness to the most rigid austerity. The paradoxical legend of Pygmalion could only be told about a sculptor.

People like to speak of Virgil's musical beauties, by which they usually mean verses like:

Saltantes satyros imitabitur Alphesiboeus
Alphesiboeus will imitate the dancing satyrs

or

Formosam resonare doces Amaryllida silvas.
You teach the woods to ring with beautiful Amaryllis' name.

Such lines have a sweetly seductive allure and draw the neophyte into the innermost recesses of the magical edifice. But the typical style of the poet's maturity is of another and a higher kind. It tends not toward ethereal undulations but toward the solidity of metal and marble. The soul of Virgil's poetry cannot be detached from its matrix, which is unalterable and unique; nor does it exist outside it. Strictly speaking, Virgil's mastery is coextensive with the Latin language, no further. Let those who will regard this as a defect; those who may as a good fortune.

The judgment of French Classicism on Virgil was that he had more "taste" than Homer. In our own terms this means that he is more of an artist. At the risk of contradicting current opinion, we would maintain that to be an artist and to be a poet are not necessarily the same thing. There are poets who are not artists. Art, in poetry, means the conscious and expert handling of language—the opposite of inspiration. Virgil spent seven years on the 2,000 lines of the Georgics. He estimated that he would need three more years to bring the Aeneid to perfection when death caught up with him. He had written both works on commission, well aware (as a letter to Augustus reveals) of the enormous difficulties involved, but trusting in effort and the knowledge of his craft. It remains a miracle that in spite of their origin these works did not end up as frigid virtuoso performances but full of vitality in their perfection.

Perfection—not force or immediacy or emotion—is the distinguishing mark of all classical works. The aesthetic appreciation of this quality is not popular today, but it is still worth contemplating. Admittedly there are dull spots even in Virgil, but then it was not granted him to give definitive shape to his work. Nevertheless, in the Georgics and the Aeneid he attains an ultimate in formal perfection, as can be seen most clearly by reference to the Stanze of Raphael. In both cases the loftiness of the style is distinguished by ideal naturalness and perfect serenity, and its specific character stands out all the more if, for comparison, we think of Michelangelo or Shakespeare with their qualities of abundance, spirit, force, urgency. We enjoy perfection for the feeling it gives of assured, knowing guidance, not for that of surprise.

Dante's famous utterance that he received "lo bello stile" from Virgil has puzzled many of the commentators because they were unable to find any external similarities in the style of the two poets. This, of course, is not the issue; rather, it is the deeper affinity in their artistic aims: the achievement of beauty and sublimity by means of the selection and arrangement of words. In this larger sense Virgil, supported by the example of the Alexandrian poets, created the model for all of Western artistic poetry. In this elevated sense he is an aesthete. For this reason he, more than any other poet, is a guide to aesthetic culture. This is how Dryden's laudatory characterization of the *Georgics*—"the best poem of the best poet"—is to be understood.

One of the most fruitful and fateful errors of Taine, and of all the historico-sociological conceptions of art that consciously or unconsciously derive from him, is to suppose that the great works are to be read as "signs" or "expressions" of their cultural milieu—or even (and this only compounds the error) to be appreciated as such. Virgil moreover would seem to confirm the rightness of this conception. But it is not enough to consider him merely as the representative of Augustan Rome. He is more than that, and his work cannot be measured by the standards that suffice for the *Ara Pacis Augustae*. He is also more than the representative of the eternity of Rome and the permanence of Latinity, however exalted and mighty he may be in this function. He must be apprehended beyond it in his absolute greatness and importance as an artist, in the sphere of the timeless, if our aim is purity and clarity of aesthetic judgment.

As a historical phenomenon Virgil is Roman and more than Roman at the same time. He is the spiritual genius of the West throughout the millennia. His mission in world history is evidenced in Dante, and perhaps after several further centuries he will demonstrate it again. At any rate, in the present turmoil and distress of our part of the globe, we cannot forbid our hope to scan the horizon for a future restorer of the Muses and the religion of the Occident.

> Si nunc se nobis ille aureus arbore ramus
> Ostendat nemore in tanto!

If only that golden bough on the tree would show itself to us now in so great a grove!

In Virgil's serene element the great spiritual and historical antitheses of our past seem to achieve an equilibrium. He contains the pure nectar of Antiquity, but he reaches beyond Antiquity as does only Plato besides him. There are Asiatic roots in the *Aeneid*, oriental prophecies in the Fourth Eclogue. Roman sculptural form is united in an unfathomable way with a prophetic, otherworldly radiance, a Sybilline piety that seems to stay upon revelation. Roman *virtus* and Greek love of beauty, mature craftsmanship and moral refinement are attested in the same material. Virgil's work is the triumph of Classicism and at the same time (consider the Tenth Eclogue) the primal fount of all Romanticism. All these forces, which would clash in isolation, attain in him a settled harmony and a rich symbolic fullness. The whole of human existence is mirrored in the wanderings of Aeneas: the weary way to a promised second homeland, far from the first.

BRUNO SNELL

Arcadia: The Discovery of a Spiritual Landscape

Arcadia was discovered in the year 42 or 41 B.C. Not, of course, the Arcadia of which the encyclopedia says: "The central alpine region of the Peloponnesus, limited off on all sides from the other areas of the peninsula by mountains, some of them very high. In the interior, numerous ridges divide the section into a number of small cantons." This humdrum Arcadia had always been known, in fact it was regarded as the home of Pelasgus, the earliest man. But the Arcadia which the name suggests to the minds of most of us to-day is a different one; it is the land of shepherds and shepherdesses, the land of poetry and love, and its discoverer is Virgil. How he found it, we are able to tell in some detail, thanks to the researches of Ernst Kapp. The historian Polybius who came from the humdrum Arcadia cherished a great affection for his country. Although there was not much of interest to be related of this land behind the hills, he could at least report (4.20) that the Arcadians were, from the days of their infancy onwards, accustomed to practice the art of singing, and that they displayed much eagerness in organizing musical contests. Virgil came across this passage when he was composing his shepherd songs, the *Eclogues*, and at once understood it to refer to the Arcadian shepherds; for Arcadia was shepherds' country and the home of Pan, the god of the herdsmen, inventor of the syrinx. And so Virgil located the lives and the poetic contests of his shepherds in Arcadia. "You Arcadians,"

From *The Discovery of the Mind: The Greek Origins of European Thought*. Copyright © 1953 by the President and Fellows of Harvard College. Harper and Row, Harper Torchbook.

he says (10.32), "who are alone experienced in song." He mentions two Arcadians "who are equal in song, and equal to giving response in turn" (7.5). He remarks on mount Maenalus in Arcadia "which ever hears the love songs of the shepherds and Pan blowing his pipe" (8.23). He calls upon Arcadia to judge a contest between the singers (4.58). The shepherds whom Virgil introduces in his earliest eclogue are not Arcadian but Sicilian (2.21): this setting comes to him from the idylls of Theocritus, the Hellenistic poet who served as the model for all Roman pastoral poetry. Since the shepherds of Theocritus, too, indulged in responsive singing and competitions, Virgil had no difficulty in linking them with the Arcadians of Polybius.

Theocritus who was born in Syracuse had written about the herdsmen of his own country. Meanwhile, however, Sicily had become a Roman province, and her shepherds had entered the service of the big Roman landlords. In this new capacity they had also made their way into Roman literature; witness Lucilius' satire on his trip to Sicily. But they could no longer be mistaken for the shepherds of song and love. Thus Virgil needed a new home for his herdsmen, a land far distant from the sordid realities of the present. Because, too, pastoral poetry did not mean to him what it had meant to Theocritus, he needed a far-away land overlaid with the golden haze of unreality. Theocritus had given a realistic and slightly ironical description of the herdsmen of his country engaged in their daily chores; Virgil regarded the life of the Theocritean shepherds as a sublime and inspired existence. If we look at the beginning of his earliest bucolic poem: "The shepherd Corydon loved fair Alexis," it has a different ring from anything comparable that Theocritus might have said. In Greek these names were hardened by daily usage; in Virgil they are borrowed words, cultured and strange, with a literary, an exotic flavour, like the names of the mythical heroes which Virgil had drawn from Greek poetry. The effect of this upon the persons of the shepherds was decisive. Later, when Virgil himself had become an example to be followed, the shepherds of European literature were called Daphnis and Amyntas, but they too were awkwardly out of place in the Cotswolds, or the Cornish heath. In the end, when Johann Heinrich Voss by-passed Virgil and re-established Theocritus as his model, he gave the protagonists of his idylls the good German peasant names Krischen and Lene.

Virgil, then, did not aspire to furnish a realistic portrayal of everyday life, but searched for a land which could harbour herdsmen named Corydon and Alexis, Meliboeus and Tityrus, a land which might be a fitting domicile for everything that seems to be implied in such poetic names. In the 10th eclogue, the latest in date of writing, which more than any other pastoral piece by Virgil stresses the Arcadian milieu, the poet Gallus has been set down in Arcady and there finds himself in the company of the gods and shepherds. The Roman god Silvanus and two Greeks, Apollo god of song and Pan the deity of the Arcadian herdsmen, express their sympathy with his unhappy love. How would this be possible in so near and familiar a setting as Sicily? This scene too has its precedent in Theocritus, but there (1.77 ff.) the gods Hermes, Priapus and Aphrodite are shown paying a visit to the mythical shepherd Daphnis, not just to an ordinary human, much less to an identifiable contemporary of the writer. Theocritus' scene is mythical, and he keeps that mythical atmosphere clear of any intrusions. In Virgil's Arcadia the currents of myth and empirical reality flow one into another; gods and modern men stage meetings in a manner which would have been repugnant to Greek poetry. In actual fact this half-way land is neither mythical nor empirical; to the Roman Virgil and his Roman public, Apollo and Pan convey even less of their divinity, as objects of genuine faith, than they had to Theocritus and his Hellenistic audience. Arcadia is not an area on the map, either; even the person of Gallus appears misty and unreal, which has not, of course, prevented the scholars from trying to penetrate through the mist and identify the historical Gallus.

The air of unreality which hangs over Virgil's poems is thus explained by the fact that he seeks to approximate the world of Theocritus and that of myth, and that therefore he manipulates the traditional mythology with a greater licence than would have been possible for a Greek. The tragedians of the fifth century, to be sure, had begun to elaborate the ancient tales and to interpret them anew, but they had nevertheless maintained the fiction that they were discussing events of the hoary past. Plato's inventions in the mythical genre are often no longer connected with the ancient motifs, but they are always profoundly significant tales, genuinely mythical in tenor and aim. Callimachus says that when he first put his writing-tablet on his knees, Apollo gave him some useful hints for his poetry. But that is obviously a joke; and when he reports that the lock of Queen Berenice was placed among the stars, he bases that on the belief of his time that a great man may after his death be received among the gods. But nobody, prior to Virgil, seriously shows men of the present in close contact, and on an equal footing, with divine beings.

When the early age, during which the Greeks had accepted myth as history, came to a close the tragic writers and the historians of the fifth century divorced the two fields from each other. Myth retired beyond the world of man, and though at first it retained its old function of providing a standard of explanation and interpretation for human experiences, tragedy turned it into a poetic counterpart of reality. With the emancipation of myth came two important changes. On the one hand the ancient heroes and events were interpreted realistically—the psychological approach to the myths is part of this trend—in order to render them more useful to men in their daily lives; and secondly new dramatic situations were invented to the end of adapting the old myths to the stage. Hellenistic poetry carried the psychological interpretation of mythical characters even further, and it made the setting more naturalistic than ever before; but as against this, it also discovered new aesthetic possibilities for the myths. From these up-to-date versions of the ancient tradition, poetry learned to turn its aesthetic energies into the glorification and embellishment of the objects of commonplace reality. In the end, Theocritus domesticated the Sicilian shepherds and made them acceptable to his sensitive art. Virgil, in a certain sense, set about reversing this order of events, and in fact he finally wound up restoring the grand form of the epic. The *Eclogues* contain the first indications of his role which was to exalt the realistic writing which served as his point of departure, viz. the idylls of Theocritus, by suffusing it with elements of myth. Myth and reality are thus once more joined together, albeit in a manner never before witnessed in Greece.

Virgil arranges the meeting between his friend Gallus and Pan and Apollo because Gallus is a poet. As a poet he is on excellent terms with the Arcadian shepherds; Virgil had transferred his shepherds to Arcadia because the inhabitants of that country, as Polybius had informed him, were especially well versed in song. The shepherds of Theocritus, too, delight in song; but the ancestry of the musical herdsman is older yet. To trace it all the way back, we must turn to the age before Homer, for on the shield of Achilles (*Il.* 18.525) we find shepherds rejoicing in the sound of the syrinx. We have already mentioned the fact that it was the Arcadian deity Pan who was responsible for the invention of this instrument. Bucolic poetry, also, is of an ancient vintage. It appears that, about the year 600 B.C., Stesichorus introduced it into the repertory of Greek literature, with a choral ode in which he told the story of Daphnis. Daphnis was loved by a nymph; but when, in a bout of drunkenness, he became unfaithful to her, he suffered the punishment reserved for him: he was blinded. This account is obviously based on a simple rustic tale, localized in the vicinity of Himera, the city where Stesichorus lived. In his version, as we might expect in a Greek poetic treatment, the folk-tale is changed into a divine myth, for Daphnis is said to be the son—or, according to others, the beloved—of Hermes, and he tends the cattle of Helios. Our information about the poem is, unfortunately, late and imperfect, but we know that an important section of it was a lament for Daphnis. From that time onward the shepherds have been in love, usually without hope of success; either they indulge in their own suffering, or they wring a poetic expression of sympathy from their friends. We cannot say for sure how Stesichorus formulated all this, but it may be supposed that he endowed the pastoral life with some of the subdued lustre which Homer allows to the figure of Eumaeus, the faithful swineherd of Odysseus. The familiar and self-sufficient world of the simple shepherd is rendered in a myth which, though evidently sprung from a folk-tale, is for all that no less real than the myths which tell of heroes and heroic deeds.

More than three hundred years later, Theocritus composes yet another lament for Daphnis. This time it is given out as a song of the Sicilian shepherd Tityrus (7.72), and again as a composition of the herdsman Thyrsis (1.66). Theocritus takes some pains to present a realistic picture of the life led by Sicilian shepherds. But in one respect they are anything rather than country folk: their mood is a literary one. Theocritus engineers a kind of masquerade; he wishes us to recognize poets of his own circle behind the rustic disguise. He adopts the classic motif of the singing and playing shepherd, and develops the scope of the pastoral poem by voicing the literary themes of the day. All this is done in a spirit of good-natured jesting; the dissonance between the bucolic simplicity of the pasture and the literary refinement of the city is never completely resolved, nor was it ever intended to be, for the whole point of Theocritus' humour lies in this dissonance. In the lament for Daphnis we read: "The trees mourned for him, those which grew along the Himera river, when he melted away like snow on mount Haemus or Athos or Rhodope or on the furthest Caucasus." This is the speech of the literati, for it is not customary with shepherds to discuss Haemus or Athos, Rhodope or Caucasus; it is the grand style of tragedy.

This high-flown diction must not be compared with the Greek geographical nomenclature with which Horace, who is our best example for this technique, equips his poems. To a Roman ear his place names do not convey the parody of tragedy, but respect for a noble tradition. And that is the spirit in which Virgil purloined his characters from Theocritus. The Roman poets use these strange-sounding names, dignified, as they thought, by the Greek passages in which they had occurred, to add to the stateliness of their speech; for the Latin tongue has no poetic diction of its own. The names help to lift the writing to a higher plane of literary art. As far as the Romans were concerned, if we may venture a paradox, all these mountains lie in Arcadia, in the land of Corydon and Alexis, of Pan and Apollo.

It would not be fair to suggest that in the Augustan period such places had already degenerated into a kind of scenic backdrop for a poetic stage which may be exchanged at will. But it is certain that they have nothing whatever to do with any real landscape outside the theatre, where you might find ordinary, nonfictional men.

When Theocritus has his shepherds enumerate these mountains, he creates roughly the same impression as when Menander puts his quotations from tragedy in the mouths of uneducated slaves. With deliberate irony he makes his Sicilian shepherds live above their intellectual means. But when Virgil read these passages and others like them, he accepted them in the spirit of the more solemn context from which they had originally come, as expressions of genuine feeling. The tension between the real and the literary world which Theocritus had exploited for its peculiar charms, is brought to nought, and everything shifts back to the even plane of an undiffer-entiated majesty.

In Theocritus, Daphnis is the shepherd from the myth of Stesicho-rus. In other works he is just an ordinary herdsman, like Tityrus or Corydon. But he is always either the one or the other. Virgil mentions him already in his earliest eclogue: there he is unquestionably the mythical shepherd (2.26). In two other passages (7.1 and 9.46) he is a common herdsman. But what is his identity in the fifth eclogue? As in other bucolic poems, two shepherds, Menalcas and Mopsus, want to stage a singing contest. They sing of the death and apotheosis of Daphnis, i.e. apparently the Daphnis of the myth. But this Daphnis had been the friend of Menalcas and Mopsus (line 52); thus he also belongs to the immediate environment of the competing herdsmen. Now at the end of the poem we discover that Virgil is using one of the two men as a mask for his own person. Once Virgil had placed his shepherds in Arcadia, it seems, it was but a short step to blend the bucolic with the mythical. This transition was, of course, facilitated by the fact that Theocritus himself had used the figure of Daphnis in both capacities.

In Theocritus, as in Virgil, the shepherds are less concerned with their flocks than they are interested in poetry and love. In both writers, therefore, they are gifted with passion and intellect, but in different ways. Theocritus' herdsmen, notwithstanding their pastoral status, often prove to be urban intellectuals in disguise. Virgil's shepherds, on the other hand— and it is charming to follow the steady progress from eclogue to eclogue— become increasingly more delicate and sensitive: they become Arcadian shepherds. Theocritus, too, stands at a distance from his shepherds; being a man from the city, he looks down upon them partly with a feeling of superiority, partly with an open mind for the straight simplicity of their primitive life. The simplicity is more ideal than fact, and so his shepherds, in spite of all realism, remain fairly remote from the true life in the fields. But this remoteness is as it should be, for a genuine summons back to nature would silence the whole of pastoral poetry; as it turned out, that is exactly what happened in a later age. Above all, these shepherds are not really taken seriously. Their quarrels have something comical about them; how different from the harsh wrangling between Eumaeus and Melanthius in the *Odyssey*! The violent head-on conflicts which we find in tragedy, even between kings, do not exist in Theocritus, and Virgil goes even further in smoothing the differences. From Theocritus on the shepherds display a courtly behaviour, and this courtliness, or courtesy, remains true of all bucolic poetry. The rustic life is made palatable to good society by its acquisition of manners and taste; if there are any embarrassing features left, the poet neutralizes them by making them appear droll, by smiling at them. Virgil is even more intent than Theocritus on toning down the crudeness and coarseness of the shepherds; as a result, he has less occasion to feel superior to them. Furthermore, while endowing the herdsmen with good manners and delicate feelings, he also makes them more serious-minded. But their seriousness differs from that of a Eumaeus; they have no strength to stand up for their genuine interests, nor do they ever clash with one another in open conflict. They are no more conversant with the true elemental passions than the heroes of the *Aeneid* were to be. And it is significant that in those ages when Arcadian poetry was in fashion, and when courtly manners were the order of the day, the *Aeneid* has always been more highly favoured than the *Iliad* or the *Odyssey*.

Virgil's Arcadia is ruled by tender feeling. His herdsmen lack the crudeness of the peasant life as well as the oversophistication of the city. In their rural idyll the peaceful calm of the leisurely evening hours stands out more clearly than the labour for their daily bread, the cool shade is more real than the harshness of the elements, and the soft turf by the brook plays a larger role than the wild mountain crags. The herdsmen spend more time playing the pipe and singing their tunes than in the production of milk and cheese. All this is incipient in Theocritus, but the Alexandrian still shows some interest in realistic detail. Virgil has ceased to see anything but what is important to him: tenderness and warmth and delicacy of feeling. Arcadia knows no reckoning in numbers, no precise reasoning of any kind. There is only feeling, which suffuses everything with its glow; not a fierce or passionate feeling: even love is but a delicate desire, gentle and sad.

Virgil, the discoverer of Arcadia, did not set out to explore new lands. He was no adventurer of the spirit who listens to the call of foreign shores. With utmost modesty he admits that he is proud to have been chosen by the Muse to introduce the Theocritean pastoral among the Romans (6.1). It was not any wish to be an innovator or reformer which caused him to swerve off the path of Theocritus. We must assume that when in his reading of Theocritus he found the grotesque tale of Polyphemus who tried to find a cure for his love in singing, the figure of the Cyclops changed under his very eyes, while he was yet perusing the tale, and turned into a lonely shepherd who voices his longing (*Ecl.* 2). Theocritus says (11.12) that the herds of Polyphemus had to make their way home by themselves in the evenings, because the herdsman forgot all else over his singing. Virgil interprets this as a picture of the golden age when the flocks were able to return to the stables of their own accord, without any herdsman to look after them (4.21). Or again: Virgil has read that during the noon heat lizards sleep in the thornbush. He had found this in Theocritus, where someone expresses his amazement that another person is up and about during that hour, "while even the lizards take their siesta" (7.22). Virgil has a shepherd who is unhappily in love sing as follows: "While the flocks seek the cool shade and the lizards hide in the bushes, I must continually sing of my love" (2.8). Thus the sensible beasts have become the happy beasts. Theocritus concludes a jocular prayer to Pan (7.111) with these words: "If you do not comply with my prayer, I hope you will pasture your flocks during the winter in icy Thrace on the Hebrus, and during the summer among the Ethiopians in the furthest south." In Virgil, Gallus mourns (10.65 ff.): "Nor will my unhappy love subside if I drink from the Hebrus in mid-winter or if I plough through the snowfalls of the Thracian winter, nor if I pasture the sheep of the Ethiopians under the sign of Cancer (i.e. in mid-summer)." The drastic punishment threatened to the shepherd's god is transformed into the sorrows of the unhappy lover who roams through the whole wide world and cannot find a hardship extreme enough to free him from his tortures. These subtle changes are numerous; little by little, without drawing our attention to it, Virgil varies the Theocritean motifs. The transformation is so slight that it took a long time before it was noticed how far Virgil had progressed in his *Eclogues* beyond the pleasantries of the Hellenistic poet. He admired and acknowledged the work of Theocritus, he dwelt lovingly on his scenes; but because he read them with the eyes of the new classicistic age, he slowly came back to the classical Greek poetry, with its earnestness, its deep feeling, its drama. Virgil had not intended to be original; he merely re-moulded Theocritus in the image of what he considered to be characteristically Greek. This was the route by which Virgil discovered Arcadia: without searching for it, without proclaiming his arrival; and so we, for our part, have no easy time in discovering that it was he who discovered the land, and what its discovery means to us.

That Virgil, in his *Eclogues*, returned to the spirit of classical art is, first of all, clear from the fact that his poems, unlike those of Theocritus, are not small clippings from the panorama of life, but well-constructed and rounded works of art. Each poem has its climaxes and its lulls; motifs light up and fade out again. Actually, as we might almost expect, this classicistic art is, in such formal matters, more demanding and exact than the classical. The Romans contribute their own native flair for disciplined structural design. Consequently the composition of the poetry written in the classicistic Augustan age is of a special perfection.

This formal beauty of the poem indicates that the work of art has attained to a greater degree of independence. The poem is no longer related to a specific situation or to any one circle of listeners or readers, or to any particular segment of reality. The process of literary creation becomes autonomous; it becomes a realm in itself, an absolute realm, detached from all that is not art and literature. Its perfect form, its grace and its sound, make it what it is. Thus, for the first time in Western literature, the poem becomes a "thing of beauty," existing only for itself and in itself.

In the course of writing his *Eclogues* Virgil turned with increasing attachment to the severe stateliness of the classical form. But the themes with which he grapples had never been treated by the Greeks. His gradual emancipation from the narrow limits of the Theocritean pastoral does not tempt him to use his eclogues for the description of great deeds or heroic fates. Actually he does not narrate facts or events at all; he is more interested in the unfolding and praising of situations. These situations are not such as had been celebrated in the archaic Greek lyric—particular occasions which help to raise the human spirit above the level of our ordinary existence. On the contrary, it is to a comprehension of this everyday life that Virgil directs his sensitive skill. Arcadia is the land of the gilt-edged weekday. Virgil's sensibility fastens upon the familiar daily activities, the constant traffic with the same routine objects, the peaceful life on the home soil. But this familiarity smacks of nostalgia. His love for the familiar things is a longing rather than happiness. For this is a land in which the mountains and the trees participate in the sorrows of the unhappy lover—a motif which Virgil inherits from the Daphnis myth—, in which animals and men are mutually linked with bonds of friendship and trust, in which the herdsmen sing songs of delicate sentiment. This is a land in which nothing is measured by its practical value, and in which men are not judged by their deeds and achievements. What matters in this poetry is that its creatures appeal to the affections, that they release in us a tender emotion. It is the dawn of a new love.

And yet, the world of pure feeling cannot escape the intrusion of contemporary events. As we read on, Virgil's eclogues contain more and more references to actual happenings. At first glance it might seem odd that topical and political themes should play a much larger role in this remote Arcadian art than in the more realistic works of Theocritus. It has been suggested that we should compare Virgil to the archaic Greek poets, to Alcaeus and Solon; that would mean that in this respect, too, through his admission of politics into the fold of his poetry, Virgil acknowledged the classical Greek authors as his models. But the politics which we encounter in Arcadia is a peculiar brand. Virgil does not venture upon an active participation in the political quarrels of his day, he is not a statesman like Solon, nor a party man like Alcaeus, nor does he recommend a political programme. In his mind, political matters are closely connected with mythical concepts; and here the combining and blending of myth and reality, which is so characteristic of the Arcadian temper, achieves a singularly impressive result.

The first time that Virgil draws contemporary politics into the orbit of his poetry, in the first eclogue, certain very specific legal and social conditions form, as has recently been recognized, the basis of his picture. But the actual plot of the poem—one herdsman wins his freedom, another is driven from his ancestral estate owing to the distribution of land to the veterans—is so deeply coloured with the dye of sentiment that the mere facts recede into the background. That a herdsman is compelled to part from his ancestral plot is seen as a curse of the restless age; that another is enabled to begin a pleasant life in his old age appears as the intervention of a saviour god who has arisen in the great city of Rome and who is putting an end to all the misery and confusion. Whenever Virgil discusses the events of his time, his judgment is controlled by a tender emotion which vibrates throughout Arcadia: the longing for peace and a home. And in the fourth eclogue, where this political yearning is even more prominent, it straightaway reaches out into the golden age and immerses itself in eschatological hopes.

These dreams of the poet place an interpretation upon history which answered to a good many expectations of the age. After the disastrous anarchy of the civil wars the desire for peace was paramount, especially among the better minds of the day. Thus Virgil's poetry reflects a genuine political reality, and it is not without significance that Virgil, at a time when Augustus was only just beginning to make his authority felt in the affairs of Rome, had already voiced that yearning for peace which Augustus was fated to satisfy. In this sense Virgil may be said to have determined to a considerable extent the political ideology of the Augustan age, and his *Eclogues* did indeed exercise an important political and historical function. Most impressive, perhaps, was their influence upon the early works of the second great poet of the Augustan age, upon the *Epodes* of Horace. Still, we should not close our eyes to the fact that certain essential aspects of political action are not considered by Virgil. It is merely the fringes of political reality which he grasps in his hands. When, in the fourth eclogue, he announces his hope that the birth of a certain boy will mean the beginning of a new and blessed era, he is hoping for a miracle. This means that, as a matter of principle, he pays no attention to the fact that politics is grounded in reality, and that it must of necessity resort to force in order to realize its objectives. Political thought thus breaks in two, ideology and *Realpolitik,* with the attendant danger that each of these two will pursue its own journey without paying much attention to the other. Virgil made it possible for those who were themselves not active in politics to engage anew in political thought and poetry. But by its very nature this political poetry could only serve to pave the way for the politically active, to support their policies and to assist them with ideas. For independent plans there was but little scope, much less for opposition.

Once before, among the Greeks, an age of political unhappiness had produced a split between theory and practice. Though Plato began his career with genuine political interests and though his social position and personal inclinations had originally destined him for a political role, he had found no room for his activities in democratic Athens; the prevailing institutions, he felt, led only to gross injustices. With bitter resignation he realized that anyone concerned about justice was out of place in the existing state. So he had removed himself to his Academy, the "Island of the Blest," where it was possible to dedicate oneself to the rule of justice—even if it was only in thought. Plato was irritated by an element which is inherent in all politics; again and again his mind is agitated by the anti-intellectual obstacles which prevent the perfection of the state: injustice, violence, and lust for power. Deeply worried how he might render those obstacles innocuous, he persists in asking the basic question: What is justice, what is the good, what is the knowledge of these? Thus the Island of the Blest, the philosophy which receives him, permits a life of clear distinctions and sharp reasoning.

Virgil, on the other hand, turns away from this harsh and evil world, he leaves it far behind, and sets out for Arcadia, where he allows no hope, not even any desire to do something about the suffering world, to lighten his sorrow and his despair. If he is striving for a better world, he does so with his emotions, not with his thought or his will. A nostalgic refugee from sombre realities, he places his hopes, not upon a just state, but on an idyllic peace in which all beings will live together in friendship and fraternity, a golden age in which the lion and the lamb will lie down side by side in harmony, in which all opposites are joined and tightly knit in one great love. Only a miracle could bring this about. Later, when he was composing the *Georgics,* he saw this miracle in the achievement of Augustus. Augustus gave back to Italy the gifts of peace, quiet and order. Virgil stepped back into politics in so much as his dreams of Arcadia seemed to have found their fulfilment; Plato, in some ways, softened his criticism of existing institutions, but he never reconciled himself to making his complete peace with political realities. In return, Virgil was always careful not to get involved in the slippery problems of political action; in fact one may presume that they never even penetrated to his dreaming ear.

Even in his last great work, in which political action is more prominently featured, Virgil clings to the standard of his metaphysical hopes in appraising the events of reality. The sufferings and wanderings of Aeneas obtain their significance from the divine guidance which in the end resolves everything into peace and order, and ushers in a golden age. This miraculous direction from above is depicted with the machinery of the early Greek epic. But in the *Iliad* and *Odyssey,* whenever the gods determine an event, they act upon their personal sympathies and antipathies, and their bias is often so pronounced that even in antiquity many took exception to it. That is one of the reasons why Virgil could not afford to adopt the conventional type of divine intercession for his own use. In the *Aeneid* we find the realization of a world scheme to which all things, the gods included, are subservient. Homer too has a Fate, the *Moira,* but it is effective only in so far as the gods cannot prevent mortals from dying; all men must die, even the favourites and the scions of the gods. But Homer knows of no higher plan in accordance with which the gods direct the fortunes of Trojans and Greeks. The gods act precisely as any healthy man with a lively disposition would act; for even the supernatural in Homer is natural. Virgil, on the other hand, has divined a deeper meaning of history; Jupiter's guidance of Aeneas is a prologue to the future development of the Roman Empire, to the glory of the Augustan age.

The dream of the golden age is as old as man's thinking about the course of the world, no matter whether it springs from a sense of bewilderment, in which case it is remembered as a paradise at the beginning of time, or whether it embodies the ideals of man's positive striving, projected into the end of history. But never before Virgil, either in Greek or Roman literature, had this Utopia been so closely interwoven with historical reality as in the *Aeneid*, or indeed earlier in the *Eclogues*.

In effect, Virgil's relation to the world is lyric; it impels him to seek out that which is dear to him, that to which his delicate senses may respond. But he does not find this in the realities surrounding him, where Sappho, for instance, had found it. He now looks for it in an area beyond the harsh facts of experience, either because the world has become too cruel and impious a place, or, which is the same thing in reverse, because his expectations in spiritual matters have increased. He looks for it in Arcadia; and even the heroic world of the *Aeneid*, with its fulfilment of the desire for order and meaning, bears the stamp of an Arcadian idyll.

The important point about Virgil's art, for the history of thought, is that he initiates an entirely new concept of poetry. Innumerable poets of the West have been the disciples of Virgil. They have viewed the task of literary creation in the light in which it was first approached by Virgil; and that this was of great importance for the nature of their poetry need not be emphasized.

In the tenth eclogue where, as we have already seen, the Virgilian Arcadia appears in its purest colours, the writer introduces his colleague Gallus. The poet alone of all mortals is permitted access to the Arcadian shepherds who are poets themselves. To be sure, not everything that is said by Gallus on this occasion may be used as evidence for Virgil's general conception of the poet and his mission, nor should we scan his lines for proof of what Virgil considered characteristic of the writing of poetry. Indeed, an ancient grammarian tells us that Virgil incorporated entire verses of his friend Gallus in the work. Still, there are a number of statements of which we can assert with some assurance that they are Virgil's own.

When Pan says to Gallus: "Amor is not affected by the tears of the unhappy lover," the poet answers: "But you Arcadians will sing of my suffering. Oh how soft should be the repose of my bones when your flute speaks of my love." In his mind he pictures to himself how happy he might be here by the cool springs, on the silken turf, in the grove of Arcadia, if he had his beloved Lycoris to keep him company. But she has gone off to the war with another. I know of no passage in the whole of Greek poetry where a man reflects upon his own death with the same sentimental sensuality. Ever since Sappho it had been customary among poets to pray for death to terminate their unhappy love; the tradition of the dying man consoling himself with the thought that his name will survive in song is even older. And the notion that it is the privilege of the dead to be mourned and lamented by their friends runs far back into the beginning of time. But that a man should indulge in a contemplation of the pity which he expects for his distress, and that he should find satisfaction in this reverie, is unprecedented. Sappho had sensed an inner urge to be linked with those close to her in feeling and thought; but this impulse was directed outward, it clove to the memory of beautiful things, the joint participation in a festival, for instance, or other similar experiences. Gallus, quite differently, trains the mirror on himself, he delights in the knowledge that others will think of him with some emotion, he dreams of a prestige which he had never enjoyed even in the happiest hours of his life. This differs, too, from the attitude of the Greek tragic hero who openly displays his affliction and appeals for sympathy, from the feelings of a Prometheus who, nailed to his rock, exclaims: "Behold my sufferings." The tragic character calls upon witnesses to testify to the injuries he has received in his struggle with the forces of the world. Instead of revelling in the sensation of his own tender fragility, he presents himself as an example of the blatant wrongs which will always occur.

It might be supposed that for this self-indulgence of Gallus, Virgil used some Hellenistic model which has not come down to us; and similar objections may well be raised on other occasions where I have cast Virgil in the role of a discoverer. True enough, we must always consider the possibility that a certain motif may have been quite common in that large body of late Hellenistic literature which is now almost completely lost. But it is significant that the self-reflexion of Gallus, as so many other Virgilian features, is already foreshadowed in an earlier eclogue by Virgil. In the fifth poem Mopsus says, while singing of the death of Daphnis, that the shepherd had selected his own epitaph (43–44):

> Countrymen, Daphnis is my name:
> The very stars have heard my fame.
> Here in the woods I lived and lie—
> My flock was lovely: lovelier I.

Virgil here follows Theocritus (1.120–21) who had written: "I am that Daphnis who here pastured his cattle, that Daphnis who watered oxen and cows." Theocritus' lines are purely factual. It was Virgil who added the references to the speaker's own glory and beauty, the sentimental concentration upon the self, for similar things are not found in Hellenistic poetry, not even in Catullus although he at times indulges in a feeling close to self-pity. The Virgilian Gallus goes to the length of picturing to himself the sad lamentations which others will sing about him. This Arcadian consolation is also an escape from life, an escape into the realm of feeling and pathos. The sensibilities of the poet Gallus are so vulnerable that he is desperately afflicted by the contradiction between his own wistful hopes and the fate which befalls him. He expects his soulful longings to be met with an equal warmth and affection, and this hope is indeed realized in the dreamland of Arcadia, despite the lack of that idyllic bliss which is the shepherd's due.

Next Gallus apostrophizes his far-away love, in verses which are bodily taken from the elegies of the real Gallus. We have here a brilliant cento, which Virgil constructed by lifting from the original distichs certain portions which would fit into his hexameters and still make sense. Thereafter Gallus continues with lines which indubitably are Virgil's own rather than echoes of Gallus' work. This is clear not only from their spirit, but from the fact that they again contain those reminiscences of Theocritus which are so characteristic of the *Eclogues*. Gallus, then, proceeds somewhat as follows: "I base my verses, i.e. my elegies, on the writings of Theocles of Chalcis, but I shall now compose them in the manner of the Theocritean pastoral. I shall suffer my misfortune in the woods, surrounded by the caves of savage beasts, and I shall cut the name of my beloved into the bark of the trees. In the Arcadian mountains I shall live, among the nymphs, and hunt wild boars." For Gallus, Arcadian poetry is tantamount to an Arcadian life, a life enacted far away from the turmoil of men.

Centuries earlier, ancient Hesiod had taken his herds up into the desolate mountains and engaged in conversation with the Muses at Hippocrene, the spring of Helicon. But Hesiod was a true herdsman, the deserted mountain crags which he climbs are real, and he is fully convinced that the Muses have summoned him to be their poet. They have appeared to him in person, to assign him his task. He looks upon his shepherd's existence as a hard necessity, not as a romantic occasion to indulge in sentiments. Gallus' desire, in the words which we have cited, to hunt wild boars, is, of course, explained by the fact that the herdsman is also a hunter: Virgil occasionally refers to this in his earlier eclogues (2.29; 3.75; 7.29). But that is not all. For Gallus does not confine himself to the mere wish for a hunt; he tries, by painting a detailed picture of the scene of the chase, the icy mountains, the rocks and the forests, to stir the hearts of his listeners. The hunt, to him, is a remedy for his love. Our tastes would deem this a rather unusual cure. Theocritus' advice that poetry and singing are the only remedies for an unhappy love (11.1 and 17) strikes us as more natural, and no doubt more people have resorted to this latter medicine than to the chase of boars. Actually, Virgil is following in the footsteps of an ancient tradition. Euripides had shown in his *Hippolytus* how Phaedra fell in love with her stepson. He is a huntsman, and so he is not interested in love. Phaedra, in her feverish dreams, imagines herself setting out for the mountains to hunt (215 ff.); only thus, she feels, will she be able to join the object of her passion: a desire which she cannot, of course, confess openly before the chorus. Virgil's transfer of this motif to the Arcadian sorrows of Gallus seems to have been understood at once by the educated Romans. For Seneca, in turn, employs certain elements from this speech of Gallus for the purpose of describing the hunt of Hippolytus in his tragedy *Phaedra* (1–48).

Finally it can be shown that at the conclusion of Gallus' speech, too, the feelings expressed are magnified and ennobled by the introduction of certain motifs from classical Greek poetry. In these words of Virgil's friend we detect the same affective quality which distinguishes the pastoral poems of Virgil more and more from those of Theocritus. Virgil stresses the element of feeling, he takes it very seriously, and utilizes the forms and formulas of the classical Greek poetry to give it voice. We would have known this even without examining the speech of Gallus. But there is something else, of vital importance, which that speech may teach us.

What sort of poet does Virgil place before us? What is his conception of the art of poetry? Whence does the poet draw his material? He follows his imagination; he gives himself to his dreams. He savours his thoughts and his longings, and records them as they come floating through his mind. Among the Augustan poets, the younger contemporaries of Virgil, it is quite common that a poet in the stillness of nature surrenders himself to his feelings, and in our modern age the creative dream and the artistic imagination are the very essentials of the poetic personality. It is, therefore, with some amazement that we should realize that this modern poet, the poet of fancies and dreams, did not exist until he saw the light of day in Virgil's Arcadia.

Hesiod, pasturing his flocks and composing his songs on the lonely slopes of mount Parnassus, does not exert his imagination, but obeys the inspiration of a deity. This is not merely a figure of speech, a way of expressing one and the same truth in two different ways, of seeing it in two perspectives, one religious, the other psychological. No, the facts themselves are distinct, although in a later epoch the concepts came to be mixed and confused in various ways. The message which the Muses impart to Hesiod and which he conveys to his fellow-men addresses itself directly to the realities of life; it provides practical suggestions for the work of the farmer and for upright action, or it explains the divine powers whose effects are felt in nature and among men. The Muses command him to announce the future and the past (*Theog.* 32), and he chooses to tell Perses "the truth" (*Works* 10). In the fifth century, when this inspiration is no longer accepted with the concrete simplicity of the older generation, the task of the poet becomes spiritualized to the point of vagueness. But the poet is, as before, expected to speak of "what is given." Even Plato, who in his *Ion* refers to the enthusiasm of the poet as a divine gift, a *theia moira*, regards this inspiration as a means of rousing the audience and transmitting the passion of the poet, not as a creative process in which the objects of the poem are themselves given life.

Invention was not unknown among the makers of tragedy, particularly among the later ones. Euripides, for example, invented Medea's murder of her children. Accordingly, all literary criticism beginning with Aristotle debated to what extent a poet may be permitted to invent his own material; the upshot was that most critics allowed only a limited amount of invention, seeing that the poet was indentured to myth. But invention is not the same as imagination or fantasy. The legendary Euripides, the solitary thinker meditating and composing his scenes in his cave on the seashore, is more like a philosopher than like an Arcadian Gallus indulging in his fancies. Euripides seeks to get to the bottom of certain matters, we might say "problems," and on occasion he will invent a new situation in order to clarify such a problem. But this invention of new motifs for the sake of creating effective dramatic situations does not rest upon the support of dreams or fancies or feelings; his kind of poetry is essentially indebted to wakeful thinking and reflexion, to a mind both active and conscious of its aims. Nor are the novel creations of the Hellenistic writers to be ascribed either to the ancient inspiration or to Arcadian dreams; they too spring from invention, an invention based on good taste and wit. They are so thoroughly committed to reason as the maker and arbiter of their art that nothing could be less characteristic of their creative skill than the darkly ebbing sub-conscious. The poetic imagination does not exist among the Greeks, except in the realm of the burlesque, as in the comedies of Aristophanes, or in the satyr plays.

In his later poems, the *Georgics* and the *Aeneid*, Virgil did not pursue the path which he had trodden in the *Eclogues*. But some of his younger contemporaries chose to travel the new Arcadian road; especially Tibullus walks as in a dream, and lets images full of feeling and delicate sorrow pass before his vision.

About six hundred years before Virgil, the early Greek lyrists had awoken to the fact that man has a *soul*; they were the first to discover certain features in the feelings of men which distinguished those feelings sharply from the functions of the physical organs, and which placed them at opposite poles from the realm of empirical reality. For the first time it was noticed that these feelings do not represent the intercession of a deity or some other similar reaction, but that they are a very personal matter, something that each individual experiences in his own peculiar fashion, and that originates from no other source but his own person. Further they had found out that different men may be united with one another through their feelings, that a number of separate people may harbour the same emotions, memories, or opinions. And finally they discovered that a feeling may be divided against itself, distraught with an internal tension; and this led to the notion that the soul has intensity, and a dimension of its own, viz. depth. Now everything that we have so far remarked about Virgil's Arcadian world may be summed up by saying that Virgil developed these three basic modes which the early lyric had ascribed to the soul, and interpreted them afresh.

Under Virgil's hands, the spontaneity of the soul becomes the swirling tide of the dream, the creative flux of poetic fancy. The feeling which transcends the individual and forges a link between many men becomes Virgil's longing for peace and his love for his country through which even the beasts and the trees and the mountains are welcomed as fellow-creatures. And finally, the dissonance and depth of the emotions unfold into the conscious suffering of the sensitive man, his awareness that his tender and vulnerable soul lies at the mercy of a harsh and cruel world.

Later on Virgil himself appears to have sensed the futility of pursuing further such an indulgence in the feelings; but the three functions of the soul which he had brought into the open: poetic reverie, unifying love, and sensitive suffering, point far into the future. It was not merely because of his prophecy in the fourth eclogue that Virgil was, in the Middle Ages, regarded as a pioneer of Christianity. His Arcadia is set half-way between myth and reality; it is also a no-man's land between two ages, an earthly beyond, a land of the soul yearning for its distant home in the past. However, in his later years Virgil avoided the regions discovered by him. For in his later poems he acquired a temper of severe manly restraint which led him to draw closer to the classical Greek expressions of feeling and thought; but many a trace of his earlier sensibility remained.

Along with his new understanding of the soul, Arcadia also furnished the poet with a radically new consciousness of his artistic role. Virgil, for his own person, was too modest to boast loudly of his achievement, but in his portrait of Gallus in the tenth eclogue he gives us a general idea of his views on the special function of the poet. The reasons, he hints, why the poet takes his stand among the gods, and why he receives the sympathy of nature, is because his feelings are more profound than those of other men, and because therefore he suffers more grievously under the cruelties of the world. Virgil does not actually spell out these ideas which were to become so important in modern poetry, but even his hinting at them is new. At the beginning of the sixth eclogue Virgil for once formulates a programme of poetic art, but, as is his manner, he is careful not to make too much of himself or his poetry. Following the traces of Callimachus, he refuses to have anything to do with the great epic—later, of course, he was to reverse himself—and he confines himself to the delicate pastime of brief compositions. But in this connexion he accidentally drops a remark which is quite unlike anything that Callimachus ever said; he expresses the hope that his lines, insignificant as their theme is, may be read by someone "captured by love." This sympathetic affection is the mark of the poet, and the poet seeks to transmit his compassion to his reader. . . .

The special importance of Virgil, which distinguishes his accomplishment from the Jewish and the Christian assimilation of Greek culture, and which places him squarely in the Roman tradition leading from Ennius to Catullus, is the fact that he uses the arts, viz. poetry, to channel the Greek heritage into the body of Roman thought. But further than that, his *Eclogues* represent the first serious attempt in literature to mould the Greek motifs into self-contained forms of beauty whose reality lies within themselves. Thus art became "symbol." Comparable tendencies do not exist in Greek literature. At most we might establish a certain similarity with the myths of Plato; but even this last comparison serves only to stress the special quality of Virgil's achievement. Plato's myths, too, had been concerned with "significance" rather than with reality. But they are not self-contained poetry; on the contrary, their objective is to illustrate something else. They refer to a specific argument which Plato would like to express rationally, but for which his language does not suffice. That is why Plato deprecates his myths and calls them mere play. In Greek literature this species of myth-making had no successors.

Arcadia was a land of symbols, far distant from the quarrels and the acrimony of the present. In this land the antique pagan world was permitted to live on without injury to anybody's feelings. Arcadia was so remote that it was no more in danger of clashing with the See of Rome or with the Holy Roman Empire than it had run afoul of the *Imperium Romanum* of Augustus. Only when Europe began to be dissatisfied with the goods handed down to her, and when she took thought upon her own spiritual substance, did Arcadia run into trouble. But that was also the time when the genuine Greece was restored to her rightful place.

ADAM PARRY

The Two Voices of Virgil's "Aeneid"

Let us . . . take care not to let ortho-
dox interpretations of the *Aeneid* obscure our sense of what it really is. The
nostalgia for the heroic and Latin past, the pervasive sadness, the regretful
sense of the limitations of human action in a world where you've got to
end up on the right side or perish, the frequent elegiac note so apparently
uncalled for in a panegyric of Roman greatness—like the passage at the
end of Book 5 which describes the drowning of the good pilot Palinurus in
dark and forgetful waters just before the Trojans reach Italy—the continual
opposition of a personal voice which comes to us as if it were Virgil's own
to the public voice of Roman success: all this I think is felt by every attentive
reader of the poem. But most readers, in making a final judgment on the
Aeneid, feel nonetheless constrained to put forth a hypothetical "Roman
reader" whose eyes were quite unused to the melting mood. *He* would have
taken the poem ultimately as a great work of Augustan propaganda, clapped
his hands when Aeneas abandons the overemotional Dido, and approved
with little qualification the steady march of the Roman state to world
dominion and the Principate of Augustus as we see these institutions mirrored in Anchises' speech in Book 6 and in Juno's renunciation in Book
12. This, we are told, is how we should read the poem. After all, what
was Augustus giving Virgil all those gold-pieces for?

So Mr. Kevin Guinach, the Rinehart translator, after putting forth
these views, adds: "From this it must not be inferred that Virgil was a

From *Arion* 4, vol. 2 (Winter 1963). Copyright © 1963 by *Arion*.

hireling. . . . It is fairer to suppose that he was an ardent admirer of the First Citizen and his policies, and sought to promote the reconstruction that August had in mind." Apropos of Dido he says: "The ancient Romans did not read this episode as tearfully as we do. . . . From the Roman point of view, Dido was the aggressor in her marriage with Aeneas, an intolerable assumption of a male prerogative." Moreover, he tells us, the Roman would have condemned her for breaking her vow to her first husband, dead these many years. Consider the case of Vestal Virgins. . . .

But what, on the simple glorification of Rome interpretation, do we make of some of the finest passages of the *Aeneid?* What we find, again and again, is not a sense of triumph, but a sense of loss. Consider the three lines at the end of Book 2 which describe Aeneas' attempts to embrace the ghost of his wife:

> Three times I tried to put my arms around her
> And three times her image fled my arms' embrace,
> As light as the winds; as fleeting as a dream.

Like the lines about the fallen warrior, these lines derive from an earlier literary tradition. And again a comparison with this tradition will tell us something about the *Aeneid*. Virgil has two Homeric passages in mind, one in the twenty-third Book of the *Iliad* where Achilles tries to embrace the hollow wraith of Patroclus:

> So spoke Achilles, and reached for him, but could not
> seize him, and the spirit went underground, like vapor,
> with a thin cry. And Achilles started awake, in amazement,
> and drove his hands together, and spoke, and his words were sorrowful:
> Ah me! even in the house of Hades there is left something of us,
> a soul and an image, but there is no real heart of life in it!

And a passage from the eleventh book of the *Odyssey*, where Odysseus in the Underworld attempts to embrace the shade of his mother:

> I bit my lip
> rising perplexed, with longing to embrace her,
> and tried three times,
> but she went sifting through my arms, impalpable
> as shadows are, and wavering like a dream,
> And this embittered all the pain I bore . . .

So the Virgilian passage first of all serves to reinforce the identification, operative throughout the poem, of Aeneas with the heroes of Homer. But the identification only sets in relief the differences. Virgil's lines are characteristic of the whole mood of his poem, the sadness, the loss, the frustration, the sense of the insubstantiality of what could be palpable and satisfying. Virgil emphasizes the *image*—the word *imago* ends the second line; and we can think of countless like passages, such as the appearance of Aeneas' mother in Book 1, not recognized until after she has fled. The Homeric heroes are made angry by these signs of what lies beyond our physical existence. Achilles *drives* his hands together, Odysseus is *embittered* that this kind of frustration should be added to his troubles. The Homeric hero, however beleaguered by fate, loves and enjoys the warmth of life, and his course of action includes a protest against the evanescence of mortality. But the sense of emptiness is the very heart of the Virgilian mood. After the three lines I have quoted, Aeneas goes on simply:

> The night was over; I went back to my comrades.

And the third of the three lines

> As light as the winds, as fleeting as a dream

receives a delicate emphasis, partly due to the two different words for *as*

> *Par levibus ventis, volucrique simillima somno*

that blurs the contours of our waking senses and gives the line a force of poignant resignation absent from both Homeric passages.

One other passage here, which I will speak of again later on. Aeneas comforts his men after the storm in Book 1 with a famous phrase:

> Forsan et haec olim meminisse iuvabit.

> Some day perhaps remembering this too will be a pleasure.

Lifted again from the *Odyssey*. But the Homeric line is quite unmemorable. Odysseus says to his men that some day their troubles now will be a memory. He means only, they will be in the past, don't be overcome by them now. Virgil has made one clear change: the word *iuvabit: it will be a pleasure*, which makes a commonplace idea into a profoundly touching one. Not I would insist, because Virgil is a greater poet, but because the kind of sentiment that stands out in the *Aeneid* is different from the kind that stands out in the *Odyssey*.

How much in general is Aeneas like the Greek heroes? We know from the first line that he is cast in the role of Achilles and Odysseus:

> Arms and the man I sing . . .

The *arms* are of course the *Iliad*, the *man* is the *Odyssey*. And the first six books of the *Aeneid* retrace the wanderings of Odysseus, the wars of the last six books follow the example of the *Iliad*. But the examples are not followed closely. The *Odyssey* goes on after its first line to tell us about the single man Odysseus; the *Iliad* goes on to describe the quarrel that was the first step in the tragedy of Achilles. The *Aeneid* moves from Aeneas straightway to something larger than himself: Rome:

> that man who was tossed about on land and sea
> and suffered much in war until
> he built his city, brought the gods to Latium
> from whence the Alban Fathers, the towering walls of Rome

Aeneas from the start is absorbed in his own destiny, a destiny which does not ultimately relate to him, but to something later, larger, and less personal: the high walls of Rome, stony and grand, the Augustan Empire. And throughout he has no choice. Aeneas never asserts himself like Odysseus. He is always the victim of forces greater than himself, and the one lesson he must learn is, not to resist them. The second book of the poem drills him thoroughly in this lesson. The word Aeneas keeps using, as he tells of the night Troy fell, is *obstipui*: I was *dumbfounded*, shocked into silence. Again and again he tries to assert himself, to act as a hero, and again and again he fails. He leads a band of desperate Trojans against the Greeks, but it all turns sour. The Trojans dress up as Greeks, an unheroic stratagem which works for a while, but then their own countrymen mistake them, and Trojans slaughter each other, while Aeneas himself ends up on the roof of Priam's palace, passive spectator of the terrible violations within. A key passage is the one in which Aeneas is about to kill Helen. At least the personal, if not entirely heroic, emotion of revenge can be satisfied. But his mother stops him, not with a personal plea, as Athena checks Achilles in the *Iliad*, but by revealing for an instant the gods at work destroying the city. Against such overwhelming forces as these, individual feeling has no place. Aeneas must do the *right* thing, the thing destiny demands, and sneak away from Troy.

One of the effects, then, of the epic identifications of Aeneas is ironic contrast: he is cast in a rôle which it is his tragedy not to be able to fulfill. Let us now consider another kind of identification: the historical ones. As well as being cast as Odysseus and Achilles, Aeneas has to be the emperor Augustus. Of many passages, this one in the third book particularly contributes to setting up the connection. Aeneas and his men coast along the western shore of Greece and stop at Actium, where there is a temple of Apollo. There they hold games and Aeneas fastens to the door of the temple spoils taken from the Greeks with the inscription THESE ARMS FROM THE GREEK VICTORS. The reason for this action in this place is that Augustus had won his great victory over Antony and Cleopatra a few years earlier at Actium. He had instituted games in honor of his victory, and he liked to identify himself with Apollo. Moreover THE GREEK VICTORS, who are now vanquished, represent the armies of Antony, who recruited his forces from the eastern Mediterranean, whereas Augustus made himself the champion of Italy. So that the victory Aeneas somewhat illogically claims here by dedicating Greek spoils prefigures the victory that was to establish the power of Augustus.

Some striking verbal parallels confirm the connection; and give us as well insight into Virgil's technique. At the beginning of Book 3, Aeneas sets sail from Troy.

> I am borne forth an exile onto the high seas
> With my comrades, my son, the Penates and the Great Gods
>
> Cum sociis natoque Penatibus et Magnis Dis.

The exact meaning of the phrase *the Penates and the Great Gods* is obscure. But it is clear that they are some sort of cult statues of Troy, destined to become cult statues of the New Troy, or Rome. The oddity of the phrase in fact helps us to remember it—the Romans liked their religious language to be obscure—and so does its remarkable thudding rhythm: *Penatibus et Magnis Dis*. This is Aeneas in his sacral character as bearer of the divine charter of Troy.

At the end of Book 8, Vulcan makes a shield for Aeneas, and on it are engraved scenes from subsequent Roman history. One of these scenes depicts the Battle of Actium:

> On one side stands Augustus Caesar leading Italians into battle,
> With the Fathers (i.e., the Senate), the People, the Penates and the
>   Great Gods
>
> Cum patribus populoque, Penatibus et Magnis Dis.

Aeneas' shield shows the future version of himself.

But Aeneas is not just Augustus. There is also the possibility of his being Augustus' bitter enemy, Mark Antony. Such is the identification we are led to make when, in the fourth book, he has become the consort of Dido, queen of Carthage. Thus the contemptuous description of him by Iarbas, his rival for Dido's love, "that Paris with his effeminate retinue," closely matches the image of Antony and Cleopatra with their corrupt eastern armies which Augustus created for Roman morale.

And Dido is Cleopatra. When she is about to die, she is said to be *pale with imminent death, pallida morte futura*. Cleopatra, in her own person, is described on Aeneas' shield in Book 8 as *paling before imminent death*, *pallentem morte futura.*

To understand the meaning in the poem of these historical identifications, we must first consider more fully the figure of Aeneas. We learn
from the second line of the poem that he is a man *exiled by fate, fato
profugus,* and we soon learn that fate has for Aeneas implications that go
beyond his personal journey through life. He is a man blessed—or is it
cursed?—with a mission. The mission is no less than to be the founder of
the most powerful state known to history; and so his every act and his every
passion, all that he does, all that he feels and all that happens to him is
in the light or under the shadow of this immense prophetic future of which
he, by no choice of his own, is the representative elected by the gods.
Every experience he passes through, therefore, has a significance greater
than the events of an ordinary man's life could possibly have. Every place
he visits acquires an eternal fame of one kind or another. Every action he
performs, every word he speaks, is fraught with consequences of which he
himself can only dimly perceive the enormity.

This sense of pregnant greatness in every detail of experience is
impressed on us too by the rhetorical exaggeration which pervades the
Aeneid, and by the unrealism of many of its incidents. Juno's wrath in Book
1 is magnified far beyond Poseidon's resentment in the *Odyssey;* Athena's
punishment of the lesser Ajax, which Juno would like to inflict upon
Aeneas, is enlarged into a cosmic destruction. When there are storms, the
waves rise up and lash the heavens. Dido is supposed to have arrived in
Africa not long before with a small band of refugees; but already the construction of a tremendous city—the later Carthage, of course—can be seen,
complete with temples and art-galleries. Aeneas is moving through a world
where everything is a symbol of something larger than itself. The layers of
literary and historical allusion reinforce this sense of expansion in space
and time which every monumental hexameter verse imposes on the reader.

The potentialities of ages and empires are alive in the smallest details
of the *Aeneid,* and Aeneas has been made into the keystone of it all. The
inconceivable destiny of Rome rests upon his shoulders. The *Aeneid* can
give a literal meaning to that cliché. So line 32 of the first Book:

Tantae molis erat Romanam condere gentem.

It was a thing of so much *weight* to found the Roman race.

Aeneas can only leave Troy by carrying his aged father upon his
shoulders. And Anchises is more than Aeneas' father. He is the burden of
destiny itself. Thus in Book 6 it is he who unfolds the panorama of Roman

history to his son who has descended to the Nether World to hear him. And at the end of Book 8, Virgil insists on Aeneas' rôle as bearer of destiny. The shield which Vulcan makes for him corresponds to the one he made for Achilles in the *Iliad.* Only Achilles' shield was adorned with generic pictures of life: a city at peace, a city at war, a scene of harvest, a scene of dancing, and so on. Aeneas' shield is adorned with scenes from Roman history, history which is future to him—it is here that we read of Augustus at the Battle of Actium—and as he puts it on, Virgil says:

> He marvels at the scenes, events unknown to him,
> And lays upon his shoulder the fame and fate of his descendants

> Attollens umero famamque et fata nepotum.

The burden may well be a heavy one to bear, particularly if the bearer of it himself is permitted only an occasional prophetic glimpse into its meaning. And when such a glimpse is permitted him, it is likely to be anything but reassuring.

> Bella, horrida bella . . .

Wars, hideous wars! the Sibyl shrieks at him when he questions her in Book 6. "You will get to Latium, all right," she tells him, "but you will wish you had never come!" *Sed non et venisse volent.* "Go, seek your Italy!" Dido tells him, and then prophesies: "Let him beg for help in his own land, and when he has accepted the terms of a shameful peace, let him not enjoy his realm, or that light he has prayed for, but

> fall before his time, and lie unburied on the sands

> Sed cadat ante diem mediaque inhumatus harena,

whereby Aeneas is included in an almost obsessively recurrent series of images of disgraceful and nameless death.

Labor, ignorance and suffering are Aeneas' most faithful companions on his journey to Rome. And at once to intensify his own suffering and lack of fulfillment and to magnify the destiny he is serving, Aeneas must witness the happiness and success of others. In the third book he visits his kinsman Helenus in Epirus, and there he sees a copy of Troy, laid out in miniature. Aeneas is at first hopeful as he asks the prophetic Helenus for advice: "Now tell me, for I have divine sanction for all I do, and the gods have promised me a happy course, tell me the labors I must undergo, and the dangers I must avoid." But a little later, when Anchises enters, and he must set sail again, Aeneas falls into despair: "May you live happy, for your destiny is accomplished; but we are called from one fate to another

. . . You have peace, you have no need to plow up the sea and follow forever the forever receding shores of Italy."

> Arva neque Ausoniae semper cedentia retro
> Quaerenda.

What this and other like passages impress upon us is something subtly at variance with the stated theme of the poem. Instead of an arduous but certain journey to a fixed and glorious goal, there arises, and gathers strength, a suggestion that the true end of the Trojan and Roman labors will never arrive. It is not that Aeneas will literally never arrive in Latium, found a city, and win his wars. That is as certain as it is that Odysseus will return to Ithaca. But everything in the *Odyssey* prepares us for a fuller end to Odysseus' labors: we are made always to expect his reinstatement in kingship, home, honor and happiness. In the *Aeneid* every prophecy and every episode prepares us for the contrary: Aeneas' end, it is suggested, will see him as far from his fulfillment as his beginning. This other Italy will never cease receding into the distance.

There is another dimension to Aeneas' suffering as the bearer of too vast a destiny. Aeneas cannot live his own life. An agent of powers at once high and impersonal, he is successively denied all the attributes of a hero, and even of a man. His every utterance perforce contains a note of history, rather than of individuality. He cannot be himself, because he is wired for sound for all the centuries to come, a fact that is reflected in the speeches of the *Aeneid.* The sonorous lines tend to come out as perfect epigrams, ready to be lifted out of their context and applied to an indefinite number of parallel situations. Aeneas arrives in Carthage and sees the busy construction of the city.

> O fortunate you, whose walls already rise!

he cries out.

> O fortunati, quorum iam moenia surgunt!

The line is memorable, too memorable perhaps for spontaneity. What Virgil has done is to turn to peculiar account what is at once the weakness and the glory of much of Latin verse: its monumentality, and its concomitant lack of dramatic illusion.

But Aeneas' failure as a hero goes deeper than the formality of his speech. As he makes his way through the first six books, we see him successively divested of every personal quality which makes a man into a hero. We have seen how the weight of his mission is made to overwhelm him at the very beginning of the poem. In the second book, he is in a situation which above all calls for self-sacrifice in the heat of battle. But this is precisely what he is kept from doing. Hector appears to him in a dream and tells him not to die for his country, but to flee. "For if Troy could have been saved," the ghost says almost with condescension, "my right arm would have saved it." We understand that Aeneas' words in the first Book, when he was overwhelmed by the storm, have a deeper meaning than the parallel lines of the *Odyssey*: "O thrice and four times happy, you who fell at Troy!" Odysseus spoke out of a momentary despair. Aeneas' words are true for all his life. His personal ties too are not kept intact: in his haste to get his father and the state gods out of Troy, he leaves his wife behind; and when he returns to fetch her, she is an empty phantom, who can comfort him only with another prophecy.

But the most dramatic episode and the one in which Aeneas most loses his claims to heroism is the fourth Book. The tragedy of Dido is lucid and deeply moving. But the judgment it leads us to make on Aeneas needs some comment. Generations of Latin teachers have felt it necessary to defend Aeneas from the charge of having been a cad. Modern readers are romantic, but a Roman reader would have known that Aeneas did the right thing. So the student is asked to forsake his own experience of the poem for that of a hypothetical Roman. Another theory is that Virgil somehow fell in love with, and was carried away by, his own heroine. But we cannot explain Virgil by assuming that he did not intend to write as he did. It is clear that on the contrary Virgil deliberately presented Dido as a heroine, and Aeneas as an inglorious deserter. Dido's speeches are passionate, and, in their operatic way, ring utterly true. Aeneas can apologize only by urging that his will is not his own. "If I had had my way," he tells her, "I would never have left Troy to come here at all." "I would never have fallen in love with you in the first place," he seems to mean. "I follow Italy not of my own choice." Of course he is right. Aeneas' will is not his own, and the episode in Carthage is his last attempt to assert himself as an individual and not as the agent of an institution. And in his failure, he loses his claim even to the humbler of the heroic virtues. For piety, in the Roman sense, meant devotion to persons as well as the state. "Unhappy Dido!" the queen about to die cries out, "is it now his impious deeds become clear to you? They should have before, when you made him your partner in rule. See now his pledge of faith, this man who carries about his gods, and his ancient father on his back." For pious Aeneas, as he is called, and calls himself, throughout, cannot maintain even his piety in a personal way.

Two later passages serve to emphasize this. At the beginning of the fifth Book, the Trojans sail to Italy, troubled by the death-fires they see back in Carthage. "For they knew what a woman is capable of, when insane with the grief of her love dishonored." The Latin is perhaps more blunt. Dido's love was literally *defiled, polluto amore,* and Aeneas is its defiler. Later, in the Underworld in Book 6, Aeneas meets Dido. He wants reconciliation now, and begs forgiveness. "I did not know the strength of your love for me," he says. Again the implication is clear. Aeneas did not know, because he could not feel the same love for her; because he is not master of himself, but the servant of an abstract destiny. Dido, speechless in anger, turns away. Aeneas is modelled on Odysseus here, and Dido's shade is the shade of Ajax in Book 11 of the *Odyssey.* Virgil strengthens the emotions this scene creates in us by recalling the one scene in the *Odyssey* where Odysseus meets a hero greater than himself, and is put to shame by his silence.

But Dido, we remember, is also Cleopatra, and we must consider the meaning of that identification. Dido-Cleopatra is the sworn enemy of Rome:

Rise thou forth from my bones, some avenger!

Exoriare aliquis nostris ex ossibus ultor!

invoking the fell shades of Hannibal; but she is a tragic heroine. Aeneas, on the other hand, could have been, and for a while seemed to be, Antony, losing a world for love. Only he must in the end be Augustus, losing love and honor for a dubious world. The *Aeneid,* the supposed panegyric of Augustus and great propaganda-piece of the new régime, has turned into something quite different. The processes of history are presented as inevitable, as indeed they are, but the value of what they achieve is cast into doubt. Virgil continually insists on the public glory of the Roman achievement, the establishment of peace and order and civilization, that *dominion without end* which Jupiter tells Venus he has given the Romans:

Imperium sine fine dedi.

But he insists equally on the terrible price one must pay for this glory. More than blood, sweat and tears, something more precious is continually being lost by the necessary process; human freedom, love, personal loyalty, all the qualities which the heroes of Homer represent, are lost in the service of what is grand, monumental and impersonal: the Roman State.

The sixth Book sets the seal on Aeneas' renunciation of himself. What gives it a depth so much greater than the corresponding book of the *Odyssey* is the unmistakable impression we have that Aeneas has not only gone into the Underworld: he has in some way himself died. He descends carrying the Golden Bough, a symbol of splendor and lifelessness. The bough glitters and it *crackles in the wind*:

> . . . sic leni crepitabat brattea vento.

It sheds, Virgil says, a strange discolored aura of gold; and it is compared to the mistletoe, a *parasitic plant, quod non sua seminat arbos*, a plant with no vital connection to the tree to which it clings. A powerful contrast to the culminating image of the *Odyssey*, that great hidden rooted tree from which the bed-chamber, the house and the kingship of Odysseus draw continuous and organic life.

Aeneas moves through the world of the dead. He listens, again the passive spectator, to the famous Roman policy speech of Anchises, a speech full of eagles and trumpets and a speech renouncing the very things Virgil as a man prized most:

> Let others fashion the lifelike image from bronze and marble;
> Let others have the palm of eloquence;
> Let others describe the wheeling constellations of heaven;
> Thy duty, O Roman, is to rule . . .
>
> Tu regere imperio populos, Romane, memento . . .

When he emerges, so strangely, from the ivory gate of false dreams, he is no longer a living man, but one who has at last understood his mission, and become identified with it. Peace and order are to be had, but Aeneas will not enjoy them, for their price is life itself.

And yet there is something left which is deeper than all this. It is the capacity of the human being to suffer. We hear two distinct voices in the *Aeneid*, a public voice of triumph, and a private voice of regret. The private voice, the personal emotions of a man, is never allowed to motivate action. But it is nonetheless everywhere present. For Aeneas, after all, is something more than an Odysseus manqué, or a prototype of Augustus and myriads of Roman leaders. He is man himself; not man as the brilliant free agent of Homer's world, but man of a later stage in civilization, man in a metropolitan and imperial world, man in a world where the State is supreme. He cannot resist the forces of history, or even deny them; but he can be capable of human suffering, and this is where the personal voice asserts itself.

Someday these things too will be pleasant to think back on

Forsan et haec olim meminisse iuvabit

he tells his comrades in Book 1. The implication is that when the great abstract goal is finally somehow reached, these present sufferings, seen in retrospect, will be more precious than it.

And so this pleasure, the only true pleasure left to Aeneas in a life of betrayals of the self, is envisaged as art. The sufferings of the Trojans, as Aeneas sees them in Carthage, have become fixed in art, literally: they are paintings. And it is here first, Virgil tells us, that Aeneas began to hope for a kind of salvation. Here he can look back on his own losses, and see them as made beautiful and given universal meaning because human art has transfigured them. "Look here!" he cries. "There is Priam; there are tears for suffering, and the limitations of life can touch the heart."

Sunt lacrimae rerum et mentem mortalia tangunt.

The pleasure felt here by Aeneas in the midst of his reawakened grief is the essential paradox and the great human insight of the *Aeneid*, a poem as much about the *imperium* of art as about the *imperium* of Rome. The images in Carthage make Aeneas feel Priam's death not less deeply, but more. At the same time they are a redemption of past suffering, partly because they remove one element of the nightmare: final obscurity and namelessness, partly because they mean that we have found a form in which we can see suffering itself clearly. The brightness of the image and the power of pleasurable vision it confers, consoles for the pain of what it represents.

The pleasure of art in fact gives value to the pain itself, because tragic experience is the content of this art. Virgil continues the scene in the art-gallery: "He spoke, and with deep sorrow, and many lamentations, fed his soul on the empty pictures."

Atque animum pictura pascit inani.

*Empty—inani—*is the key-word here. Consider again how many times Virgil creates his most touching scenes by dwelling on how something substantial becomes empty and insubstantial: the phantom of Creusa, old fallen Troy, the apparition of Venus in Book 1, the shade of Dido in the Underworld, the lost pledge to Evander, the outraged life of Turnus. *Inanis* is the very word that describes the tears Aeneas sheds upon leaving Carthage and Dido: "His mind was unmoved; the tears he wept were empty." That is, *of no avail.*

Mens immota manet; lacrimae volvuntur inanes.

Aeneas' tragedy is that he cannot be a hero, being in the service of an impersonal power. What saves him as a man is that all the glory of the solid achievement which he is serving, all the satisfaction of "having arrived" in Italy means less to him than his own sense of personal loss. The *Aeneid* enforces the fine paradox that all the wonders of the most powerful institution the world has ever known are not necessarily of greater importance than the emptiness of human suffering.

THOMAS GREENE

The Descent from Heaven: Virgil

The loss of Virgil to the modern world is an immeasurable cultural tragedy. For we have lost in him not only one of the greatest of world poets but also the master of European poetry. Ignorant of him, we are ignorant of aspects of other poets we think we know better. Virgil's earlier poetry was taught in Roman schools even before his death, and from then on, from the first century to the nineteenth, he was generally at the core of European education. More than the Bible (so little read in so many places at so many times), far more than Homer, Virgil has been *the* classic of Western civilization. This has been true partly because he is more fitly a poet of maturity than of youth, because his work continues to educate as the understanding ripens. Fully to know him, one must know him long. If he teaches the schoolboy style, to the man he imparts nobility.

The very word *nobility* is suspect in an age which has seen the decline of Virgil's influence. The word has overtones of snobbery and social privilege, and its moral associations suggest today an offensive pretentiousness, a shallow posturing, a cardboard dignity, qualities wholly un-Virgilian which he would have considered vulgar. Nobility in Virgil is concerned with authenticity, labor, and humility; it involves above all a spiritual generosity and an incapacity for triviality. Second-rate imitators of Virgil (we shall encounter some later) have tried to achieve nobility by the ar-

From *The Descent from Heaven: A Study in Epic Continuity*. Copyright © 1963 by Yale University. Translations by Robert Fitzgerald from the *Aeneid*, New York: Random House, 1983.

tificial exclusion of commonplace things, but he himself wrote cheerfully about fertilizers. Our own century, reacting against that artificial exclusion, has embraced the commonplace and the trivial, so that a whole generation of poets has felt obliged to strew their work with the bric-a-brac of recent civilization. The same misplaced conscientiousness leads Day Lewis doggedly to measure out his clichés for each line of the *Aeneid:*

> To speak with brutal frankness
> And lay all my cards on the table—please take to heart what I'm saying—
> I never had the right to promise my daughter . . .

The high style of the original Latin is earned by the high style of its author's feeling—style which cannot easily be imitated but to which one rises slowly, out of respect and emulation. In those rare places where the *Aeneid* courts the danger of flatulence, where the trumpets begin to sound a little too sonorously, Virgil's native magnanimity almost always saves him. Thus when, in the eighth book, Venus anticipates her gift of arms by a series of thunder crashes and a celestial vision of the gift, the potential emptiness of this grandiloquence is filled by the subsequent speech of Aeneas:

> Ai!
> What carnage is at hand for poor Laurentines.
> What retribution you will make to me,
> Turnus. Many a shield, many a helm,
> And many brave men's bodies you'll take under,
> Father Tiber. Let them insist on war,
> Let them break treaties!
>
> (8.537–40)

Aeneas' joy at this encouraging omen is tempered by pain for his enemies' future suffering. That pain is the token of his authentic generosity, not the hollow goodness of a wooden paragon. The pain is *in character;* it is related to other things in Aeneas which hurt him and his mission and which might be regarded as faults. Virgil's nobility lies in his capacity for writing at a high moral level without losing verisimilitude or dramatic intensity. His generosity is spontaneous and human, and so it never dishonestly ignores the cost or the regrets that generosity may involve.

Why has Virgil become so inaccessible? It would appear that the decline of classical education cannot wholly be blamed for his remoteness, since Homer is still read and appreciated in translation. But Virgil in our time has not found his Lattimore, and there is a question whether his poems will ever yield themselves to translation as gracefully as the *Iliad.* It is very hard to understand anything important about Virgil without his language. Perhaps he is also neglected because the *Aeneid*, as a whole, is not so supremely great as the *Iliad*, and thus Virgil seems to run a negligible second best. The comparison with Homer is regrettably unavoidable, because Virgil invited it and built it into his poem, but in fact the *Aeneid* is so different from the Homeric poems that comparisons are often unfruitful. Despite appearances, and despite the author's own conscious intent, the *Aeneid* is unique among epics.

Perhaps the taste for Virgil is unfashionable because he has been identified with the literary Establishment against which the Romantics reacted—as a later generation of rebels reacted in our century. The individual admiration of a Chateaubriand or a Wordsworth—or an Eliot or a Valéry—has not sufficed to obliterate the stigma of neoclassic associations, a stigma intensified by Tennyson's homage. But these historical circumstances would not have sufficed to discredit Virgil did he not fail to supply what we habitually demand from poetry. He is never, for instance, a comic poet; there is a little horse play in the fifth Aeneid, but not much, and not very funny. He is generally serious, but he is not tragic in any very recognizable fashion—not tragic like Sophocles or Shakespeare. I shall have to speak below of his oblique relation to tragedy. But these wants might be excused if at least the texture of his verse were roughened with irony. Yet here too, alas, he fails. Homer seems closer to the modern world because his ironies are so terrible. When Achilleus taunts the tears of Patroklos who is weeping for his beleaguered comrades, when Achilleus compares him to a little girl, there is a bitter irony for the reader who anticipates Achilleus' own flood of tears for his friend's approaching death. And when, just before his fatal wounding Patroklos taunts his victim Kebriones for the gracefulness of his plunge to death, there is a tragic irony in the fine, gay sarcasm of the doomed victor. Virgil was not given to this Sophoclean cruelty, not, however, because he was ignorant of that complexity in life which irony commonly underscores. Virgil was aware of it, perhaps too aware for the gentleness of his temperament. He was not as *hard* as Homer, and he would have found the Homeric form of tragic irony intolerable. His only form was the straightforward, more bearable sarcasm of Roman oratory, the sarcasm to which Mercury has recourse in his most important epiphany to Aeneas. Before any more generalizations, we ought now to consider that passage.

The gods have frequent occasion to intervene in the action of the *Aeneid*; the superior gods both appear in person (in particular, Venus, Juno, and Apollo) and dispatch emissaries or agents like Iris, Juturna, Opis, and so on. Mercury is dispatched three times by Jupiter—first in Book One (297 ff.), to render Dido hospitable to the storm-weary Trojans, and twice in Book Four (222 ff. and 556 ff.) to command Aeneas' immediate departure from Carthage. Of all these interventions, only one is described very circumstantially, and only one follows closely the Homeric theme. This is Mercury's second flight. This account is ample; all the others are bare. Virgil may well have chosen to imitate once only this particular convention, and then selected this crux of the narrative in which to do it.

Jupiter's attention is called to Aeneas by his son Iarbas, a Libyan king who has sued unsuccessfully for Dido's hand. Iarbas has heard gossip of Dido's pseudo-"marriage" with Aeneas, an arrangement contrived by Juno with Venus' approbation. Iarbas complains to his father that Dido has yielded to "this second Paris, wearing a Phrygian bonnet to tie up his chin and cover his oily hair, and attended by a train of she-men." This complaint succeeds in turning Jupiter's eyes upon Carthage:

> Pleas like this
> From the man clinging to his altars reached
> The ears of the Almighty. Now he turned
> His eyes upon the queen's town and the lovers
> Careless of their good name; then spoke to Mercury,
> Assigning him a mission:
> "Son, bestir yourself,
> Call up the Zephyrs, take to your wings and glide.
> Approach the Dardan captain where he tarries
> Rapt in Tyrian Carthage, losing sight
> Of future towns the fates ordain. Correct him,
> Carry my speech to him on the running winds:
> No son like this did his enchanting mother
> Promise to us, nor such did she deliver
> Twice from peril at the hands of Greeks.
> He was to be the ruler of Italy,
> Potential empire, armorer of war;
> To father men from Teucer's noble blood
> And bring the whole world under law's dominion.
> If glories to be won by deeds like these
> Cannot arouse him, if he will not strive
> For his own honor, does he begrudge his son,
> Ascanius, the high strongholds of Rome?
> What has he in mind? What hope, to make him stay
> Amid a hostile race, and lose from view
> Ausonian progeny, Lavinian lands?
> The man should sail: that is the whole point.

Let this be what you tell him, as from me."
He finished and fell silent. Mercury
Made ready to obey the great command
Of his great father, and he first tied on
The golden sandals, winged, that high in air
Transport him over seas or over land
Abreast of gale winds; then he took the wand
With which he summons pale souls out of Orcus
And ushers others to the undergloom,
Lulls men to slumber or awakens them,
And opens dead men's eyes. This wand in hand,
He can drive winds before him, swimming down
Along the stormcloud. Now aloft, he saw
The craggy flanks and crown of patient Atlas,
Giant Atlas, balancing the sky
Upon his peak—his pine-forested head
In vapor cowled, beaten by wind and rain.
Snow lay upon his shoulders, rills cascaded
Down his ancient chin and beard a-bristle,
Caked with ice. Here Mercury of Cyllenë
Hovered first on even wings, then down
He plummeted to sea-level and flew on
Like a low-flying gull that skims the shallows
And rocky coasts where fish ply close inshore.
So, like a gull between the earth and sky,
The progeny of Cyllenë, on the wing
From his maternal grandsire, split the winds
To the sand bars of Libya.
                 Alighting tiptoe
On the first hutments, there he found Aeneas
Laying foundations for new towers and homes.
He noted well the swordhilt the man wore,
Adorned with yellow jasper; and the cloak
Aglow with Tyrian dye upon his shoulders—
Gifts of the wealthy queen, who had inwoven
Gold thread in the fabric. Mercury
Took him to task at once:
                   "Is it for you
To lay the stones for Carthage's high walls,
Tame husband that you are, and build their city?
Oblivious of your own world, your own kingdom!
From bright Olympus he that rules the gods
And turns the earth and heaven by his power—
He and no other sent me to you, told me

To bring this message on the running winds:
What have you in mind? What hope, wasting your days
In Libya? If future history's glories
Do not affect you, if you will not strive
For your own honor, think of Ascanius,
Think of the expectations of your heir,
Iulus, to whom the Italian realm, the land
Of Rome, are due."
                    And Mercury, as he spoke,
Departed from the visual field of mortals
To a great distance, ebbed in subtle air.

(4.219–78)

Virgil's copy of Homer was open as he wrote this passage, but the innovations he has made in the theme are considerable. Both his indebtedness and his originality are most easily studied in the middle section beginning "Dixerat," a word which is itself a rendering of the Greek "*I ra.*" The line that follows—"Ille . . . imperio" echoes but does not follow precisely Homer's formulaic statement of Hermes' obedience. The next three lines, however, ("et primum . . . portant") do follow word for word Homer's praise of the marvelous sandals. Virgil's treatment of the staff, in turn, is a significant expansion of Homer's two lines. Homer had alluded only to the staff's power of inducing and waking from sleep. Virgil repeats this idea in three words but chooses to emphasize rather Mercury's role as *psychopompus,* guide to the Lower World—guide both for the newly dead into that world and for ghosts who are summoned from it. The key phrase in this sentence is the last—"lumina morte resignat" ("unseals eyes from death")—which might be applied to either of these duties. We shall want to consider below the effect of this expansion. Let us note here that the following line, which ostensibly continues to describe the staff, forms in fact a transition to the act of flight:

                    This wand in hand,
He can drive winds before him, swimming down
Along the stormcloud.

(4.245)

This fine image owes its felicity largely to the juxtaposition of *turbida* and the verb *tranat* which contains a suggestion of swimming and thus of effortless, unbroken movement through the swirling clouds.

From this point the passage becomes increasingly Virgilian. The powerful image of Atlas is original and so is the description of the overdressed hero, although the simile which separates these two constitutes a modification of Homer's corresponding cormorant simile. Mercury speaks with curt sarcasm and disappears as he concludes, with a virile abruptness much more Roman than Greek, an abruptness which will typify the very close of the poem. Mercury's speech is more or less his own, but it does contain many phrases used by Jupiter ("tantarum gloria rerum"; "celeris . . . per auras"; "Quid struis, aut qua spe . . . ?") and one line of his speech (273) is quoted verbatim from Jupiter's except for the shift to the second person. Virgil remembers but does not imitate Homer's word-for-word repetitions of entire speeches.

All of Virgil's innovations in this passage are made in the same spirit: they introduce a moral dimension into the action while maintaining, or heightening, the grandeur of the god's movement. Virgil is concerned with conferring a certain metaphysical prestige upon right conduct. Aeneas' conduct as the god finds him appears exemplary but is in fact misguided. It represents an evasion, a futile rehearsal of his duty to found the Roman state which was destined to impose order upon the world. Aeneas' evasion stems not so much from any love for Dido as from a dreamy willingness to indulge himself under her opulent, oriental hospitality. Mercury's role as *psychopompus* is relevant because through his descent he is symbolically unsealing the eyes of a man asleep or dead. The instantaneous effect of his epiphany upon Aeneas resembles an awakening or an unsealing of eyes:

> Amazed, and shocked to the bottom of his soul
> By what his eyes had seen, Aeneas felt
> His hackles rise, his voice choke in his throat.
>
> (4.279–80)

The chthonic associations of Mercury's staff anticipate as well the literal death of Dido, a death which his descent is to bring about. Mercury's mission is actually to send a soul to the Lower World, even though the allusion in its context seems irrelevant. Aeneas is to encounter Dido as one of the "pale shades," when he visits the underworld. Thus the lines devoted to the staff have a two-fold reference—to Aeneas and to Dido— even though Virgil leaves their ulterior meaning unstressed.

This transformation of Homeric elements is characteristic of Virgil's procedure throughout. He imitated the episodes and characters and speeches and similes of Greek epic—in particular of Homer—to a point which scandalized some of his early readers. But precisely at those points where he appears most derivative, he is most Virgilian. The broad context of the *Aeneid* metamorphoses the derivative passages and acculturates them to the world of a distinctive, Roman, far more self-conscious imagination. Similes which in the *Iliad* retain a kind of independence from their context, find

themselves grafted more firmly and dependently upon the new poem, acquiring now a new moral and symbolic richness. It is a pity that so many
of Virgil's imitators during later antiquity and the Renaissance followed his
practice but missed the dimension of originality which justified it.

The Virgilian stamp is set upon Mercury's descent partly through
the vigorous description of Atlas on which it hinges. The Atlas image is
one of those which allows itself most easily to be translated into moral
equivalents. There is, to be sure, a slender mythological pretext to justify
its appearance, since Atlas was said to be the father of Maia and grandfather
of Mercury. But the important justification for the image lies in the contrast
between Atlas and Aeneas. The great shaggy ice-bound figure sustaining
the sky is an *exemplum* of heroic self-denial, of austere exposure to the
elements for the sake of the world community. Atlas embodies the qualities
which Aeneas has temporarily forgotten. As we first encounter him, Aeneas
is exposed to the violence of the elements, enduring as Atlas endures and
as Romans would learn to endure. In the *Aeneid* as in the *Georgics*, the
human lot depends upon weather. Only a god like Mercury is master of
the elements; as he descends the poet remembers that mastery which is
symbolized by the sandals and staff. But Aeneas, who can only be the
victim of the elements, now takes cover from them in Dido's splendid
palace. His reprehensible instinct of self-indulgence is visible in the cloak
she has given him, the cloak made of Tyrian purple interlaced with golden
threads. This cloak and the idle sword, studded ostentatiously with jasper,
point the contrast with Atlas' huge battered head. They represent as well
Dido's unnatural and possessive hold upon him. Aeneas appears the dandy
which Iarbas has scornfully pictured him to be, and this evasive rehearsal
at Carthage is an act of cowardice. Thus Mercury's sarcasm:

> Is it for you
> To lay the stones for Carthage's high walls,
> Tame husband that you are, and build their city?
> Oblivious of your own world, your own kingdom!
> (4.265)

Because of Aeneas' unrelenting servitude to fate, *pulcher* is a word to be
used with stinging reproach.

The value placed by the *Odyssey* on beautiful artifacts and on the
cultural refinement they manifest is here suspect. There are historical and
sociological reasons (as well as reasons private to the poet) why such a shift
in values should have occurred. Virgil was writing, not for an audience
whose achievement of culture was precarious and thus uncritical, but for

an audience whose traditions of austerity were threatened by power, luxury, and corruption. As a result the questions to be posed about Virgil's places are not those viable for his predecessors. In the *Odyssey* one asks "How barbarous or how refined?" In the *Aeneid* one asks "How austere or how decadent?" The beautiful thing was too familiar to be marvelous, as it once had been. The romance of culture had been lost, as Roman eyes were opened to its supposedly insidious seductiveness. The characteristic ritual of the *Odyssey* is the ceremony of hospitality—a ritual of courteous indulgence. But the rituals Virgil admires are the communal habits of work and piety. Dido's brilliant reception of the weary Trojans—with its swirl of ornate gold and silver and fine cloths and music and hecatombs to be feasted on beneath the glowing candelabra and the inlaid ceiling—is a dangerous ritual. It contrasts unfavorably with the simpler hospitality of Pallanteum, where Aeneas spends the night on a pallet of bearskin and leaves.

But if Virgil admired primitive plainness, he did not really admire archaic unrestraint. His primitivism is the backward-looking idealism of a Roman, nothing like the naive serenity in nature of a Homeric Greek. The bird to which Mercury is compared in the *Aeneid*:

> Like a low-flying gull that skims the shallows
> And rocky coasts where fish ply close inshore.
> (4.254)

is less vivid than the cormorant, its Homeric equivalent, because it has less wild freedom, less rapacity; its genus is not specified—it is simply "a bird," *avis;* moreover it is a timider bird, haunting the shore rather than crossing seas like the cormorant—and like Mercury. Thus Virgil's bird is less natural and less "real." It is given life by no detail comparable to the salt upon the cormorant's wings. Virgil was not truly at home in the world of untamed nature; he did not feel that fellowship with wild animals which one divines even in those Homeric similes that pit men against animals. He came to the *Aeneid* from writing a great handbook for domesticating natural unruliness.

His largest poem is a handbook for political domesticating—"sub leges mittere orbem." It is a guide as well for the domestication of the self, which also knows its wild beasts. *Empire* is the key idea—empire over the world, over nature and peoples, over language, and over the heart. The respective struggles for command over these various realms imitate and illustrate each other. In the end it is hard to say which *imperium* shows the strictest control—the government of Caesar Augustus, or the hexameters which celebrate it, or the terrible moral discipline which Caesar's ancestor is brought to obey.

II

The character of Aeneas has frequently been criticized, and perhaps most frequently for his conduct after Mercury's descent. The fourth book of the *Aeneid* being its best known (although the second, third, sixth, and eighth are at least as fine), Aeneas is remembered as a paragon of deserters, a "master-leaver," to use Enobarbus' phrase. Aeneas is supposed to be un-feeling, wooden, ungrateful, and worse—a cad. The alleged betrayal—the act of a rotter—stands out, and the presentation of his character through the rest of the book, more subtle and understated, counts for less.

Nobody today, I imagine, is going to try to *clear* Aeneas, if only because such an attempt would falsely imply that Aeneas is everywhere admirable. Virgil of course is forever judging his hero, indeed holding up such high standards to judge him by that one is inclined to protest their inhuman strictness. No one will want to absolve Aeneas, but the cliché criticisms, to mean anything, need a context of understanding they do not always receive. First of all, Aeneas' character in Book Four never gets out of hand; it cannot be blamed on the poet's narrative clumsiness or gross moral insensitivity. For better or worse Virgil wants Aeneas to appear as he does. The rest of the poem is there to attest to the powerfully controlling imagination and the almost painfully rigorous moral sense. Virgil has chosen to assign his hero the role of the cad, a little upstage, colorless, and ap-parently composed, while downstage the heroine tears her passion to mag-nificent tatters. The Dido drama demonstrates Jackson Knight's remark that "Virgil always sees two sides of everything." He does see them and feel them; that is the reason one can speak of the "painfulness" of his morality. In Book Four he allows one side alone its full pathos, knowing that the weight of the remaining eleven books suffices to right the balance. But such nice artistic calculations are wasted upon the hasty or sentimental reader.

A second qualification to the cliché attacks concerns Aeneas' emo-tional depth. Whether or not he is in love with Dido—probably he is not—Aeneas is not cold. He would suffer less if he were. The depth of his feelings constitutes the most important thing about him, the thing to start with in speaking of him; it is what makes him interesting and complicated, what leads him to err and disobey, what underlies his nobility. For just as Virgil's nobility is genuine because his generosity is native and human, so the nobility of his hero escapes appearing factitious because it has real emotional substance. Aeneas has dramatic life because his feelings are lifelike: they are impure and fragmentary, confused and intermittent; some of his motives ripen and others wither in the course of the poem. Thus when Mercury leaves him, a malicious reader might find his first response too conventional, too rehearsed:

> Amazed, and shocked to the bottom of his soul
> By what his eyes had seen, Aeneas felt
> His hackles rise, his voice choke in his throat.
> (4.279–80)

but the succeeding line introduces that division of impulses which is the mark of human feeling and above all the mark of Aeneas' feeling:

> he now
> Burned only to be gone, to leave that land
> Of the sweet life behind.
> (4.281)

Already in the very phrasing of Mercury's disappearance:

> And Mercury, as he spoke,
> Departed from the visual field of mortals
> To a great distance, ebbed in subtle air.
> (4.277)

there is a flicker of Virgilian melancholy, of loneliness and regret at the brevity of the gods' apparitions which recalls the more accentuated pathos when Venus leaves Aeneas in Book One. Here in the later scene we know the hero well enough to impute that fleeting regret to his own sensibility although the poet does not explicitly lead us to do so.

Aeneas' emotional intensity is particularly striking in the quality of his religious feeling, that feeling which leads him against his will away from Carthage. His critics tend to discount this strain in him, and yet it is powerfully realized in the poem. Aeneas is not only stolidly pious, in the English sense, or *pius* in the much richer, humane, Latin sense, but he is religious in a more inward way. He is not only punctilious in his duties to the gods and in the divinely-sanctioned duties to those about him. That is his *pietas*, his conscientiousness, but the more remarkable thing about him is the fervor which informs his conscientiousness, a fervor which has no counterpart in the Homeric poems. Aeneas is forever open to a capacity in earthly things for assuming divinity, and he comes to have an intuition of a transcendence in human history. He has occasion in the poem to make several prayers, and in these, curiously, he emerges almost more convincingly and dramatically than anywhere else, as his language becomes most charged and eloquent. Thus the opening of his beautiful prayer to Apollo in the Cumean cave:

> O Phoebus,
> God who took pity on the pain of Troy,
> Who guided Paris' hand, his Dardan shaft,
> Against the body of Aiacidës,
> As you led on I entered all those seas
> Washing great lands, and then the distant tribe
> Of the Massylians at the Syrtës' edge.
> Now we take hold at last of Italy
> That slipped away so long. Grant that the fortune
> Of Troy shall have pursued us this far only!
> (6.56–62)

Weariness, gratitude, pride, melancholy, faith are mingled here, although translation strains out the poignance of their merging. The prayer exemplifies too that association of Virgilian religion with geography which makes part of its charm, as well as those associations with tradition and festival which the unquoted remainder will introduce.

The charm and beauty of Virgil's religion are actually far more winning in his accounts of human worship, where he is most himself and most spontaneous, than in the heavier, more perfunctory scenes on Olympus, the councils and disputes, where the derivations from Homer are least successful. Virgil's gods, tending as they do to embody abstract principles or forces, court the risk of transparency, and Homeric mystery starts to fade into Virgilian machinery. The descent of Mercury, which lies open to the charge of perfunctory imitation, is saved by those accretions of dramatic meaning we have already noticed. In general, Virgil is at his weakest with his gods, particularly while they remain on Olympus, and this weakness can be attributed to his lack of belief in them as they are thus represented. Virgil's faith must have been like his hero's: inward and intuitive, taking sustenance from places known, from ritual and tradition, from tree and bush and earth. His faith must have been vague in some respects, blurred around the edges, shot with doubts, but his fervor, his openness to some transcendence, were very vital and enriched the dramatic substance of his hero.

It can be granted that Aeneas remains a little muted as a character; he is deep but he is not brilliant. Virgil may well have been incapable of creating a figure as brilliant as the Achilleus of the *Iliad* or the Odysseus of the *Odyssey*. He had no supreme talent for the color and variety of personality. His genius was not quite of that temper, and this is one of the main reasons why he is not to be ranked with Homer, Dante and Shakespeare. Having granted that, one has then to recognize that Virgil does turn Aeneas' greyness to artistic advantage in the *Aeneid*. For there is an artistic wisdom, as many great writers have discovered, in subordinating the dramatic interest of a protagonist to the interest of those lesser characters he meets and of those events through which he passes. Thus in the *Divine Comedy* the characters of Dante and Virgil acquire their dramatic life much more gradually and subtly than the vivid, spontaneous souls they encounter, and this graduation of revealed drama ultimately lends a firmer, deeper, soberer power to their respective lives within the poem. Thus Mann introduces the protagonist of *The Magic Mountain* by emphasizing his mediocrity, and we come to appreciate the intelligence of his choice of heroes as the macabre story develops. Thus Joyce dismayed Pound by displacing Stephen Dedalus from the center of his novel for a nonentity. Aeneas is not mediocre or simple, but there are places where he is flat, and needs to be flat, if Virgil's emphases are to fall as they should. The *Aeneid* does not hinge so much on personality as upon experience, events, and history. Aeneas' occasional flatness actually helps the reader to lose himself within the hero, to experience what the hero experiences; it is easier to imagine one's self into a neutral character than an eccentric one.

The poem is partly about the moral ambivalences which personality entails. The strongest, most vital personalities in the poem—Dido and Turnus—are defeated and humiliated, while Aeneas comes to succeed only as he gives up his selfhood. He has to surrender the pride and willfulness and energy which his two great victims refuse to surrender and so pay for with their lives. But Aeneas has to surrender still more than that; the deeper selfhood which situates one in a historical and social context, that which gives one a role and makes *pietas* possible. About this deeper kind of identity there are no ambivalences in Virgil's mind: it is the good that makes life possible. When Troy falls, Aeneas loses that identity, that situation in a context, and when he loses it, he tries to die. He is preserved to create another context, another social fabric elsewhere—which he individually is never to enjoy, having created it. He will scarcely have time to descend from his Mount Pisgah. That is his real loss. Troy falls to rise elsewhere, but in him, in his life, it remains fallen. That is why he is so weary, so reluctant, hesitant, and erring, why he lacks the marvelous, Homeric vital energy. He has no place.

It is touching to watch his attempts to reduplicate the fallen city—building his futile Aeneados and Pergamea, envying the miniature Troy of Helenus and the illusory Troy of Dido. Fortunately, perhaps, he does not learn the fullness of his loss all at once, as he gropes through this third book which is so moving and so underestimated. But when after the severest stroke—Anchises' death, Aeneas is swept off-course by the tempest, his *cri de coeur* vents the whole bitterness of his desolation. It is significantly his first speech in the poem, and one of the most brilliant of the Homeric adaptations.

> Triply lucky, all you men
> To whom death came before your fathers' eyes
> Below the wall at Troy! Bravest Danaan,
> Diomedes, why could I not go down
> When you had wounded me, and lose my life
> On Ilium's battlefield? Our Hector lies there,
> Torn by Achilles' weapon; there Sarpedon,
> Our giant fighter, lies; and there the river
> Simoïs washes down so many shields
> And helmets, with strong bodies taken under!
> (1.94–101)

The general sense of the first sentence recalls the words of Odysseus in another storm, but the most interesting phrase—*ante ora patrum*—is new. The nostalgia for Troy embraces a nostalgia for the heroic comradeship of Hector and Sarpedon, for such beloved landmarks as the Simois, but most of all for the city of fathers, the city of beloved customs and familial bonds, with a living history of generations and a past flowing into the present. In such a city it is easy to know one's role, and if one's role is to die, even that is relatively easy. One remembers the pathos of Sarpedon's death in the *Iliad*, "far from the land of his fathers"; Aeneas' pathos is to have no land and no father, nor the death which those twin losses bring him to desire.

The nostalgia Aeneas vents at our first sight of him is like a burden of which he has to free himself. He has to stop looking over his shoulder. He is still doing it as Book Five opens: holding his fleet for Italy but looking back at Carthage and the pyre of Dido:

> Aeneas held his ships firmly on course
> For a midsea crossing. But he kept his eyes

Upon the city far astern, now bright
With poor Elissa's pyre.

(5.1–4)

In the next book, at the Cumaean temple, he pauses to admire the reliefs
in which Daedalus has depicted the old stories of Crete, only to earn the
sybil's reprimand:

The hour demands
No lagging over sights like these.

(6.37)

Not *these* sights do the times demand, but rather such visions of the future
as Anchises himself will show his son at the end of the same book. From
that experience, Aeneas learns to put his burden down. He has borne it
heretofore as he once bore Anchises from the rubble of Troy. He has another
burden, the burden of the future, which he now more knowingly shoulders
in the latter half of the poem. It is all on the shield which his mother gives
him; as he takes it up, pleased though uncomprehending, he bears the glory
and destiny of his race.

taking up
Upon his shoulder all the destined acts
And fame of his descendants.

(8.731)

Aeneas' identity no longer derives from tradition—Yeats' "spreading
laurel tree"—but from the chilly glory of the nation he may not see. He
is no longer a son; he must remember he is a father, as Jupiter and Mercury
have urged ("Ascanium surgentem et spes heredis Iuli respice.") The beloved, defeated, human past is exchanged for the bright, metallic future.
By the close of the poem, Aeneas is becoming the faceless, official person
his new identity requires him to be, the complete and finished *imperium*.
His former personality is fast waning, and if in the final brutality, the knifing
of Turnus, he reveals a flash of his older impulsiveness, his personal loyalty
to Pallas and Evander, he also reveals—the impassivity of the public ex-
ecutioner. The marriage with Lavinia will be the one ritual of his life
conducted without feeling. If Aeneas' name is related to the Greek *aineo*
(as has been suggested), he becomes at last fully the character his name
suggests—"the consenting." Beneath his increasingly effectual activity lies
the passivity of acceptance.

No one could possibly be more sensitive to the cost of Aeneas'
sacrifice than the poet himself, who hated the violence he felt it necessary
to commemorate. It is worth repeating: "He always sees two sides of every-

thing." Just as he allows his hero no moment of indulgence without reproof, so he never allows himself the luxury of the ambivalent. Apparent loss always turns out to be real gain, but so apparent gain turns out—perhaps in spite of him—as profound loss. That is why this poem of celebration and hope reads so often like an elegy. The trees which Virgil praised and loved and imbued with sacred symbolism, the trees which, "rooted in one dear perpetual place," represented that living and growing stability he needed, these—the ashes, oaks, pines, and cedars of the poem—are repeatedly being felled for the pyres of soldiers. Nothing in the *Aeneid* is more elegiac than these litanies of falling timber: for Misenus—

> Into the virgin forest,
> Thicket of wild things, went the men, and down
> The pitch pines came, the bitten ilex rang
> With axe blows, ash and oak were split with wedges,
> Mighty rowans were trundled down the slopes.
> (6.179–82)

and later for the dead of the first battle in Italy:

> And so they made a twelve-day truce, while peace
> Should hold between them, Teucrians and Latins
> Mingling without harm as they traversed
> The wooded ridges. Lofty ash-trees rang
> With strokes of double-bladed axes, pines
> That towered starward toppled and came down,
> And men with wedges all day long
> Split oak and fragrant cedar logs, or hauled
> The trunks of mountain ash on groaning wains.
> (11.133–38)

When Troy falls like an ash tree in the great central simile of Book Two (2.624–31), the resonance of its crash never ceases to echo in heartbreaking rhythm. The perpetual elegiac note of the *Aeneid* never turns to tragic, because tragedy involves the confrontation of loss and he purgation that follows acceptance. Virgil wants always to exalt the loss even as he winces at it. He denied himself even the luxury of tragedy. . . .

Few poets have asked so much of their heroes. Of all the celestial descents in the classical epic, none symbolizes so strong a pressure on the human will as Mercury's descent to Aeneas at Carthage. In the *Iliad* the celestial messengers commonly intervene to prompt or suggest, and seldom represent a categorical imperative. Priam can debate with Hekabe whether to follow Iris' admonition; Hermes as a guide is gentleness itself. His descent in the *Odyssey* simply removes an obstacle from the path of the free human will. Apollonius' Eros descends to inflame, actually to weaken the will. But Virgil's Mercury asks that the self be made an *imperium*. Mortality, the great Enemy of the *Iliad*, is very little at issue here, and time is no longer enemy at all, but friend. The true enemy is the unguided human spirit, and the deepest awe is for *its* overcoming.

The corpus of Virgil's poetry possesses a unity which few poets' work attains. In a sense the *Aeneid* requires the *Eclogues* and even more the *Georgics* because it presupposes a quiet reverence for Roman life that modern readers lack. It only gives us glimpses of the felicity which justifies Aeneas' effort. Virgil seems to have taken for granted that his audience would respond to the names of Roman families and ceremonies and places. He assumes that we too love the rivers and trees and farms of Italy, whose serenity justifies centuries of violence. If one does not share that love, even in one's imagination, then one ought to read the earlier poems before returning to the epic. The piety toward family and community, whose *exemplum* is Aeneas, is complemented in the *Georgics* by the pious but pragmatic and unsentimental bond to the soil. One returns to the *Aeneid* grateful for the simpler, sturdier, more cheerful poet, enlivened by a kindliness that tempers duty. That poet has not vanished from his greatest work, but one could wish its bleak nobility to be graced by a mellower, unpremeditated joy. For without that, all empire is as sounding brass.

KENNETH QUINN

Did Virgil Fail?

My starting point is familiar ground:
a review of the evidence for supposing that Virgil thought his epic a failure.
It constitutes, I shall argue, a *prima facie* case, entitling us to proceed. The
next step is to see whether we can plausibly conjecture what reasons Virgil
had for believing he had failed. The next, to consider how far we should
accept his reasons as valid criticism of the poem.

No reader, I hope, will anticipate that he is going to be asked to
write the *Aeneid* off as simply a failure. It is my opinion that the *Aeneid*
is, beyond argument and beyond mistake, a very great poem. But that
opinion is not incompatible with a growing awareness of serious flaws in
the poem's structure. If he senses such flaws, the critic's duty, surely, is to
draw attention to them. I think there *are* major structural defects. I shall
suggest they are the result—not of bad craftsmanship, or incompetence—
but of successive, fundamental changes in design. My thesis is that these
changes created problems which Virgil found it increasingly difficult—and
perhaps in the end impossible—to overcome: the more he revised his plan,
the more success eluded him.

The prima facie case

The evidence for what Virgil thought about his poem rests on two main
sources. There is his own statement that "he thought he must have been
just about mad to attempt the task"; and there is a tradition at least as old

From *Cicero and Virgil: Studies in Honor of Harold Hunt,* edited by John R. C. Montagu.
Copyright © 1972 by A. M. Hakkert, Amsterdam. Translations by Robert Fitzgerald from
the *Aeneid,* New York: Random House, 1983.

as the middle of the first century A.D. according to which it was Virgil's dying wish that his epic should not be published, and that the manuscript should be destroyed.

The first is the better attested. Our authority is Macrobius, who claims he is quoting an actual letter from Virgil to Augustus. As evidence it does not amount to much. The letter was written, it seems, when Virgil had been working at his poem for five or six years, and was to continue working for five or six more before death intervened. It is very much the sort of letter a conscientious poet, feeling his poem far from complete, might write to an emperor who was plainly eager to assume the twin role of patron and hero of a national epic.

The tradition that Virgil on his deathbed asked that his poem should be burnt deserves to be taken more seriously. That was five to six years later, when the poem, according to Donatus, lacked only the finishing touches. The story that the manuscript was preserved from the flames by the personal intervention of the emperor is mentioned by several writers. In modern time it has captured the imagination of the Austrian novelist Hermann Broch, who reconstructed the last eighteen hours of Virgil's life in great detail in his *Der Tod des Vergil*.

Such is the *prima facie* case. At the least, it provides grounds for believing that Virgil considered his epic unfit to be published. The poem was published, however, more or less, it seems, as Virgil had left it. There is some justification, therefore, for looking for things wrong with it; some major weakness, or major weaknesses, in the poem's structure. If Virgil thought this poem simply bad, then he was mistaken: great artists are not always good judges of their own work—their standards are too high. But if he thought that his poem, though good, had something, or some things, seriously wrong with it, or fell seriously short of what he had hoped to accomplish, that is a different matter.

Suppose we set alongside the tradition about Virgil's deathbed wishes the statement a little earlier in Donatus that Virgil planned, when he set out for Greece on that last journey, to spend three years more exclusively on getting his poem the way he wanted it. The poem as we have it looks virtually complete. The famous 60-odd half-lines apart, it is not obvious where extensive revision was called for. We can imagine that Virgil was a perfectionist. But he was also, we gather, a steady, methodical worker. Twelve books in ten or eleven years is not fast, but it is not the performance of a dilettante; three whole years wholly devoted to revision ("triennioque continuo nihil amplius quam emendare") looks like an evasion—as if Virgil (always supposing he is correctly reported) were being not wholly honest, perhaps with himself.

A failure as poetry?

But if there is a *prima facie* case for supposing Virgil too dissatisfied with his poem to feel it was worth preserving, there is no evidence why he was dissatisfied. Hermann Broch has built his intuitive reconstruction around the concluding words of Virgil's letter to Augustus, but that is hardly criticism. There is of course a minority among modern critics who have not been exactly slow to find evidence of all manner of failure in Virgil's poem. Mr. Robert Graves's picture of Virgil, the incompetent, servile botcher, is hard to reconcile with Hermann Broch's sensitive artist dedicated to an ideal so unattainable that the mere pursuit of it was "a blasphemous presumption." But on the whole the *Aeneid*, as poetry, has stood the test of time. Only Virgil's bitterest detractors wish to dismiss the poem as poetry. Among the rest there is general agreement that Virgil managed to solve the problem of how to write a poem in the epic tradition at a point in time where that tradition seemed worn out, devoid of interest for an original, creative poetic artist. In the main, the only serious reservations about the poetry of the *Aeneid* are those made by critics who have misunderstood Virgil's use of Homer; or who have been ill-equipped to understand a poem that is in one respect a sustained exercise in the poetry of allusion, in another what I have called the exploitation of form, or who expect what no poet feels obliged to provide—full, plain, explicit statement of his meaning, exact agreement between what is said in one place and what is said in another.

A failure as a poem?

But though most modern critics would agree, many enthusiastically, that Virgil deserves the highest praise as a poetic artist, they are less willing to allow that the *Aeneid* succeeds as a poem. Those who express the strongest misgivings include many of the *Aeneid*'s warmest admirers—as poetry. They find evidence—not of incompetence, and not usually of anything that could be labelled simply as failure—but of an unresolved and possibly irresolvable conflict within the poem or perhaps within the poet himself.

The theory that something went wrong which the poet could not put right seems to have originated among Romantic critics, disposed to believe in an unconscious Virgil working against (and superior to) the conscious Virgil. It went off at an interesting tangent some thirty-five years ago, as a result of a provocative article by Francesco Sforza, from which Virgilian criticism has never fully recovered. Sforza argued that Virgil was emotionally committed to the opposition to Augustus, and either sabotaged his own poem or made it a kind of concealed accusation of Augustus. He argued his case forcefully, but the case is one that can really only be made by heavy-handed misconstructions of the ambiguities and implications characteristic of any sensitive poetic structure. Many would still agree, however, with Professor Maguinness that "the problem raised by Sforza is not by any means an unreal one, though his own solution is so paradoxical as to be most improbable *a priori.*" Few take seriously Sforza's political explanation of failure. But by pointing to the apparent discrepancy between the poem's ostensible aim and our instinctive reaction to much that seems implicit in the narrative, Sforza strengthened the old sentimental, Romantic view that the poem went wrong because of Virgil's instinctive sympathy for the losing side. It is a view which, in varying forms, has recently acquired fresh currency and it deserves consideration.

Suppose we start with *Aeneid* 2. The Book succeeds admirably as an exciting narrative of how Troy fell; it is a wonderful demonstration of the sureness of Virgil's dramatic instinct, and of that urgent sense of economy which enables him to tell a story quickly and in a way that stresses the pity and the horror of human suffering. At the same time the Book seems to me to succeed on two other levels: as an assertion, all the more convincing because it is discreet, of Rome's historical destiny; and as a study in the futility of what I have called the Heroic Impulse—the urge to meet every crisis with an act of unreckoning physical courage.

It is this third level which makes even those most enthusiastic about the poetry of the *Aeneid* uneasy about the *Aeneid* as a poem. They have nothing but praise for the clarity of Virgil's insight, the courage with which he exposes the shallowness of the heroic ideal; for them, it is one further sign of Virgil's civilized maturity. But this quality of Virgil's poetic sensibility seems to them destructive, or at best deeply hostile, to what they take to be the poem's ideals.

These are the critics who approach the *Aeneid* willing, or at any rate prepared, to admire its hero (they may have little taste for heroic poetry as such, but they can't help liking Virgil, any more than they can help liking the poetry of the *Iliad*)—and are surprised to find Aeneas so unadmirable a hero. In Book 2 he seems to them to lack common sense; in Book 4 common decency. And when in the final scene in the poem Aeneas strikes down in a sudden, blazing fit of anger the defeated opponent who kneels before him, they find it disturbingly hard to reject Professor Putnam's view that "it is Aeneas who loses at the end of Book XII, leaving Turnus victorious in his tragedy", Turnus in Book 12 seems to fulfil so completely the prescription for the tragic hero, Aeneas so incompletely. It seems to them that something *must* have gone wrong. Just as they feel that something must have gone wrong when they want to pity Dido in Book 4, and to despise the lover who deserts her with so little show of affection, or even understanding. They feel their sympathy well up for Camilla, for Pallas, for Lausus, even for Mezentius, hardly less than for Turnus and for Dido: why not for Aeneas?

Personally I feel such readers expect too much of the poem, both as a heroic epic and as a defence, by implication, of Augustus. They are apt to assume that anything in the poem which does not imply unmixed approval for Aeneas' actions must be a sign that something has gone wrong—not a sign that Virgil wished to be honest and was willing to imply an honest man's reservations about particular actions, or reasons for actions, of a side he believed, for all that, to be in the right. Where Sforza saw sabotage and Maguinness and others have seen involuntary sympathy for the underdog, I suggest we should see a planned component of the poem, an unfaltering integrity in the poet.

Virgil's reaction to the brutality of war and to the heroic code was no doubt the hypersensitive reaction of a man who had lived through and detested war; who had seen the cruel harm done on countless occasions by men believing they were dying nobly when they were throwing their lives away to no purpose. But this hypersensitivity does not mean we should condemn his imaginative realization of war's brutality. Though himself no soldier, though hardly cut out for hero-worship, he could not help knowing what war was like and how heroes behaved: it was part of the common experience of his time. At most we might make the kind of reservations we make about D. H. Lawrence's reactions to industrial ugliness. The fact that Lawrence was clearly the sort of man to feel this revulsion in an extreme degree does not invalidate the revulsion. It is part of the artist's job to react, to the edge of morbidity, to things to which our reaction is blunted by common sense. This quality of Virgil's poem helps to make it so wholly adequate a reaction to the feelings about war latent in the society in which he lived, instead of an épopée de cabinet.

I cannot agree, therefore, with those who assert that Virgil's sympathy for Turnus or for Dido shows that something has gone wrong, or even that Virgil treads an uneasily faltering path between conflicting sympathies. I have argued the case of Dido elsewhere. The case of Turnus is perhaps less straightforward, but when Professor Putnam claims that the poem ends with Turnus, not Aeneas, as its hero, I feel this is misreading by simplification both Virgil's intentions and Virgil's text. There were doubtless those at the time who admired Antony in the hour of death, just as there were those doubtless who admired Cleopatra. Admiration blunts judgment no less than common sense. Transcending both is the poet's capacity for intuitive identification and sympathy. Virgil extends sympathy to Turnus and to Dido—his Antony and his Cleopatra: sympathy, but not admiration. . . .

Structural conflict

To write a successful poem to so complex a formula is not an easy matter. The mature conception of his theme which we have postulated can hardly have come to Virgil early, all in one piece, before he set out to write his poem. More likely it took shape as he wrote, forcing on Virgil a constant reassessment of his task.

It seems to me at least not improbable that the *Aeneid* started as a more or less conventional historical epic (conventional in the attitudes expressed and implied, as well as in theme), and then became, by a process of constant revision, the vehicle of a complex, mature attitude such as that we have described. I think it not impossible that Virgil began to feel, during this process of revision, that he had gone too far, and changed his poem once again—and kept on changing it, till he despaired of getting it right. It must have been clear to him, it may even have been made clear by others, that the degree of honesty he aimed at, while it might satisfy his conscience and spell success for his poem with a more reflecting audience, made it unacceptable to others—above all, perhaps, to Augustus himself. Did he then, impelled by prudence, by plain hints from above, by a desire to write a poem that *would* be understood, break the new harmony of his artistic structure? Did misgivings, then, about what he had done, shame at the harm he had done his poetic structure, the sacrifice of integrity involved, the sensed need to make even greater concessions to propaganda, despair of getting Augustus to accept a truthful poem—did all or any of these leave Virgil unwilling to bring his poem to completion or see it published?

Now if there is anything in this theory at all, some of Virgil's reasons for feeling he had failed, though they properly concerned him, concern us, as critics or readers of his poem, less. The problem of a poem already too honest in its portrayal of what happens to men's motives and character and to the ideals of a leader in war, is of this order. The fact that some reviewers of my *Critical Description* have felt that I was interpreting the *Aeneid* as an antimilitaristic poem, or even a poem surreptitiously attacking Augustus, suggests that Augustus too could have felt that Virgil conceded too much, or even have mistaken honest defence (one that attempted to deal with the problems of leadership in war) for attack. Augustus' reactions to the portions of the poem which were read to him may have left Virgil feeling that he had gone too far for Augustus—and not far enough for his own conscience.

However, such speculations are only marginally our concern. They deal with aspects of the poem that may have left Virgil feeling he had failed—his intentions were not understood by those he felt he was defending. To us this is more like success than failure. Our concern is not with politics, but with the things Virgil did not get right in his poem, or the harm he did the poem by revision. His sense of despair may well have been sharpened by the feeling that what he had written puzzled and disappointed those he hoped would understand. But was it prompted also by a feeling that he had written a poem that, even properly understood, was somehow all wrong?

I think we can point to serious faults, ways in which the structure was put off balance, perhaps, and never recovered. As one gets to know the poem, one is troubled by two things: the first is a shift of attitude towards the war of Books 7–12; the second is a shift of attitude towards the poem's hero. It becomes hard to shake off the feeling that these are major structural uncertainties; they involve each of the basic themes of the poem, the arma and the vir; they seriously compromise the poem's integrity.

Two views of the war

The clash is plain if we set Jove's words in the Council of War in Book 10 alongside his words to Venus in Book 1. Jove's speech to the gods in council compares unfavourably as poetry with his prophecy of Rome's future to Venus. But worse than that is that in Book 10 Jove claims that he forbade the war which in Book 1 he foretold to Venus as part of fate's plan for her son. How can he argue now that the time will come when Rome will fight a just war against Carthage, (10. 11 *adueniet iustum pugnae tempus*), that then hatred and rapine will be legitimate (14 *tum certare odiis, tum res rapuisse licebit*), whereas the war now being waged is a war that should never have happened?

I suspect that the two passages represent separate stages in the composition of the poem, and reflect different versions of the plan to which Virgil worked. Book 10 is based, I suggest, on the hypothesis of a "wrong" war, forbidden by Jove, between the Aeneadae and the Italians; Book 1 is based on the hypothesis of a war which was part of fate's plan. The two hypotheses are not exactly incompatible. Jove can know that his prohibition is fated to be disregarded, and plan accordingly. But there is no hint of this in the poem, no sign that the conflicting hypotheses have been reconciled within the poetic structure. It can hardly have escaped Virgil's notice that this was necessary, but it has not been done.

Set alongside Jove's words in Book 10 Virgil's description of the gathering forces of war in Book 7 (582–4):

> They came in from everywhere with cries for Mars.
> Nothing would do but that, against the omens,
> Against the oracles, by a power malign
> They pled for frightful war.

These two passages seem to me left over from an earlier poem, which perhaps comprised only 7–12. In the poem as we have it, the war which is part of fate's plan predominates. Alongside Jove's prophecy to Venus in Book 1 we can set what the Sibyl tells Aeneas in Book 6 (84–97): there the war is already something that can be foretold in detail. Aeneas replies (6. 103–5):

> No novel kinds of hardship, no surprises,
> Loom ahead, Sister. I foresaw them all,
> Went through them in my mind.

He means, probably, that he has been told by Helenus what is to come, though actually Helenus says he will leave detailed explanation to the Sibyl (3. 458–60):

> She will inform you of the Italian tribes,
> The wars to come, the way you should avoid
> Each difficulty, or face it.

Anchises' briefing of Aeneas is merely mentioned in passing (6. 890–2). But it is clear by the time of Aeneas' meeting with Evander in Book 8, when the thunder crashes out and the arms of Vulcan flash in the sky, that Aeneas knows what lies ahead, though he tells Evander that it is his mother, not his father, who has told him (8. 530–40):

>   The others
> Sat still, mystified, but Troy's great captain
> Recognized the sound, and knew the promise
> Made by his goddess mother. Then he said:
> "My friend, you need not, truly need not ask
> What new event's portended. I am the man
> Whom heaven calls. This sign my goddess mother
> Prophesied she would send if war broke out,
> And said, too, she would bring out of the sky
> Arms made by Vulcan to assist me. Ai!
> What carnage is at hand for poor Laurentines.

> What retribution you will make to me,
> Turnus. Many a shield, many a helm,
> And many brave men's bodies you'll take under,
> Father Tiber. Let them insist on war,
> Let them break treaties!"

The fated, inevitable war preponderates in short. It is of course a necessary hypothesis for the poem as we have it: the concept of Aeneas the man with a mission, the whole concept of Rome's mission as set out by Anchises in Book 6, and by Vulcan on the shield of Aeneas in Book 8, depend on a fated war. And a fated war obviously provides a much more humane symbol for the civil war which ended with Actium.

It suggested perhaps a further step away from Virgil's original plan. The symbol becomes even more humane, if we make the fated war between Aeneas and Turnus, not a war between right and wrong, but a war between two fallible human beings, with both of whom we can sympathize, but who are allotted contrary destinies. Turnus is then the man whose character and motives we can admire, though he is committed to a course of action which is contrary to fate's plan and must therefore fail (and which we can see must rightly fail, because it places force and impulse before reason and compassion, because it represents *discordia*). While Aeneas, to put the matter bluntly, is now the man who must often be seen to do the right thing for the wrong reason.

Two views of Aeneas

This broader view of Aeneas and the concept of fate's plan as complex and extending far through time accounts for the first half of the poem—which came second, I suspect, in the poem's genesis; and coming later (and perhaps interesting Virgil more), it tended perhaps to outweigh 7–12 as poetry, despite Virgil's claim, *maius opus moueo* (7.44). In 1–6 Aeneas becomes a kind of Stoic hero, as has often been pointed out, destined to undergo a series of moral *labores*—a sort of moral Hercules. But here we begin to notice signs of a second structural uncertainty. Perhaps if Virgil had kept to his original plan, he might have made Aeneas the conventional epic hero, the conventional symbol of an idealized Augustus. But as he elaborated his symbol of a more rounded Augustus—not the victor in a war in which both sides shared the guilt, but the humanely fallible champion of the cause that represented the working out of Rome's destiny—he took fright, perhaps, at his own temerity in abandoning panegyric for honest justification. To avoid a poem that looked too much like a *roman à cléf*, did he then make his hero a composite symbol—sometimes Augustus, sometimes Julius Caesar? Book 4, for example, fits Julius well, but does not fit Augustus at all: Dido is of course both Virgil's Calypso and Virgil's Alcinoos, but it is obvious that she is Cleopatra, too. Then there is Ascanius. He is not Virgil's invention of course—he is in Livy, too, for example. But the use Virgil makes of him seems confusing. The charming youngster of Books 4, 5 and 7 is hard to reconcile with the child of Book 1 and the youthful commander of Book 9. It almost looks as if he is being prepared for the role of the young Octavian, without ever quite assuming the part, even when his father says to him in Book 12 (434–5):

> Learn fortitude and toil from me, my son,
> Ache of true toil. Good fortune learn from others.

More puzzling is the discrepancy between the version of the line of descent from Aeneas given by Jove to Venus in Book 1 and echoed at 8. 47–8, and that given to Aeneas by his father in Book 6 (760–80). One would have supposed that such things would all have been worked out in Virgil's original plan—the prose draft that we are told about so specifically. These are more like the inconsistencies of a poet who has no plan, or who drastically revises his plan after his poem has taken shape.

Let me tie together this very tentative analysis of what may have gone wrong with an outstandingly good and mature and difficult poem.

It seems to me at least worth considering seriously whether Virgil perhaps started with what became Books 7–12, a poem about a wrong war and a typical epic hero, with Augustus cast in the role of that hero. The impossibility of an honest poem on such lines sent Virgil, I suggest, in a fresh direction. The first shift was perhaps to a poem about Aeneas, the ancestor and the symbol of Augustus: a conventional epic hero, the victor in a war which the other side should never have started; the speech of Jove in Book 10 looks like a survival from this stage. But this first shift was followed by, practically entailed, an epic on a grander scale, in which the war is part of fate's plan—the first step toward the grandeur that was to be Rome.

As he worked at this new poem, can we not imagine that Virgil became interested in a more maturely conceived hero, struggling to rise to the level of the task thrust upon him against his will, to act as an enlightened, humane, civilized human being; but also falling short under stress of this ideal, and then (because he is the instrument of fate's purpose) doing sometimes the right thing for the wrong reason, or for motives that leave him and us uneasy? Understandably Virgil will now be drawn to match against his more mature hero a more mature opponent. Then another change of plan. To Virgil's *Iliad* is added Virgil's *Odyssey*, the story of the moral *labores* of Aeneas.

But this humane Aeneas, though he added enormously to the stature of the poem, added greatly also to Virgil's problems. He forced into an epic poem concepts for which the epic tradition was ill prepared. Once we are invited to look at the hero in this new light, as a person with claims upon our moral sense, it is difficult not to extend this attitude to the poem generally. Dido can stand it, so can Turnus. But the epic narrative is hardly on the same plane. How can fate be on the side of the foreign invader in a war of conquest? The invader is a refugee returning to his ancestral home; he is the instrument of fate; the Italians act unreasonably; it is better for Italy if the two cultures are blended. All this is true, but in a way it only makes things worse: the more Virgil appeals to our moral sense, the more that sense is outraged by a story whose fundamental data are so out of keeping with the use Virgil seeks to make of it.

It is not necessary to suppose that my reconstruction of how the *Aeneid* came to reach the form in which it has come down to us represents more than a rough approximation to the truth. We need only allow that something like this occurred. We can then imagine that Virgil felt, each time he recast his poem, that he had both made it a better poem (more the expression of a mature, civilized sensibility) and a poem which it was more impossible than before ever to get right.

ADAM PARRY

The Idea of Art in Virgil's "Georgics"

Edmund Wilson says, a little clumsily but suggestively, in *Axel's Castle*: "How can the *Georgics*, the *Ars Poetica*, and Manilius be dealt with from the point of view of the capacity of their material for being expanded into 'pure vision'?"

Wilson singled out T. S. Eliot's phrase "expansion into pure vision" for attack. Eliot meant that poetry should present the sort of unencumbered aesthetic experience that we find in music. If a poem seemed to urge a particular set of values, or way of life, or philosophy, it was merely presenting that prosaic material as an "object of contemplation." But the philosophy or doctrine itself must be "capable of expansion into pure vision." Lucretius falls down, Eliot suggested, because his Epicureanism was too poor in feeling ever to become "pure vision."

To this Wilson made the common reader's objection that great poetry often does in fact attempt to persuade us of something; we cannot really separate the philosophy from the poetry; or assess the degree to which a given philosophy can be "expanded into pure vision." The three Latin works he cited seemed to him to clinch his case. His question was rhetorical, and the implied answer was "no way."

Wilson therefore applied to the *Georgics* a simple historical relativism. The modern reader finds the agriculture puzzling and tiresome; the Roman reader must have liked it. But if we keep the notion of "vision" while enlarging it to mean more than a purely aesthetic experience, we

From *Arethusa* 1, vol. 5 (1972). Copyright © 1972 by *Arethusa*.

may find that Eliot was after all closer to the truth. By this I mean some picture of life, some dramatized attitude, that may work through such vehicles as agriculture, prescriptions for good writing or astronomy, but finally rises above the details to be valid for all activities and for men of all periods of history. Such a vision would be a product of all the disparate parts of complex literary works; it would at the same time shed light on and explain the literary work as a whole. It has seemed to me that the Virgilian vision in the *Georgics* was finally one of the function and value of human art. And this paper is an attempt to define the idea of art in the *Georgics*.

Of the three works acknowledged as authentic of the greatest of the Roman poets, the *Georgics* may well contain the finest expression of Virgil's poetic art. At the same time, they are, and are likely to remain, the least popular and the least accessible. The pastoral poems, or the *Eclogues*, have the advantages of simplicity and brevity. The *Aeneid* too, the most sweeping and powerful of Virgil's poems, is simpler in expression, possibly even simpler in thought, than the *Georgics*. That the *Aeneid* is heroic narrative, telling a continuous story, in a manner deriving directly from the most perspicuous and accessible of all poets of the Western tradition, Homer, and a narrative moreover centrally concerned with the Roman historical experience, ensures it a popularity which the more difficult and didactic poetry of the *Georgics* will certainly never attain. The *Aeneid* is perhaps not a less subtle and complex poem than the *Georgics*. Its strange amalgam of triumph and sadness, of confidence and nostalgia, of the martial tones of Roman and Augustan achievement, and of the poignant notes of personal loss and renunciation, has hardly been fathomed by ancient or modern criticism. But the *Aeneid,* like the *Eclogues* in a very different way, can be read and enjoyed in a simple fashion. It tells a story, a compelling story, a story of travel and experience, of sacrifice and victory. The poems can be read for that story, and what most of us would regard as its deeper meanings, its characteristic mode of taking back what it gives, of mixing personal regret with Roman hope, can, without a positive distortion of perspective, be left to be apprehended by the reader, as, shall we say, overtones and undertones, further vistas to be felt almost subliminally, not requiring, in order for us to reach any adequate understanding of the poem, to be fully analyzed and raised to the level of conscious and explicit critical exposition.

Not so the *Georgics*. Portions of that work, many of the individual descriptions of natural phenomena, or the constantly recurring digressions mythological and otherwise, such as the one on the Roman Civil Wars at the end of book 1, or the praise of the farmer's life at the end of book 2, even the baroque invocations to the gods, to Augustus, and to Maecenas at the beginning of books 1 and 3, can be appreciated in a simple way for and of themselves, particularly since in these and other passages the sheer art of words reaches a height and a degree of finish greater than anything else in Virgil. As a collection of pieces worthy of inclusion in anthologies, the *Georgics* offers no difficulty. It is the total thrust and meaning of the work, the way in which all the many descriptions and short narratives, natural, mythological, historical and philosophical, the expressions of different attitudes, sometimes in apparent contradiction to each other, are orchestrated into a complex but unified vision of the world, which is hard for us to grasp. The *Georgics* is ultimately about the life of man in this world, about a kind of art in living which can confront the absurdity and cruelty of both nature and civilization, and yet render our existence satisfactory and beautiful. All its rich and diverse ingredients are expressed and arranged to conduce to this vision, a vision less cosmic and explicitly philosophical, but finally as comprehensive and purposeful as that of the poem which may, more than any other, have been Virgil's model, the *De Rerum Natura* of Lucretius.

Virgil's three works are each ostensibly modeled on one of the classical (to Virgil and his audience) works of Greek poetry, the *Eclogues* on the bucolic poems of Theocritus, the *Georgics* on the *Works and Days* of Hesiod, and the *Aeneid* on the Homeric epics. As the *Georgics* is in itself the least accessible of Virgil's works, so the *Works and Days* is the least accessible of his three models—or at least if Theocritus seems harder than Hesiod, the greater difficulty is mostly due to the former poet's use of dialect. It is not merely that the Hesiodic poem and its Virgilian descendant belong to a genre of literature which seems strange to the modern world: the didactic poem. It is also the didactic content itself. The pastoral vision of nature has still its living manifestations: the willed simplicity and the waving fields of grain in *Bonnie and Clyde* may have more of a connection with Theocritean and Virgilean pastoral vision than at first sight occurs to us. But a long poem—four books of between 500 and 600 lines each—in an intricate language dealing with the details of agricultural practice in 35 B.C.: that is something far enough from us to give us pause, and to incline us, following the lead of so many classicists, to talk about the consummate art of Virgil's *Georgics* when the occasion arises, but to confine our reading and effort to understand to a few splendid anthology plums. The agricultural mode does not seem to us a natural expression of poetry. To show that the idea is not wholly alien, I suppose one could cite something like Knut

Hamsun's *The Growth of the Soil*, a work which does not spare the laborious details of the farmer's life, and yet—like Virgil—contains a vision which goes beyond the mere assertion of the superiority of the life attached to the living earth and far from the corruptions of metropolitan, or even smalltown, civilization.

I cite the difficulty and the remoteness of subject of the *Georgics* primarily to explain why one of the finest poems of all antiquity is one of the least known; and further to indicate how much worth study it is: the deepest beauties of the poem are a little like the value of the natural existence itself, as Virgil defines it: man's livelihood is hidden in the earth by the harsh but wise counsel of Jupiter . . . to be gained therefrom by labour and assiduous art.

One feature of both the excellence and the complexity of the *Georgics* it shares with the other great didactic Latin poem, that of Lucretius. What we may, for lack of a better term, call the *philosophical* aspect of the poem, the network of ideas and attitudes which makes up its essential vision, is not separable from the detailed description of natural phenomena or from the specific instructions offered to the hypothetical tiller of the soil to whom the poem is addressed. The characteristic Virgilian attitudes toward labour and joy, toward all the conditions of existence, in fact, pervade the poetry; and many of the most beautiful passages are also the most didactic. Book 1. 160–7 may illustrate this double aspect of the poem:

> Dicendum et quae sint duris agrestibus arma,
> quis sine nec potuere seri nec surgere messes:
> vomis et inflexi primum grave robur aratri,
> tardaque Eleusinae matris volventia plaustra,
> tribulaque traheaeque et iniquo pondere rastri;
> virgea praeterea Celei vilisque supellex,
> arbuteae crates et mystica vannus Iacchi.
> omnia quae multo ante memor privisa repones,
> si te digna manet divini gloria ruris.

This passage comes shortly after an important section, to which I shall refer later, in which the poet urges the necessity of constant, intelligent labour in extracting life from the soil. The next step, and here Virgil follows Hesiod fairly closely, is to say something of the tools which make this labour possible. The corresponding passage in the Greek poet is, at least in part, simply practical: Hesiod there tells us what tools we need and actually how to make them. But Virgil talks of tools to illustrate his point: they represent the element of *art*, an element largely absent from the Hesiodic original.

> Now I must tell you what arms are possessed by the tough farmer, without which the crops cannot be sown, and cannot grow: the ploughshare first,

and the heavy tree of unbending plough; the slow rolling waggon of the Eleusinian mother; sledges, harrows, and the unbalanced weight of the hoe; the humble wattle-work equipment of Celeus as well; wooden hurdles, and the mystic winnowing-fan of Iacchus. All these things you will take thought to lay up beforehand, if the godlike glory of the fields is to be yours, and you worthy of it.

The tone of this short paragraph is firmly didactic: the gerundive *dicendum* and the second person future *repones* for the imperative at the end of 167 catch the business-like and peremptory note of the true agricultural treatise. Note also the expressiveness of 164: the alliteration and the double *-que* construction give the sense of a Greek catalogue, and of the specialization of the farmer's tools: the heavy last part of that line is more than a conventional or ornamental circumlocution; the hoe or mattock is unusually and harshly heavy; it is also unbalanced, with the weight in the head.

The farmer's equipment thus set out in detail is modest: the ["humble equipment"] carries an implicit contrast to the expensive furniture of the town-dweller. At the same time these things are *arms*: the farmer has the manly virtues of the soldier, and like his plough, he must be hard: *duris agrestibus arma*. But these arms, the emblems of his austere and honest life, all have divine connections: Demeter had the first waggon; and such a waggon is used in her rites at the Eleusinian mysteries; Celeus, father of Triptolemus, was taught by her, and taught the rest of mankind how to till the fields; the winnowing-fan is simple and practical, but it is also prominent in the mysteries of Bacchus: the phrase anticipates the celebration of the magic of the vine in book 2. The penultimate line, though maintaining the stern instructive tone, has the alliteration and assonance which accounts for so much of the amazing music of Virgilian poetry. Then the last line gives, so to speak, the reward of all the labour implied by the preceding. It reveals the vista of godlike splendour and satisfaction that makes the drudgery worth it. The release and assertion of this line surprises, but is made to follow naturally from the enumeration of the farmer's means, and that is one of the principal points of the poem.

Another passage: this time from book 3, the book devoted to livestock (49–71):

Seu quis Olympiacae miratus praemia palmae
pascit equos, seu quis fortis ad aratra iuvencos,
corpora praecipue matrum legat. optima torvae
forma bovis cui turpe caput, cui plurima cervix,
et crurum tenus a mento palearia pendent;
tum longo nullus lateri modus: omnia magna,

pes etiam; et camuris hirtae sub cornibus aures.
nec mihi displiceat maculis insignis et albo,
aut iuga detrectans interdumque aspera cornu
et faciem tauro propior, quaeque ardua tota
et gradiens ima verrit vestigia cauda.
aetas Lucinam iustosque pati hymenaeos
desinit ante decem, post quattuor incipit annos;
cetera nec feturae habilis nec fortis aratris.
interea, superat gregibus dum laeta iuventas,
solve mares; mitte in Venerem pecuaria primus,
atque aliam ex alia generando suffice prolem.
optima quaeque dies miseris mortalibus aevi
prima fugit: subeunt morbi tristisque senectus
et labor, et durae rapit inclementia mortis.
semper erunt quarum mutari corpora malis:
semper enim refice ac, ne post amissa requiras,
ante veni et subolem armento sortire quotannis.

Whether a man raises horses out of admiration for the Olympian victor's palm, or whether he raises stout bullocks for the plough—let him select above all the bodies of the mothers. The best shape of a cow is fierce, an ugly head, an oversize neck; and all the way down from her chin to her lower legs hang her dewlaps; long flanks, the longer the better; everything big, even the hoof. And beneath her twisted horns, shaggy ears. No objection to one with white spots, or one that resists the yoke, or now and then threatens with her horns, and looks more like a bull than a cow, and standing high all along her length, sweeps as she walks her hoofprints with the end of her tail.

The age of the goddess of childbirth, and of lawful union, is over at ten years, and begins after four. Outside these limits, she is neither capable of reproducing, nor strong enough for the plough. Meanwhile, then, while their rich prime of life still lasts, let loose the males; be the first to give over your cattle to Venus, and by generation replenish the stock of the young. The best days for unhappy mortal beings are the first to flee away; then come sickness, and unhappy age, labour and trouble; and the unpitying hardness of death takes all away. There will always be some whose shape you want to change; keep replacing them; don't wait till the stock is gone and you miss them; be beforehand, and choose each year the young to breed for the continuation of the herd.

The picture of the ideal cow here is particularly fine. The sharp edge of Virgil's observation expresses a connoisseur's professional delight in the best product of its kind. The massive ugliness of the beast—*turpe caput—plurima cervix—nullus lateri modus*—defies the simple-minded aesthetics of the inexperienced and suggests a new and more functional beauty.

The single points are made with almost staccato accuracy, but with no less expressiveness for that: note how after the first three brief features, the fourth, describing the extravagant length of the animal's dewlaps neatly fills a whole line (53); and how another whole line, of more formal and heroic structure, appears at the end of the description (59), as if, like a judge, Virgil has looked over the animal and now lets it grandly walk off.

No Latin poetry is more inventively and variously expressive of external phenomena than the Georgics; but what I want to bring out in this didactic passage is the *suite* of thought: "For both horses and cows, breeding is important. Breeding depends especially on the physical characterstics of the mother; e.g., here is the best kind of cow. There is also a right age for breeding; it is soon over. So take advantage of that short period, and keep up the numbers and the standard of the breed." That is the bare argument of the passage as a whole, but Virgil's feeling for animal life, and its relation to human life, leads him to introduce an entirely different, and tragic, note. The phrase *laeta iuventas* in 63 appears conventional, a formulary phrase, when we first come to it, but it and the mention of Venus, the divine source of love and generation, again a convention that becomes more than that, leads to lines of sudden poignancy 66–68, lines which, as readers of Boswell remember, Dr. Johnson said were the saddest of all ancient poetry. The limits of the proper age for breeding, a practical matter of husbandry, is transformed by Virgil's quick thought into a melancholy reflexion on the transience of happiness and life itself. But this again is no mere ornament or indulgence; the clear thought that underlies the transformation is the characteristic contrast between the evanescence of the individual and the continuation of the race. Though contrasted, there is an indissoluble connection: if the race, the process of life, is to continue, the individual must be selected, and the brief moment allotted must be seized and exploited; otherwise the race itself will decline or disappear. But even if it does not disappear, the irreducible value of the individual life is lost, and that loss is inconsolable. Hence the famous lines 66–68 are not really comprehensible outside their context, where they are at once a warning and a lament.

The Georgics begins with a series of indirect questions (1.1–5):

> Quid faciat laetas segetes, quo sidere terram
> vertere, Maecenas, ulmisque adiungere vitis
> conveniat, quae cura boum, qui cultus habendo
> sit pecori, apibus quanta experientia parcis,
> hinc canere incipiam.

What makes the crops grow rich, under what constellations to turn the earth, Maecenas, and to graft the vine to the elm, what care we should give to oxen, what is the management of cattle, and what sort of experience is needed for thrifty bees: these are the subjects of my song.

These words in fact outline the subjects of the four books as we have them: book 1 concerns the seasons of the year and how they are marked by the heavenly bodies: it is the book closest in subject to Hesiod; book 2 deals with care of trees and the grapevine; book 3 with livestock; and book 4 with bees. These subjects, however, offer only a small idea of the true contents of the books. Thus book 1 includes the fundamental passage concerning the fall of man from the Saturnian Golden Age, and it moves at the end from the signs given by the stars to the farmer to the apocalyptic warnings in the heavenly bodies of the Roman Civil Wars. The Civil Wars are over, but wars elsewhere continue: *saevit toto Mars impius orbe* (1.511).

It is a dark and pessimistic book, ending with a Lucretian sense of inevitable movement into disorder and destruction. Book 2 is the happiest book and ends with the famous praise of the Italian countryside. 3, dealing with animals, and hence closer to the human condition, is yet darker than 1. Unlike trees, animals are subject to passion, and passion leads to tragedy. At the beginning of a passage describing the destructive and irresistible power of *amor*, Virgil specifically includes mankind (3.242–4):

> omne adeo genus in terris hominum ferarumque
> et genus aequoreum, pecudes pictaeque volucres,
> in furias ignemque ruunt: amor omnibus idem.

The whole race of men and of beasts, and the race of fish and cattle and varicoloured birds—all rush into frenzy, into the fire of passion—amor is the same for them all.

Specific directions towards the end of the work concerning the treatment of disease in livestock bring Virgil to speak of a great plague of cattle which destroyed vast herds. The model here is the despairing end of Lucretius' poem, which is in turn based on Thucydides' description of the plague at Athens. The plague is inevitable, Virgil says, and its effects final. All the animals died, and the bodies were contaminated, so that those who wore clothes made from their skins contracted the sacred disease, and were themselves devoured by it. The transition at the end from animals to men makes explicit the symbolic purpose of the whole book. All existence, including human, is doomed, despite even our best labours, to annihilation. And in the face of the nightmare destructions of the race, the whole subject of the poem, the value of care and ingenuity and work, is called into question (3.525–6):

> quid labor aut benefacta iuvant? quid vomere terras
> invertisse gravis?

What does this labour avail them now? What their services? What reward for having turned the heavy earth with the plough?

It is left to the fourth book to find a resolution of the tension of the first three between the joy and beauty of nature and its ultimately destructive power, a tension which we saw in the passage concerning the breeding of cows, in the brief turn from directions for the maintenance of the herd to the irreparable loss of individual happiness and life. In that passage, collective survival seemed at least a counterbalance to individual loss. The relation of such an equation to the feelings of a Roman in the closing years of the Civil Wars need not be elaborated. But that melancholy assessment, as I said, is replaced by the vision at the end of the book, of the total destruction of the herd, of life itself.

The solution in book 4 appears at first to be the unique character of the bee. The description of the life of bees filling the first half of the book is done with—on the whole—accurate observation and felicitous humor. The bees, unlike plants, have intelligence and motion. They have, more than any other animal, a complex social structure, a structure which Virgil's description makes sound analagous to that of men. But within the analogy, Virgil shows his awareness of the differences. On the one hand, bees are small and in a way insignificant: "I hold up for your admiration, Maecenas, the spectacle of the small beings"—*admiranda tibi levium spectacula rerum* (4.3). And as they lack passion, so they lack power: lines 67 and following describe with a delightful mockery of human effort, a battle of bees. They circle around the *praetoria* (75) of their leaders, and there is martial clangour imitating that of the war trumpet. Yet if you toss into their midst (86–87) a small handful of dust, the battle instantly ceases, and these great combats are reduced to quiet. On the other hand, bees are superior to all other animals, including men, because of their collective instinct, their completely social orientation. Each does his job without protest or reluctance. Their obedience is perfect. They are a faultless social organization, offering in this sense a corrective model to the chaos of human society. This perfect subordination of the individual to the group and specifically to the *rex*, the apian analogy to the *princeps*, seems to bespeak a divine influence. In one passage Virgil speaks, in a manner anticipating the Pythagorean statements of *Aeneid* 6, of how the movements and life of bees show us the pervasive presence of god in nature. This presence is not confined to bees: divinity moves through all nature, and from it— "cattle great and small, men, all wild beasts, each one as he is born, acquires the subtle elements of life" (4.223–5):

> hinc pecudes, armenta, viros, genus omne ferarum,
> quemque sibi tenuis nascentem arcessere vitas.

The passage is especially noteworthy because in book 1, observing the remarkable sense of weather to be observed in some birds, Virgil had denied that this was due to any particular infusion of divine intelligence. Here we find that all living things derive their being from a divine source; but bees are especially symbolic of this, because of their devotion to the collective good. Since they and other living things derive from a living source and return to it after individual death, the sum of life appears constant; "Nor is there any place for death; ever alive they fly off to take their place among the throng of heaven" (4.226–7):

> nec morti esse locum, sed viva volare
> sideris in numerum atque alto succedere caelo.

Using Lucretian language, *viva volare*, Virgil has adopted a Platonic idea— see the first argument of the *Phaedo*—to assert a collective immortality. But though this idea is here phrased in general terms, it is still centered on the image of bees. And does even their ideal social instinct ensure them continuing life? The Platonic-Pythagorean generality does not really solve the essential problem posed in the *Georgics* as a whole: partly because death is an observed fact, partly because bees are ultimately not an adequate image for humanity.

Virgil continues the argument by reverting to the didactic: *labor* is necessary here too, and we learn how to care for the hive and keep it clean and how to remove the honey, the honey which Virgil refers to in the first line of book 4 as "the heavenly gift of honey," *mellis caelestia dona.* But bees too are subject to sickness. The analogy here is first to the diseases of livestock so vividly described in book 3. The poet, however, passes over this logical step, and equates the sickness of bees directly to that of men: "But if (for life brings to bees our sufferings too) their bodies languish with dread sickness . . ." (4.251–2):

> Si vero (quoniam casus apibus quoque nostros
> vita tulit) tristi languebunt corpora morbo . . .

Remedies for various maladies follow. The course of thought retraces that of book 3, ending with the possibility of the incurable sickness that destroys the entire hive: "But if all at once the entire race is extinguished, if there is nothing left from which to create a new generation" (4.281–2):

> Sed si quem proles subito defecerit omnis
> nec genus unde novae stirpis revocetur habebit . . .

Here the poem takes a final and unexpected turn. An ancient tradition recorded by Servius tells us that Virgil's poem originally ended with the praise of his friend Cornelius Gallus, the one who is the subject of the tenth *Eclogue*. Gallus was appointed prefect of Egypt at about the time when Virgil is supposed to have finished the *Georgics*—30 B.C. Afterwards, he fell into disfavour with Augustus, and in 26 B.C. committed suicide. After his disgrace, Servius tells us, Virgil replaced the original ending of the work by the Aristaeus story which now ends it—presumably in a second edition if the tradition of first publication is correct. The question is important aesthetically as well as for literary history, because if the story is true, then the judgment of those who have considered the Aristaeus episode an inorganic addition to the body of the *Georgics* appears to receive some support.

The story, at least taken at its face value, seems, almost certainly, to be untrue. Several arguments beside the problem of dating can be brought against it. One is simply that if it was true, and if the original book 4 was approximately as long as the preceding three books, the praise of Gallus must have occupied more space than all the passages praising Augustus and Maecenas put together. This would have been most tactless, and Virgil as well as Gallus might have had to commit suicide. Another reason is that the Aristaeus episode, or something like it, is necessary to the sense of the work. What may have happened, and what could account for the story, is that originally Virgil included, at the beginning of the episode, a few lines in praise of Gallus which were afterwards excised. That would help to explain the emphasis on Egypt with which the episode begins. Having posed the question of total extinction of the race, the poet says that "it is time now to set forth the discoveries of the Arcadian shepherd—i.e., Aristaeus. Then he says that this *art* is practiced in Egypt. The country of Egypt is richly described in a climactic sentence of 8 lines, ending with the words, "this whole land finds sure salvation in the *art* of which I am about to tell you (4.294):

> omnis in hac certam regio iacit arte salutem.

The description of Egypt and its exotic neighbours (287 f.) is functional, as Klingner saw [F. Klingner, *Virgil*, Zürich and Stuttgart, 1967.], in that it helps to remove the focus of attention from the real world of Italy to the mythical and magical realm where life can be created from death. But the choice of Egypt in the first place may well be due to Gallus.

The Aristaeus episode is an [epýllion, (a "miniature epic")], and while it plays a vital part in the economy of the whole work, it is obviously written in a different key from the rest of the poem, and has a considerable degree of autonomy. Lines 281–314, which purport to describe the actual process of bougonía, the generation of bees from the rotting carcass of a young bull, form a transition from the didactic poem to the rich involution of the myth of the epýllion proper. It is doubtful that Virgil actually believed in this remarkable process; but it would make little difference if he did.

The bougonía must take place in spring, and as such it is symbolic of the regeneration of life in springtime. Virgil stresses this in three unusually beautiful lines (4.305–7):

> hoc geritur Zephyris primum impellentibus undas,
> ante novis rubeant quam prata coloribus, ante
> garrula quam tignis nidum suspendat hirundo.

> This is to be done when the West wind first begins to move the waves, before the fields come out in new colours, before the talkative swallow hangs her nest on the roof-beams.

The way in which the two conjunctions ante . . . ante are placed at the beginning and end of 306, leaving 307 clear for the swallow to hang her nest, with the adjective that gives life to the scene, garrula, in the emphatic position at the beginning of the next line, which ends with the sonorous name of the bird, is true Virgilian art.

The epýllion proper begins with line 315. The perfection of its form and its truth to type reminds us of how much Virgil was, after all, a neoteric poet. The shepherd Aristaeus has lost all his bees by sickness. He implores his mother, the sea goddess Cyrene's help. She tells him to go capture the elusive deity Proteus. When Proteus is finally pinned down, he tells Aristaeus that he must expiate his fault in causing the death of Eurydice. Proteus then tells the whole elegiac tale of Orpheus' descent into the underworld to regain Eurydice, his losing her a second time, his return to earth to mourn her continuously until his own death at the hands of jealous Thracian women. Proteus then vanishes, Cyrene takes over, giving her son specific and ritual directions how to create a new hive of bees from the rotting carcass of a cow, after having made expiating sacrifice. Aristaeus does as he is told, a new hive appears, and the poem ends on the note of renaissance and pastoral paradise regained.

The first lines contain the epic invocation of the Muses and the inquiry after the divine causation. This introductory passage embodies, in transformation suitable to the tone of the work, scenes from both *Iliad* and *Odyssey:* the lamenting Aristaeus, complaining that he is denied even that little honour due him, is Achilles of *Iliad* 1, while the catalogue of nymphs matches those who rise from the sea to mourn Patroclus in *Iliad* 18. The capture of Proteus as the story continues is of course taken from the fourth *Odyssey.* But the allusions are not merely Homeric. Aristaeus visiting his mother in the world under the sea is from Bacchylides' dithyramb on Theseus, where that hero is welcomed into the depths by Amphitrite. And Eurydice, in the story within a story, as she says farewell to her imprudent husband and is drawn back to death, is the dying Alcestis of Euripides' play. . . .

The Hesiodic and Alexandrian quality of the *epýllion* appears particularly in the catalogues which fill the poem. Besides the muster (336–344), we have the sources of the great rivers in the underworld (367–373), a theme which Eric Havelock has ingeniously shown to derive from early Greek geographical speculation, and to have echoes as late as Coleridge:

> In Xanadu did Kubla Khan
> a stately pleasure dome decree,
> where Alph the sacred river ran
> through caverns measureless to man,
>   down to a sunless sea.

And the Orpheus-Eurydice story itself contains two more geographical catalogues: 460–463, at the beginning, the Thracian lands that weep for Eurydice, and matching it in a corresponding position at the end, 517–9, the lands traversed by Orpheus, lamenting her now twice lost.

> solus Hyperboreas glacies Tanaimque nivalem
> arvaque Riphaeis numquam viduata pruinis
> lustrabat . . .

These, and the many other geographical references in the episode, are designed to express both the universality and the exotic splendour of the story. The sort of rich and rare and highly wrought language of these passages in particular show Virgil in his most lyrical, and his most Alexandrian, mood. The theme of the Orpheus story—more than in any other ancient version of the myth—is lamentation and death. The *imperium* of art here is entirely in the threnodic mode. But this dense expression of grief, these unremitting plangent notes, are elevated into what is almost a symbol of music and art by Virgil's employment in them of every possible lyrical device: the magical and exotic notes of Greek names and Greek metres, of anaphora, alliteration and assonance. Consider 460–6:

> At chorus aequalis Dryadum clamore supremos
> implevit montis; flerunt Rhodopeiae arces
> altaque Pangaea et Rhesi Mavortia tellus
> atque Getae atque Hebrus et Actias Orithyia.
> ipse cava solans aegrum testudine amoreum,
> te, dulcis coniunx, te solo in litore secum,
> te veniente die, te decedente canebat.

The chorus of Dryads, of her age, filled with their cries the mountain tops; the summits of Rhodope wept, and lofty Pangaea, and Rhesus' land of Mars, and the Getae, and the Hebrus, and from the Attic cliffs, Orithyia; while he went solacing his bitter love with the hollow lyre, singing you, sweet wife, alone on the shore by himself, singing you, as the day arose, you, as the day declined.

Line 463 contains at least three elements alien to Latin metrics: the hiatus of the first syllable of the second dactyl; the long syllable in Hebrus before -br-; the unlatin short second *a* in Actias; and the drawn-out spondaic ending in the single final word, Orithyia, with its unlatin vowels. Note also the *tour de force* of assonance in 465–466: the alternating *o*'s and *u*'s of 465 succeeded by the repeated *e*'s of 466. The language, that is to say, in fairly direct fashion, presents Orpheus as the essence of poetry as well as of grief.

The construction of the *epýllion* too shows a conscious symmetry to a degree beyond anything else in the *Georgics* or the rest of Virgil's poetry. The form of the *epýllion* often depends on an *aítion*: that is, the poem purports to be an explanation of the origins of a custom, usually a religious rite still continued in the poet's day. This is expressed in the first line, 315: "What god, Muse, fashioned this art for us?":

> Quis deus hanc, Musae, quis nobis extudit artem?

The whole passage ends with the first successful practice of the art of *bougonía*. The concluding lines 556–558, which by mentioning weather, trees, and grapes, as well as the bees born from an animal, also sum up the subjects of the whole poem: "The bees buzz in the animal's belly, but burst forth from its broken ribs, are borne aloft in a huge cloud, and settle in supple branches in a grape-like cluster":

> liquefacta boum per viscera toto
> stridere apes utero et ruptis effervere costis
> immensasque trahi nubes iamque arbore summa
> confluere et lentis uvam demittere ramis.

The matching of beginning and end is the outer layer of an intricate nested structure: 317–332, the pastoral god Aristaeus complaining to his mother of the loss of his bees, corresponds to the Aristaeus scene at the end, successfully carrying out the *bougonía*.

The passage from line 333 to 424 is dominated by Cyrene, receiving her son into her watery kingdom and telling him how to discover the cause of his affliction from Proteus. It corresponds to 530–547, where Cyrene tells Aristaeus after the speech of Proteus how he can expiate his fault. Lines 425–452 describe at length the appearance of Proteus surrounded by his faithful seals, and Aristaeus' capture of him. That corresponds to two lines, 528–529, where Proteus goes back under the foaming sea. Proteus' oracle occupies the centre, 453–527, and this oracle is itself chiastically disposed: beginning with the death of Eurydice, ending with the death of Orpheus, those sections, 453–463, and 516–527, are followed and preceded respectively by the first and second scenes of Orpheus' lamentation—465–466 and 507–515; and these in turn by Orpheus regaining Eurydice (467–484), and losing her again (485–506). The turning point, where Orpheus looks back a moment too soon to see if Eurydice is still there, and so loses her forever, is in almost the exact centre of the Orpheus-story. "He stopped, and right there, at the edge of the world of light, oh god, forgetting himself, yielding to desire, he turned back to look."

What is the point of this art of such extraordinary richness and intricacy? Klingner properly compares Catullus 64, the long poem on the marriage of Peleus and Thetis. Here too we find the Alexandrian device of a story within a story, two myths joined by an ingenious and unexpected, if somewhat arbitrary, transition. Moreover, the two myths in that poem, like those of our text here, are joined closely in form, but embody contrasting moods. The marriage of Peleus and Thetis is all joy and success: human life virtually raised to the level of the divine. The Ariadne story embroidered on the wedding present is tragic. Two aspects of existence are symbolized by the two intertwined myths of the poem. But, Klingner points out, the poem also contains a suggestion that the outcome of the two myths is the same, and not in contrast. The marriage of a mortal, Peleus, to a goddess, Thetis, is paralleled by the suggestion at the end of the poem of the marriage of a mortal woman, Ariadne, to a god, Bacchus.

Klingner wants to find a similar higher resolution of the two contrasting stories of our poem, the regeneration of life for Aristaeus, and the inevitability of death for Orpheus. He tries to find this resolution in the Pythagorean sense of the continuation of all life on a superterrestrial plane as a compensation for the tragic loss of individual life, an idea which, as we saw in the passage on the breeding of cows (39–40 above), occurs elsewhere in the poem. Klingner misses this passage, but compares *Aeneid* 6, where the individual deaths of Icarus and Marcellus at the beginning and end of the book are balanced by the sense of unending Roman history merged with religious philosophy in Anchises' speech. The resolution here in the *Georgics* and in the *Aeneid* is less clear than that in Catullus' poem, and perhaps this refusal to work out a comforting equation is itself characteristic of Virgil.

But I should like to suggest another sort of resolution. In book 1 of the *Georgics*, Virgil takes over from Hesiod the idea of the fall of man from the Golden Age as Jupiter's punishment of man's intellectual challenge to the gods (1.121–3): "The father himself wanted for men no easy way of agriculture, and he was the first to see that art must move the fields . . ."

> pater ipse colendi
> haud facilem esse viam voluit, primusque per artem
> movit agros . . .

But Virgil varies the Hesiodic theme. In Hesiod, Zeus' punishment is ultimately a good thing, because it necessitates *work*, and work is man's way of achieving justice. For Virgil, work, *labor*, is important, but not so much because it embodies justice. Rather, because it in turn necessitates *art*. Virgil's whole poem, in contrast to that of Hesiod, stresses the beauty and variety of human experience raised to the level of art. Art, *ars*, is at once an intellectual and an aesthetic achievement. To continue the passage in book 1, 125 ff.:

> ante Iovem nulli subigebant arva coloni;
> ne signare quidem aut partiri limite campum
> fas erat: in medium quaerebant, ipsaque tellus
> omnia liberius nullo poscente ferebat.
> ille malum virus serpentibus addidit atris,
> praedarique lupos iussit pontumque moveri,
> mellaque decussit foliis ignemque removit,
> et passim rivis currentia vina repressit,
> ut varias usus meditando extunderet artis
> paulatim . . .

Before Jupiter was, no farmers tilled the soil. Nor was it right to mark the fields or part them with boundaries; all sought life in common, and earth herself bore freely all, so that no one needed to ask. Jupiter added poison to serpents, ordered wolves to prey on other animals, made the sea a place of storms; he struck the honey-dew from the leaves, took away fire and stopped the flow of wine in rivers, *so that* need and experience would *fashion* the several arts, little by little . . .

The whole process of agriculture in which Virgil takes such delight is one of the *variae artes* which men have fashioned by experience and design. Note the key word *extunderet* in 133—'hammer out'—a word which properly suggests the sculptor's creation of a statue. The sculptor's, or metalworker's craft, I suggest, is a bridge between the farmer's and the poet's art. Nature, for which Virgil feels so vivid a passion, is to be understood and appreciated through art, and the assimilation of the farmer's lore and the poet's song is furthered by their common subject, the natural world.

At the beginning of the *epýllion*, line 315, these key words reappear. And the verb is repeated in Aristaeus' lament (4.326–328):

> en etiam hunc ipsum vitae mortalis honorem,
> quem mihi vix frugum et pecorum custodia sollers
> omnia temptanti extuderat, te matre relinquo.

See how this one honour of my mortal life, which with such pains my care of crop and herd, after long experience, had *fashioned*, is taken from me, though I am your son!

He is angry because his art, which he has fashioned with such effort, appears to be of no avail.

The lesson which Aristaeus must learn to make his art viable, to attain by it a kind of immortality, is a lesson of poetry. Proteus in fact does not tell him how to regain his bees: that practical matter, the religious rite of expiation, is left to Cyrene. Proteus instead sings a song, and the song is about the singer *par excellence*, Orpheus. The grief of Orpheus is irredeemable, despite the regeneration of bees that follows it, except that it becomes the subject of song; and the song in turn becomes the condition for the recreation of life. The grief is elevated to the highest art, and in that art, the epitome of all human art and craft, lies the true immortality of the poem, the resolution of man's confrontation with the absolute of death.

DOUGLAS J. STEWART

Aeneas the Politician

In his 1961 lectures from the Oxford Chair of Poetry Robert Graves labeled Virgil the "anti-poet"—in Graves-peak, roughly, the Anti-Christ—and denounced him for "pliability . . . subservience . . . narrowness; his denial of the stubborn imaginative freedom that the true poets who preceded him had valued; his lack of originality, courage, humour, or even animal spirits. . . ." Graves' performance, long awaited as the most spectacular clash of humors in a generation, was really rather tame, if not conventional. Most students of Virgil had heard that litany before, based as it is on the almost cliché image of the poet in the modern era, a shaggy rebel touchy to the point of oaths or tears at society's supposed attempts either to curb or ignore his personal feelings. How very different Virgil's role as a court poet, living on state funds and writing, on commission from Caesar Augustus, an epic poem that was not about the feelings of anybody in particular, but the destiny of a supranational empire. The case against Virgil is just too simple: a toady, a propagandist, a man afraid of conflict and direct statement.

That of course is the trouble: the case is *too* easy, simply because a 15-year-old could make it. After reading Graves once, I found myself wondering what Virgil might have to say, if *he* were elected Oxford Professor of Poetry, about our modern poets (and critics). One thing I am sure he would stress is the deplorable political naivete of poets who seldom seem to know the first thing about politics, and rarely have exercised their "stubborn imaginative freedom" to explore the inner nature of *institutions* and the complex fate of men who are called upon to manage them.

From *The Antioch Review* 4, vol. 32. Copyright © 1973 by *The Antioch Review*, Inc. Translations by the author.

There is nothing wrong with the literature of personal experience and the feelings; that indeed is what most literature has always concerned itself with. And it is difficult for a writer to come to grips imaginatively with the political element in life. Finally, institutions may well be both corrupt and corrupting. But none of these considerations proves *a priori* that literature cannot tackle a political subject, or that it cannot be successful, which is to say convincing to the reader, in doing so. And the task Virgil set for himself in the *Aeneid* was to write literature about institutions and the political vocation. He did not try to write imitation Homeric epic, or second-rate Apollonian romance, or philosophical cryptograms based on Stoic matter in Lucretian forms. Whatever Augustus was expecting from Virgil, one thing he certainly did *not* get was a patriotic hymn of praise for Rome, nor indeed is Rome the specific subject of the poem. Much less did he get simple propaganda favoring his own regime. The essential subject of the *Aeneid* is the "education" of a political leader.

As we shall see presently in greater detail, the most persuasive boast Roman culture could make was that it had objectified and codified the conditions of creating political leadership, which gave it title to rule the world. That being the claim, Virgil determined to produce in full detail a dry-eyed study of how that process occurs, using the persona of Rome's legendary founder, the Trojan hero Aeneas. Virgil's first insight was relatively simple, if hard for emotional people to absorb: that a politician, normally, is neither a gangster nor a hero, but a frequently puzzled player of a fiendishly complicated game most of the rules of which change by the hour. A typical politician may find this fascinating or heartening, but to others a politician at work must seem a dull fellow, because most of his "adventures" are infinitesimal mental acts of deduction, appraisal and equivocation, seldom even verbalized, or not candidly so. The knowing or threatening look, the muffled conversation, the equivocal speech are perhaps the politician's most typical outward expressions of his feelings and functions, hardly comparable to the sweeping gestures or lofty oratory of an epic hero. In Homer, especially in the *Iliad*, heroism is for the human characters; politics is for the gods. Though the heroes have technical political roles as chiefs and kings, they seldom remember to fulfill them—except perhaps Agamemnon, who fills his incompetently, as Thersites reminds everyone. Making a politician out of Aeneas, who began his "career" as a Homeric hero, required the displacement, if not the disappearance, of Aeneas' epic personality, because a politician has very little time for a private set of feelings. To state this perspective would not of course make Robert Graves any happier with Virgil, because Graves like so many others limits the focus of real poetry ("true poets") to the personal realm; but all one can say in reply is that Virgil understood much better than his detractors what kind of poetry he had chosen *not* to write and how and where the *Aeneid* had to differ from the poetry of personal life.

The *Aeneid* is a study of the preternatural strains and anxieties a political vocation brings to mere natural man, and the ultimate surd presented to us when we consider the problem of political leadership: is such a thing possible at all; can one be both a human being and a leader; and will it not turn out that the claims of nature and politics will be mutually contradictory? Poetry of the more usual pattern, with its involvement in the fate and aspirations of the individual, stands at a great distance from politics, whose concern is the fate of groups—and indirectly the fate of individuals who act as their agents—and Virgil understood this better than anyone else. Eventually, it may be, poetry with its "higher" morality must come to judge even politics. But the right word is *eventually.* Not too quickly or too rashly, as is usually the case. And Virgil understood this too.

One source of the impatience even subtle readers experience with Virgil and all Latin literature is a curious system of retreat and apology that threads its way through the works of most Roman writers. They all seem so terribly conscious of having come, collectively, upon Greek literary themes and forms late in the day, *arrivistes* blundering in upon a cultural dialogue that had been going on a long time without them, as though the subjects of discussion, though old in fact, are new to them. They also seem embarrassed and distinctly modest about any contribution they could possibly make to the discussion already well under way. The poet Horace in one poem stakes his claim to immortality on his ability to make the rude Latin language dance in Greek meters, a very modest claim indeed, and probably not even an honest one, but that is all he *dares* to say, because no one would believe anything more. Lucretius grumbles about the *egestas,* the poverty of Latin for discussions of philosophy, and *claims* to be doing no more than versifying the ideas of Epicurus (though that too is probably false). Sallust apologizes for the absence of respectable Roman historiography by arguing that in Rome men competent in public affairs took part in them rather than wrote about them, unlike Greece where, if anything, the political genius of a writer like Thucydides exceeded the magnitude of the events he had to write about. Even Ovid, though evidently troubled and annoyed by the cautious, imitative tone of his fellow writers, found no better means of asserting his own originality than by farcical imitation of the imitators. The most famous of these apologetic texts—or so it is usually interpreted—is the great prophecy of Anchises in *Aeneid* VI. In lines 847–853 Anchises (actually his ghost) foretells to Aeneas just which of the civilized arts it will be granted to Rome itself to practice, once Rome takes its ordained place on the world stage, and which must be conceded to subject peoples like the Greeks. The lines appear to acquiesce in a straight trade-off between Greek and Roman skills: let the Greeks (called simply, "the others") seek fame and excellence in the fine arts and the like, provided only that the Romans understand that their own fame will be secured through the exercise of the arts of legislation, politics and at least a modified form of imperial warfare:

> excudent alii spirantia mollius aera
> (credo equidem), vivos ducent de marmore vultus
> orabunt causas melius, caelique meatus
> describent radio et surgentia sidera dicent:
> tu regere imperio populos, Romane, memento
> (hae tibi erunt artes), pacique imponere morem
> parcere subiectis et debellare superbos.

Others, I dare say, will hammer out breathing bronzes more subtly, and draw living faces out of the marble; they will speak more eloquently, map the course of the heavens with instruments and predict the comings and goings of the stars. But you, a Roman, remember how to rule nations. These will be your arts: to enforce the habit of peace, to spare the conquered, but war down the proud.

(847–853. Oxford Classical Edition, 1969, ed. by R. A. B. Mynors.)

It is remarkable how much Virgil gives away here. I call attention to the phrases "breathing bronzes" (spirantia aera) and "living faces out of marble" (vivos . . . de marmore vultus). With more than a touch of the true artist's sadness he is admitting that by the turn of the fates the Greeks have been selectively and abundantly blessed with the ability to create an approximation of life from that which is naturally non-living (spirantia and vivos are key words here and much stronger than Virgil's usual metaphors), and that is the program and aspiration of all art, one may say.

This passage, as noted, is part of a pattern that frequently earns all of Latin literature the scorn of critics and scholars as a second-rate and "derivative" historical phenomenon. But this passage in particular has had a more specific, unbalancing effect on Virgil's individual reputation, because it has been used to call into question his respect for his own art, or even his attentiveness to what he was doing. Supposing it agreed that a Horace or a Sallust were but second-raters—at least they worked earnestly and believingly to the best of their ability. These lines have sometimes been taken to mean that Virgil had no stomach for his project, and it has even been thought that they amount to a moody, half-conscious resignation of the spirit from the whole enterprise. This interpretation is especially tempting to over-eager critics who read more than is there into the first half of the "bargain" conceding pre-eminence in the arts to the Greeks, and have seen much less than is there in the second half claiming political pre-eminence for the Romans. This in turn is intimately linked with the essential issue of what kind of poetry Virgil thought he was trying to write.

First of all, one may note that in the catalogue of Greek superiorities Virgil omits mention of poetry, his own medium. Yet poetry was obviously the supreme accomplishment of the Greeks. This omission can be given several explanations, all of them correct in their way. First, Virgil did not need to praise Greek poetry, since he was in the very act of imitating it, the highest form of praise. Second, and more important, no matter how humble one may feel, it would not do in the middle of a *Latin* poem to say too explicitly that the Greeks win all the prizes for poetry, too. It would simply jar the poetic frame too crudely, and the poem one was writing would perish in the saying of it. And third, though Virgil was in some ways a shy and self-critical man, I doubt he really failed to understand his own gifts. And surely he hoped by means of his own poem to render the case between Greek and Latin poetry not so entirely one-sided as it was before his coming.

But there is yet another way to explain this omission, and it brings us back to the opening question: what sort of poetry can one write about material that is, in the judgment of most people, so unpoetic so as to seem positively anti-poetic? And how is it to be made credible, given this very suspicion? Virgil's complex answer to this puzzle grows out of this passage. The first step is to admit that *by and large*, poetry and politics *are* antithetical and then to write poetry that portrays just why this is generally true.

Virgil says in the prophecy of Anchises that the Roman genius best expresses itself in the arts of politics. He also states, in effect, that politics is essentially alien to the whole realm of the arts. He omits any mention of poetry here because he realizes that he has undertaken an almost impossible task in the *Aeneid*, to celebrate and justify a political quest and a political event, and to do it within the rules of art itself, not those of politics. Having accepted responsibility for this hybrid enterprise, Virgil—if not the world's greatest poet then surely its most *tactful* poet—immediately understood that to intrude the quarrel between poetry and politics just here would be to spoil the effect and reduce the results to a conundrum about his own personal position on politics and the Augustan settlement. As we have seen, Virgil did not escape posterity's inquisition on this subject, though the questions have normally been posed with unVirgilian crudity: Was Virgil sincere? Was he hostile to his political assignment? And so on. So put, they are simply beneath intellectual consideration because Virgil himself obviously understood them, found the means to escape the false dilemma they posed, and passed on to his real work. The real question for us is: How did Virgil so manage his efforts that he could speak truth about his theme, politics, without foisting on it the often irrelevant petulancies of the artist, and without at the same time letting the expediencies of the politician (Augustus, or the whole herd collectively) make him descend indecently to propaganda. It was at once a terrifying exercise in restraint and an extravagantly ambitious program.

In practical terms this program meant that Aeneas, who begins as just one more epic "hero," must be conducted by the poet through a series of brain washings until he has developed into something totally different, a political leader, who is no hero at all. This, however, will entail a progressive estrangement of the poet from the hero, a loss of contact between the increasingly political figure of Aeneas and the mechanisms easily available to a poet for assessing character and penetrating the psyche.

Politics is very difficult for literature to portray, for except at extreme moments of either heroism or tyranny it displays very little of the sharp features of individual personality, which are what literature wants to find in life. Politics usually takes a little from the personalities of many people, and not much from the personality of any one man. On the other hand, it gives very little scope to the personality of any one man, or offers little room for the development of the individual personality. I think Virgil grasped this frustrating state of affairs very early on, yet determined grimly to follow its implications to the end. The *Aeneid*, as a result, is perhaps the one really successful, though unappreciated, literary portrait of a politician's life and education.

Politics, sadly, is quite mute at its real center, the heart of the politician, the structure of his loves and cares. Literature, the carrier of fame and thus of historical approbation—at least as all poets believe—has rarely if ever solved the problem of handling quotidian politics with insight and conviction. If we look to Shakespeare we find that to make politics artistically tolerable he was forced to reduce it to mere crime (*Macbeth, Julius Caesar, Richard III*) or to gross quarrels over succession (*Richard II, Hamlet, Lear*)—the *coup d'état* in its various manifestations. These models are negative and suggest that politics can provide literature only with pathological material . . . which is largely true. Literature normally can only deal effectively with the boundary moments *between* regimes, the assassination, the *coup*—or with certain types of tyranny, because tyranny, as Tacitus made clear, treats *all* events as real or potential boundary moments. It is only when politics disguises itself as the individual concern of life-or-death that literature can normally get it in clear focus. Yet Virgil is probably the one clear exception to this rule: he really taught himself to understand politics in its standard operations, and created the epic of a political man— an agent, not a hero.

The typical politician does not spend his time thinking about assassination, *coup d'état* or tyranny. He enjoys most what we call "administration," *i.e.*, the marshalling of usually reluctant forces and factors— men, materials and money—into concerted action to produce a permanent and visible result, a "fixture" of some sort, that will survive on the landscape, both as a permanent addition to society's collection of amenities (or vanities) *and* as a witness to the fact that the politician responsible did not live entirely in vain. (Power comes in as a *means* to this end.) In other words, most politicians do not consciously think of power *per se* but of serviceable memorials to their skill at creation. Here is where the politician gains *his* immortality. Any Roman reading the prophecy of Anchises would instantly have understood that the background assumption of the passage was one of vicarious immortality gained through political achievement.

But fame requires a repository, a reliquary, an *object* in which it resides. Works of art are their own reliquaries and works of thought repose in written documents, books and treatises, verbal continuities speaking for themselves. The most obvious object a politician leaves behind him is the public building, the great monument in stone and steel. This is why politicians have engaged in an ages-long love affair with the construction industry. True, some politicians have believed that constitutional reform in the broad sense, a re-integration of a people's needs with their public law, is as good as, or better than, a building program. But they have not been in the majority, and even they have never entirely scorned the importance of buildings. For example, in the year 1800 one would have to say that the two shrewdest politicians living were Jefferson and Napoleon. Both effected massive changes in the political thought and basic law of their nations—both were thought of as law-givers—yet both men also with their left hands, as it were, were avid builders and possessed an almost professional eye for architectural style and proportion. It is probably only with Bentham that the idea began to grow that institutional re-design is *more important* than buildings, both *pro bono publico* and for the political leader's reputation. (Although, as I shall note shortly, even here Virgil may have anticipated history.)

Virgil, I suggest, having agreed to write an "epic" about a political leader, did the responsible thing: he studied political leaders to see how they really operated. He learned, if he had not known before, much of what I have been discussing: the typical politician is not really on easy terms with the poet; his ideals and aims are elsewhere. Despite the claims of ancient poets that politicians desire their attention because poetry alone confers immortality, in their actions politicians prove that they think other-wise. Politicians may be happy to hire the services of poets—in modern terms, journalists—to celebrate the regime for short-term public-relations purposes, but when the question is true immortality, politicians instinctively vote with the other side: a building or a program beats the poet's faint praise (or the historian's awe) every time. Thus Virgil set himself the chore of writing about a "hero" who would himself have very little use for, or interest in, the services of a poet like Virgil. The *Aeneid* then begins to sound very much like a series of long-distance telephone calls between a distracted central character and an intelligent poet whose fidelity to truth makes him understand why it is increasingly difficult to keep Aeneas on the line.

At the 31st line of the first book of the *Aeneid* Virgil, in his own voice, utters a remarkably quotable and intuitive line, *Tantae molis erat Romanam condere gentem.* "Such struggle would be needed to found the Roman nation." *Tantae molis,* to be sure, does mean "such struggle," and the line is a Stoicized expression of the extreme demands that duty will impose upon Aeneas as, like Hercules, he goes about his largely unpleasant labors. But *molis,* before it acquired the ethical sense of "struggle" had the primary physical meaning of "building stone" or another very large and heavy object solid and immovable enough to serve as the foundation of an enduring public building. And, appearing with the verb *condere,* "to lay down" or "fix" (in the ground), it makes a pretty clear case that the dominant image in Virgil's mind was that of building on a monumental scale.

I dwelt above on the fact that Roman culture contained a large admixture of defensive maneuvers whereby the supremacy of Greek culture was admitted, while spokesmen for Roman culture agree to compete only for secondary honors, those of re-doing Greek achievement in Latin phrases. Virgil, obviously, subscribed to this view, but only to a degree. Quite apart from his own self-respect, he realized that he had a different problem here—

in fact one diametrically opposed to that accepted by most Roman writers: he was not trying to domesticate Greek ideas in Roman terms, but to discover the essence of Roman ideas and feelings and naturalize them in the Greek style, *i.e.*, in a verse form, the epic, that was foreign to Roman culture. (The older Roman "ipics" of Naevius and Ennius were fabulized "annals" or history, not especially mythic.) I think he understood his own capacity to do just this, while also realizing, perhaps, just what the cost would be in critical incomprehension. Virgil, in contrast to other poets who never seemed to question the fact that they were educated in Greek terms to think like Greeks, deliberately reversed the pattern and successfully internalized true-to-character Roman enthusiasms and then sought to create freely with them in a Greek medium. This he largely succeeded in doing. The dominant ideal in the minds of upper-class Romans was the desire to appear in history as important and creative politically, and the surest token of political creativity is long-lasting public construction, as the careers of the great Roman magnates, from Appius Claudius Pulcher to Augustus himself make clear. As recorded in Suetonius (*Vita Divi Augusti*, 28) Augustus boasted that he found Rome brick and left it marble, and in his own record of his reign (*Res Gestae*, 19–21) Augustus gloats over the long list of buildings begun, finished and repaired in his reign, though he makes no mention of having sponsored the greatest of all Latin poems—as I have noted, when it comes down to cases politicians vote with the contractor and the architect, not with the poet. It just happened that this particular poet, Virgil, shrewdly noted this very fact and proceeded to elaborate his epic upon this basic understanding of the ways of politics.

The poem opens and wastes no time in lodging in the reader's mind the dominant image of construction, the heavier the better, the romance of public buildings, the most essential Roman image that could be set forth. The point is obviously to suggest to the perceptive reader that nearly all of the epic, and hence Greek-style, "adventures" of the story are a throwaway: they are never crucial. And in fact the most important passages in the *Aeneid* are those times when the poem reneges on pursuing an "epic" story to an epic conclusion, such as Aeneas' headlong flight from Dido (with nothing like Odysseus' doubts or complaints about Calypso) or his dropping out of action just when there is the chance to make the great epic speech. Even though the *Aeneid* is modeled, superficially, on both *Iliad* and *Odyssey*, and at a deeper level, follows the *Odyssey* in being the story of a man forced to introspection in order to find out who he is through the agency of his experience, in the last analysis it is not much like any "epic" before or since.

I have said that Aeneas began his heroic "career" in Homer's *Iliad*. I used that odd word "career" for a purpose, to imply that for him heroism was not to be a way of *being*, but simply a profession for a time. And that profession is aborted in *Aeneid* II (606 ff.): in a desultory skirmish with a band of Greek looters on the night Troy is taken, Aeneas is suddenly commanded by his mother Venus to break off the engagement and flee, because he has other *work* to do: "do not fear the commands of your mother, nor refuse to obey my orders" (*tu ne qua parentis/iussa time, neu praeceptis parere recusa . . .* , words which will never read quite the same to me after *Portnoy's Complaint*). Aeneas obeys instantly. He is no Achilles proclaiming to *his* mother his resolve to follow the heroic code until it kills him. Nor is Venus a Thetis: she simply will not stand by wringing her hands to see her boy killed for no purpose: he is destined to a political career as the founder of a new state, and she is determined that we will have it. The tone suddenly drops in this passage to the practical, if not the bourgeois. Epic assumptions are destroyed and Aeneas is propelled by his mother— playing a Roman matron on the model of the great political matriarchs like Cornelia—into the new world of policy, calculation, and caution. From here on he is searching for a new role to assume, and by the time he reaches Carthage he is already half a politician. At the sight of the rising walls of Carthage he bursts out to Achates: "*O fortunati quorum iam moenia surgunt!*" (I, 437). Walls, structures, are now of primary concern to him because they are the surest tokens of social reality and continuity. Real epic heroes are not interested in buildings but in deeds of the moment. In her speech to Aeneas prevailing on him to abandon Troy, Venus had dwelt on the horror of seeing mighty buildings destroyed (II, 608–612) and implied that this was even worse than the destruction of people. She was teaching him a lesson about the permanence of society as represented by its buildings— buildings as a prerequisite for all civilized life, and even for life itself. And through his subsequent experience Aeneas will be forced to learn at first hand the malaise of an unhoused, nonpolitical existence, to the extent that he quickly becomes an almost fanatical apostle of the civic life and the concrete artifacts upon which it depends.

Aeneas' ejaculation *O fortunati* came as he was gazing on the temple of Juno, his arch-enemy, and on the frescoes adorning its walls which told the story *of the destruction of Troy! Sunt lacrimae rerum* and all that. But none of this matters to him at this moment. Here is the most positive civic achievement known to him, the erection of great public buildings which somehow protect a people while encouraging them to believe in their own survival despite any challenge time may hurl upon them.

But a politician is more than a builder. He is a leader of people (not, as the phrase usually has it, a leader *of men*—readers often forget that Aeneas led a band of men *and women* from Troy). And a leader, except in the simplified terms of *warfare*—another boundary situation—is no hero. He is simply one who organizes other people's energies. He leads (often) by pretending that a given common aim is both realizable and beneficial, though he personally may doubt the first and not even understand the second. Those who have searched the *Aeneid* for a second Achilles and found only the "priest" of Yeats' story, have simply misunderstood the arena in which the "hero" is operating. All those flat, dull speeches of encouragement, all that weariness, that general hangover quality Aeneas both experiences and communicates when he looks out upon the world, are the politician's special burden. He must pretend to enthusiasms he does not feel, repress emotions he does feel, and generally behave not as a free individual but as the incorporation of a society's needs, a trust-officer for other people's future. The heraldic badge of the *Aeneid* is the vignette of Aeneas carrying his lame father and leading his small son away from the ruins of Troy. It sums up precisely the fate and role of Aeneas: go-between, maker or agent of continuity, link between past and future, doubly burdened by both. And finally of course the politician has the misfortune—and the wretchedness—of accepting responsibility for the actions of his subordinates. Aeneas must face the grim results of his son's ill-timed hunting expedition, and of the foolish bravado of Nisus and Euryalus. This is a world totally different from that of Achilles, whose sense of role is so personal as to be infantile: he quarrels with a superior, retires from action, delegates command to an inferior, and then reacts to the inferior's defeat only in terms that reflect his personal feeling of outrage and loss. A real leader, a politician, has no time for the ego-cultivation of an Achilles (Virgil might say); he is just a center around which effective historical action *may* take place. That is, if he's lucky, if he can hang on, hope for the best, and keep his power intact for as long as possible.

For such reasons as these Aeneas the politician is always on the point of escaping from the status of a literary character under his creator's control, into another world where the poet cannot easily follow. Again and again he turns his back on the kinds of action and self-expression that literature can normally take into its forms. His abandonment of Dido is the prime case in point. Virgil, and Aeneas, have been attacked a thousand times because Virgil has Aeneas, after one warning from Mercury, drop Dido with no complaints and no arguments, and certainly with no dramatic expressions of his passion or the loss he is incurring. Thus Aeneas is cold

and calculating, a cad, a jellyfish, without backbone or balls—so the in-
dictments run. But they are not to the point. Any politician with a capacity
for introspection would instantly understand even this as simply an extreme
case of what politics *always* demands from its practitioners, a readiness to
deny and ignore the promptings of mere nature when policy, the duty of
role-playing, the communal purpose demand it. True, the average politician
suffers little more than the loss of regular dinners with his family, but the
possibility of greater sacrifice is always there, as the fateful careers of two
Kennedys have instructed us. The Dido story is a metaphor for what any
politician must be prepared to do: to sacrifice every last personal tie, if
necessary, to help keep the political enterprise going, to maintain the quest.
Literature has never found this sort of thing very palatable, either because
it is devoted to exploring the *private* passions of man, or because it holds
an implicit ethics denying the validity, if not the reality, of the abstruse
and probably corrupt doings of politics. Literature may be right, and politics
wrong, in the final judgment. But insofar as politics exists and there are
politicians to observe, Virgil is saying, it is proper to present what politics
really is like and how a politician lives, since that is what Aeneas was.

I suggested above that Virgil anticipated the modern conviction
that social programs, intangible institutional reforms (*e.g.*, Social Security),
are even more significant monuments to a political career than memorials
in stone. As evidence, consider the prophecy of Anchises in Book VI,
already cited to make a narrower point. What Anchises declares, in effect,
is not just how Greek and Roman cultures should compose their differences
in a viable scheme that carries on the best of both; he also enunciates a
new constitutional principle: *parcere victis et debellare superbos*, "spare the
conquered and war down the proud." This, if finally understood, would
accomplish the total conversion of Aeneas from a bloodletting epic hero
to a wise philosopher-king. For it says that warfare, that plaything of epic
heroes, is to be conducted *solely* under the guidance of cold-eyed impersonal
policy. To a large extent Aeneas' own character manages to conform itself
to this principle even though the following of principle so intently tends
to obliterate and bury that character, which is only "rescued" by a horrid
paradox at the end. It is noticeable that Aeneas begins to curtail all instinctive, natural reactions and replace them with political calculation, in
the better sense. And for this the poet rewards him by switching from the
epithet *pius*—which implied, in the first six books, his subjection to paternal
and ancestral control, that of both Anchises and Venus—to the epithet
pater, father, indicating his acceptance of, and title to, full responsibility
and political authority in the last six books. Likewise, Aeneas ages signif-

icantly in the last six books: we can no longer imagine him appearing as a lover. In the words of Professor Clausen: "We see him, middle-aged and a widower, bound to pursue his reluctant way from Troy to Italy, from a past he has lost to a future he will never possess." The last phrase sums up a politician's vocation about as well as anything can. Aeneas becomes cautious and stiff; he develops a resistance to emotional appeals, whether to fear or vanity. And he becomes caught in the categorical imperative of politics: preservation of the leader's *person* is inextricably involved with the accomplishment of his *purposes,* to an extent that even he can grasp only in rare moments.

The *Aeneid* ends with the murder of Turnus. It *is* a murder precisely because it would have been a piece of behavior perfectly normal for an epic hero on the Homeric model. But it comes long after Aeneas has been taught, and has accepted, the new constitutional principle which subjects war, and all other behavior, to the demands of a rational, and humanitarian politics: *parcere victis,* "spare the conquered." Critics hostile to Virgil seem to blame this atrocity on the poet himself. Yet Aeneas does no more than what Achilles does to Hector, and Hector is admirable while Turnus most certainly is not. Yet a charge must be made: Aeneas is wrong. His act is one of excess. And worse, it is a *personal* act.

Political leaders cannot afford to act on personal grounds. Aeneas is no Achilles; he does not occupy that primitive sphere in the shame culture which countenances a permanent adolescence forever clamoring for attention and given to smashing the furniture if it does not get it. Aeneas is simply subject to different and higher standards, standards to which he with at least partial understanding, has lent himself. It is not even an excuse that he has considerable human grounds for his act. Turnus is a narrow, violent, and rather stupid egomaniac (*he* is an Achilles), and he had savagely killed the most unoffending and ideal human type who appears in the *Aeneid,* Pallas, the saintly son of Evander. The disparity between their characters can hardly be measured. Moreover Virgil supplies an extra irony. Pallas is clearly portrayed as a cadet-leader from the younger generation, possessing all the qualities of incipient leadership that would make him Aeneas' ideal successor. And any half-competent politician spends at least half his time worrying about the problem of capable and acceptable successors. In politics continuity is always *the* problem. It may be that Aeneas saw Pallas, rather than his own son Ascanius, at least for a few hopeful moments, as his own successor, *via* the procedure of adoption. This procedure was common among the great political families of Rome. Augustus was the adopted son of Julius Caesar. The saintly Marcellus was, likewise, the adoptive heir of Augustus, and the untimely and horrid death of Pallas at the hands of Turnus is perhaps a literary parallel with the untimely and regrettable death of Marcellus. Yet even this does not excuse a political failure, which is what the murder of Turnus is. Aeneas has multiple motives, but a multiplicity of motives does not constitute a reason for political action, not for a politician. The new constitutional order demands that he restrain himself—even as he had been restrained by Venus from killing Helen in Book II—and that he substitute policy for spontaneous, natural human action.

Aeneas fails the final political test, yet, paradoxically, he reasserts his humanity at the same time. Why? The answer is not that Virgil is an obtuse and disoriented writer. Rather he is a poet who is also a shrewd and reliable witness of the real world. Aeneas is shown in the last six books growing in political consequence and command. Meanwhile his personality deteriorates and fades. His motives are less and less subject to scrutiny as those of a simple human being. Yet in the end he fails as a politician because human nature finally breaks through. But it is too late, and the wrong moment. His world and his vocation have changed, but at the last moment he himself betrays the new system he has instituted. Virgil shows us that the tension between natural man and civic man will probably never be fully resolved. This point is given excruciating prominence in Book VI, near the end of Anchises' prophetic vision of the panorama of Rome's history. Of Brutus, the first consul after the overthrow of the Etruscan kings, Virgil writes:

> consulis imperium hic primus saevasque securis
> accipiet, natosque pater nova bella moventis
> ad poenam pulchra pro libertate vocabit,
> infelix, utcumque ferent ea facta minores.

He first will receive the power of the consulate and the dread axes, and he, as father, will call his sons, plotting revolution, to due punishment, for the sake of dear liberty—a wretched man—or so lesser men will think who retell these things.

(819–822)

The phrase "wretched man, or so lesser men will think . . ." is the exact description of the terrible paradox of the political leader, the sensitivities of natural man meeting the leader's self-imposed duties to his society rather than to his blood and feelings. It is a tragedy, and tragedy quite beyond the matter of individual griefs, that political leadership, though indispensable, so often seems to end up in a situation in which a leader, having systematically educated himself to reject the promptings of mere nature, will either go a step too far and use policy in such an unnatural way that he disgusts other men, even if they appear to benefit from his acts, or else he will suffer a momentary lapse and abandon policy for a natural act at precisely the wrong point. The former was the fate of the first Brutus, who horrified the ancient Romans quite as much as the second Brutus horrified Plutarch and Shakespeare by killing Caesar; the latter is the fate of Aeneas. Virgil has planned the moment carefully: he has brought back personal motivation at the point where it is at one and the same time politically unacceptable, *but artistically necessary and conclusive.*

The politician is yet always a human being, even if the unique pressures of his profession tend to persuade him that this is not true. He cannot always see every problem presented to him as though it were a simple theorem in the geometry of power and of responsibility for the community. Usually his own humanity and weaknesses will at some point invade his behavior and this, though acceptable to art, will be disastrous for politics. It is not always the general dehumanization of politics that makes our collective social life especially dangerous, but sometimes its sudden *re*-humanization at the worst possible moment on an unpredictable schedule. The politician's existential risk is twofold, and probably intolerable for complete mental health: either he will lose his humanity entirely and become a robot or a fanatic, or he will reassert it at precisely the wrong moment, as Aeneas does, only to put everything wrong.

The ambiguity of critics and criticism when facing the *Aeneid* is simply a copy of the ambiguity an observer like Virgil must have felt in studying the careers of successful Roman politicians like Scipio, Sulla, Julius Caesar or Augustus. How can one do justice to a man who is both an individual and the embodiment of the *res publica?* It really can't be done. Virtually no one can stand the strain, ultimately, of both roles. Virgil's alleged and much-discussed demurrer against the Augustan system, if it exists, is not to be found at some superficial level like distrust of imperialism or autocracy. He is hardly interested in such abstractions. His entry into the political problem of Aeneas is effected at a much deeper point: he sees the acceptance of political leadership as a crucial denial of natural human feelings, which in the long run will probably rebel, and the eventuating crisis will destroy the characters of all but the strongest. Leadership is a necessary good—or evil, perhaps—but hardly ever can it provide ethical or personal satisfaction for the chosen vehicle. *Fata dederunt:* Aeneas often silences grumblers with such a phrase, but it only quiets lesser folk. For him all it means is that he personally has no escape and no prospect of contentment. What the fates have really granted is his own unwilled yoking to an enterprise that systematically overrules the feelings, or else guarantees that expression of natural life and feeling will bring him only gigantic troubles and endanger his civic aims. This honest and sympathetic account of the politician's dilemma in no sense makes the *Aeneid* an artistic failure. Far from it: it makes the poem a perfect portrayal of one of mankind's most serious and besetting problems, which no other literary work I know has expressed so convincingly.

J. WILLIAM HUNT

Labyrinthine Ways

Aeneas stood motionless, a fierce figure in his armor; but his eyes were restless, and he checked the fall of his right arm. And now at any moment the plea of Turnus, already working in his mind, might have prevailed on his hesitation; when suddenly, there before him, he saw slung over his shoulder the accursed baldric of Pallas and his belt inset with glittering rivets, which he had known of old when they had belonged to his young friend whom Turnus had brought low with a wound, and overcome. This baldric Turnus now was wearing over his shoulder, and the trophy was fatal to him. Aeneas' eyes drank in the sight of the spoils which revived the memory of his own vengeful bitterness. His fury kindled and, terrible in his rage, he said: "Are you to be stolen hence out of my grasp, you who wear spoils taken from one whom I loved? It is Pallas, only Pallas, who by this wound which I now deal makes sacrifice of you; he exacts this retribution, you criminal, from your blood." Saying this and boiling with rage Aeneas buried his blade full in Turnus' breast. His limbs relaxed and chilled; and the life fled moaning and resentful to the Shades.

Aeneid 12.938–52

Three vivid pictures of concrete action stand out memorably in the whole expanse of the *Aeneid:* the sword buried in the breast of Dido, the magic shield raised on Aeneas' shoulder, and the sword buried in the breast of Turnus. In the tripartite scheme of the twelve books, these three pictures occur as the final scenes in each of the three main "acts" of the *Aeneid* trilogy—books 1–4, a tragedy of love;

books 5–8, a tragedy of vocation; books 9–12, a tragedy of war. Each of the pictures culminates that particular book which closes each section of the epic, and which belongs in a special way to one of the three chief characters: Dido in the palace at Carthage in the fourth book, Aeneas at the site of Rome in the eighth book, Turnus on the battlefield of Latium in the twelfth.

Each picture focuses graphically the essential destiny of the three main figures of the poem, presenting a central light balanced on either side by darkness and death. When fused together in a unified vision of the whole epic, the three scenes indicate the relationship to Aeneas of the Dido and Turnus patterns, as a trinity of forces in a tragic parable of the human soul. As Aeneas' pursuit of a vision of glory brings ruin upon queen and prince alike, so their destruction frames and qualifies the final form his glory assumes. His future is founded upon a burial of their hopes.

One of the clearest functions of the twelfth book is to draw attention to the parallel fates of Dido and Turnus, by means of the repetition of many themes and images already seen in the fourth book. The thematic and imagistic echoes of Dido's death which surround the closing duel with Turnus emphasize Aeneas' final memory of both events together, each occurring so close in time to his central vision of glory. Both in leaving Carthage and in reaching Italy, Aeneas envisions only good; but Dido falls victim to his pursuit of the vision, Turnus to its realization. Only this haunting awareness of the guilt and pain implicit in both transactions fully poses the question of the *Aeneid,* the epic question with which the direct voice of the poet opens and closes the poem:

> I pray for inspiration, to tell how it all began, and how the queen of heaven sustained such outrage to her majesty that in her indignation she forced a man famed for his true-heartedness to tread that long path of adventure, and to face so many trials. Can the gods in heaven be capable of such rancor?
>
> (1.8–11)

> What god can now set forth for me in story all the horrors, all the various deeds of death, and tell how the chiefs perished, when all over the field of battle first Turnus, then Troy's hero in his turn, drove them fleeing? Jupiter! did you indeed ordain that nations who were to live together afterwards in everlasting peace should clash in such violence?
>
> (12.500–504)

While the parallel imagery of Dido and Turnus, therefore, suggests that much of Virgil's meaning lies in the balanced and alternating patterns, his fuller meaning lies in the framing by both patterns of the distinctive central section. This is why it seems at least as appropriate to speak of the

Aeneid as displaying three panels in the manner of a triptych, as to speak of it as unfolding three acts in the manner of a trilogy. The principal point, in any case, is that although the story must unfold in time its meaning emerges in a kind of spatial memory—i.e., its organic sense emerges only when the three parts are held together in a simultaneous vision. If the disparate themes and images were unified into a mental complex grasped spatially as a whole, the pattern of related meanings would fuse in an instantaneous impact, a genuinely comprehensive view whose apprehension would give the true form of the poem.

The twelfth book brings these parts together, as effectively as any single book of the epic can do so, by presenting the final triumph of Aeneas in such a way that not only Turnus but Dido also is present—Turnus concretely in the narrative, Dido implicitly in the recurring imagery. In a sense, it is as though the final book, telling of Turnus' last hours, also retells the last hours of Dido. As the epic sweeps to its climax, the verses repeatedly hint that Aeneas, unable to escape the memory of his final days in Carthage, will also be unable to escape the memory of his initial days in Italy. As his sword pierces the breast of Turnus, Aeneas seems to be reenacting Dido's death as well, and he stands at the end in victory bitterly won, burdened forever by a double indignity.

The twelfth book falls conveniently into three parts—preparations for the duel (1–215), its brief suspension by an outbreak of general fighting (216–697), and the final single combat of the two heroes (698–952). The first and third parts are each interrupted in the narrative by a sudden change of scene from earth to heaven. In the first part, while Latinus and Aeneas are praying before the altar set up on the dueling ground, Juno summons Juturna, the deified sister of Turnus, and asks her to save her brother by hindering the proposed combat. In the third part, when Juturna's efforts to reawaken the war have failed and the duel is under way, Jupiter prevails at last upon Juno to yield to his will and cease to oppose the Trojan fortunes, and he sends earthward one of the Furies to execute his judgment upon Turnus. Both divine interludes recall the two similar scenes in the opening book, when Juno first appealed to Aeolus to cause the storm off Carthage which opened the entire plot, and when Jupiter first prophesied to Venus the unfolding Roman destiny which has controlled the entire plot. Juno has known from the start the "plan of the spinning Fates" (*sic volvere Parcas* [1.22]) to be accomplished by a "people whom she hates" (*gens inimica mihi* [1.67]).

Despite all her opposition, through the agencies of Aeolus and Iris and Allecto and Juturna, the "day of the Fates and the malevolent force [Trojan victory] has finally come to pass": *Parcarumque dies et vis inimica propinquant* (12.150). But the destiny which Jupiter confided to Venus can only become effective with the acquiescence and cooperation of Juno. When the two supreme divinities finally settle the course of the future history of Italy by a compromise honorable for both Trojans and Italians, their reconciliation balances the initial prophecy, and intention can become actuality. Juno, enraged and unrelenting throughout the epic, assents with happiness to the final terms of peace, and reverses her will in the climactic line: *adnuit his Juno et mentem laetata retorsit* (12.841).

Both divine interludes in the twelfth book symbolize effectively the events enacted on earth—Juno through Juturna stimulating to action the natural forces and psychological processes already at work within the desperate Latins, and Juno with Jupiter dramatizing not only the larger issues at stake throughout a long and tragic tale of opposition but also the fulfillment of promise at the "moment of final decision": *ventum ad supremum est* (12.803). The second scene on Olympus thus resolves the tension which has bound together the whole expanse of the action: *saevae memorem Junonis ob iram* (1.4). But the last hundred lines of the twelfth book are not an anticlimax, for what has been symbolized in heaven must be enacted on earth. Turnus must still be defeated, for he represents disunion and strife, and a dread messenger is sent from Jupiter to effect Turnus' destruction by paralyzing his energies.

On the natural level of the action, the turning point of the twelfth book is the death of the Italian Tolumnius: "Tolumnius the seer himself fell, who had been the first to discharge a spear against their adversaries" (12.460–61). At the conclusion of the speeches of Latinus and Aeneas ratifying their compact in full view of all the captains, Juturna in the disguise of Camers has stirred up the Rutulians with pity for Turnus' unfair lot and with a passion to fight for him. She then displays a sign in the sky—an eagle, attacking a flock of swans and seizing the leading swan in its talons, is successfully routed a moment later by the united attack of the whole flock. The seer Tolumnius interprets the sign as an omen of Latin victory. Assuring his men that Aeneas will also take to flight if they will all close ranks and fight together, Tolumnius hurls the first spear and general conflict ensues. The altar is dismantled, Latinus flees back to the city, and a moment later Aeneas is wounded by Juturna (12.320–23, 813–15).

While Aeneas is away behind the battle lines, Turnus "burning anew with the sudden fire of hope" (*subita spe fervidus* [325]) ranges victoriously over the field and disaster seems imminent for the fleeing Trojans. But the tide of battle turns again when Aeneas comes back miraculously healed, and Tolumnius is one of the first Latins to fall. From that point, the exact center of the book, the Latins flee in their turn, and the Trojan success increases until Aeneas charges the walls of the city itself. To save the city from destruction, Turnus returns from the field and agrees to fight the interrupted duel. Longing for a city is one of the leading themes of the *Aeneid;* and it is a major part of the tragedy it unfolds that for Rome to rise four other cities must fall or at least undergo the most critical suffering— Troy (death of Priam), Carthage (death of Dido), Latium (death of Turnus), Pallanteum (death of Pallas).

Troy is the only city whose ruin is fully narrated, but many themes and images of the fourth book, which recur in the twelfth, are associated in each case with the siege of a city, for the fates of Carthage and Latium are closely connected to the falls of Dido and Turnus. The long preparation and final act of Dido's suicide is compared throughout with the shock of the capture and burning of a city; and, between the opening scene of the Dido episode in the first book and its climax in the fourth book, there intervenes Aeneas' recounting to her of the fall of Troy.

As Francis Newton has shown in his study of the fourth book's imagery, the fall of Aeneas' own city, like the fall Venus plans for Dido, was accomplished by deceit and by the will of certain gods. The metaphors of the conquest of Dido by the stratagems and weapons of Cupid and Venus culminate in the closing simile of the captured city, which rests upon the imagery of warfare woven into the whole narrative:

> Lamentation and sobbing and women's wailing rang through the houses, and high heaven echoed with the loud mourning (at the moment of Dido's death); as if some enemy had broken through and all Carthage, or ancient Tyre, were falling, with the flames rolling madly up over dwellings of gods and men.
>
> (4.667–71)

Again, in the actual warfare of the twelfth book, Venus once more is the direct inspiration prompting Aeneas to move against the walls of Latium at the height of the general fighting:

> Then the mother of Aeneas, goddess of rarest beauty, prompted him to move against the defence-walls and wheel his army quickly towards the city, to alarm the Latins by threat of sudden disaster.
>
> (12.554–56)

The simile of the bees, used to portray the panic and turmoil of the Latin defenders within the walls, recalls its first use to portray the happier ferment of activity by the Carthaginians when Aeneas first beheld the rising walls of Dido's city a year before:

It was like the work which keeps the bees hard at their tasks about the
flowering countryside as the sun shines in the calm of early summer, when
they escort their new generation, now full grown, into the open air, or
squeeze clear honey into bulging cells, packing them with sweet nectar;
or else take over loads brought by their foragers; or sometimes form up to
drive a flock of lazy drones from their farmstead. All is a ferment of activity,
and the scent of honey rises with the perfume of thyme.

(1.430–36)

As when a shepherd has tracked bees to their home in some volcanic rock
containing many a hiding place, and fills it with acrid smoke; the bees
inside, in desperation, hurry everywhere about the waxen fortress, hissing
loudly as they whet their anger, while the reeking smoke rolls black about
their home; the rock resounds darkly murmuring within, and fumes escape
to the open air.

(12.587–92)

Placed as they are at the beginning of the episode in Carthage and
at the end of the fighting in Italy, the two similes serve a double function.
The recurrence itself, in keeping with many other passages in the twelfth
book, focuses both tragedies together in the mind at the end of the poem;
and the contrast between both reveals the different relation of Dido and
Turnus to each city. The queen's death directly causes the plight of Carthage. On the contrary, the plight of Latium directly causes the prince's
death. Dido dies and a city is destroyed; Latium is on the point of destruction
and Turnus dies to save it. The despair of the queen and the valor of the
prince both end equally in death. The significant point is that their parallel
disasters result from one or the other of the two chief qualities for which
Aeneas is most praised throughout the epic: *insignis pietate et armis*, which
may justly be rendered—devotion to his mission (Dido), and strength to
execute it (Turnus).

Images of fire are also prevalent in each book, both external flames
and the fire of inner passion. Venus inflames Dido, entwining the fire of
passion about her very bones, an invisible fire which grows steadily to the
point of helpless frenzy and culminates in the real flames of her pyre.
Professor Newton writes:

The image of fire dominates the close of the book. Mercury's words
threaten danger to Aeneas (a second boat-burning) if he does not sail at
once. The image recurs in Dido's speech as she looks after the departing
ships; she thinks at first of summoning her Tyrians (to bring firebrands)
but turns instead to her imagined revenge, the *faces* and *flammae* she might
have used on the Trojan camp. Then she solemnly invokes the flaming
sun and other gods to hear her curse. The climax of the curse is in the

hatred between Carthaginian and Trojan. Fire and warfare are to be the means of Dido's vengeance upon the people whom she hates, and the fires of hatred are to replace the fires of love. . . . The passion of Dido's will not die but will live as fire and sword (wound) to avenge her. In the simile of the captured city, which shows the significance of her death and knits up several images in one, the final impression is one of swirling flames, (4.670–671); and the blaze of fire (her funeral pyre) reflected on the city's walls is, fittingly, Aeneas' last view of Carthage.

There is a similar progression in the twelfth book from the inner fire of Turnus' passionate fury to real flames threatening the walls of Latium. The book has opened to show Turnus "blazing with an implacable anger" (*implacabilis ardet* [12.3]) which mounts ever higher despite the pleas of Latinus and Amata to give up the duel. This opening scene in the palace ends by linking his fury and his love together in a single image of fire, as Turnus fixes his eyes upon Lavinia, and burning love "makes all the hotter his passion to fight": *ardet in arma magis* (71). Even his sword is a magic one forged by Vulcan, "the god whose might is fire": *ignipotens deus* (90). When Aeneas is wounded at the altar, Turnus is depicted as burning once again with a "sudden fire of hope" (*subita spe fervidus* [325]), and at the height of the general conflict both heroes are compared to forest fires released from different directions (521–22). Aeneas' own imagination "kindles" (*accendit* [560]) at the thought of attacking the city directly as the only way for him either to force all the Latins to acknowledge defeat or to compel Turnus himself to return and fight him alone. He commands his men to fetch firebrands and to "exact restoration of the truce by the argument of flames": *foedus reposcite flammis* (573).

In the climax of the fire-imagery at this point, metaphors of fire and madness are joined together in the frenzied suicide of Amata as she sees the flames approaching the palace, and in the immediately subsequent madness that overcomes Latinus when he hears of her death and beholds his city falling in flames. The many verbal similarities in the accounts of the two suicides of Amata and Dido are striking, in each case intensified by the madness of uncontrolled passion and its intimate connection with the fall of a city. Thus Amata's final act, as well as the surrounding imagery and poetic overtones, brings Dido once again vividly into the context of the final book at the very moment when the scene shifts again to Turnus.

In Turnus' heart, as in the heart of Dido, are mingled shame and a consuming passion for revenge, and love and madness and misery blending (4.531–32; 12.666–68). He realizes also that his return to the duel will mean his death, and he admits to Juturna that his decision is in a way insane and in effect suicidal: "let me do this one mad deed before I die" (*sine me furere ante furorem* [680]). The grip of madness on queen and prince alike is stressed repeatedly in both books by the same epithet, *demens* or *amens*, "frenzy" or "helpless bewilderment"; and their parallel mood is chiefly expressed in metaphors and similes of fire, an encompassing fire framing the epic at both ends in the opening and closing panels, and in the mind of Aeneas an irremovable fire from which the light of his final triumph can never be dissociated.

In the closing lines of the forth and twelfth books (the suicide and the duel), three further parallel similes occur which are connected exclusively with the deaths of Dido and Turnus, i.e., the wounded deer, the bird of ill omen, and the nightmare. The simile of the wounded deer actually comes early in the fourth book, but images related to it pervade the whole book and culminate in the actual wound causing Dido's death. The first wound is the one inflicted earlier by Cupid, mentioned again in the fourth book's opening lines as a deep "wound of love's invisible fire draining her life's blood" (*vulnus alit venis et caeco carpitur igni* [4.2]) and suggested immediately after by Aeneas' "countenance and words transfixed within her heart": *haerent infixi pectore vultus/verbaque* (4–5).

The wound is again closely linked to fire as Dido seeks relief from her infatuation in prayer and sacrifice to the gods: "the flame ate into her melting marrow, and deep in her heart the wound was silently alive" (4.66–67). Professor Newton comments:

> The echo of *pectore vultus* (4.4) in *pectore vulnus* (4.67) is unmistakable; in the earlier expression we are justified in seeing that the expression and words of Aeneas were metaphorically the barbs of love which remained fixed in the wound. This interpretation is borne out by the simile which follows quickly (the third and principal one in which Dido is compared to a wounded deer):

>> Poor Dido was afire, and roamed distraught all over her city; like a doe caught off her guard and pierced by an arrow from some armed shepherd, who from a distance had chased her amid Cretan woods and without knowing it has left in her his winged barb; so that she traverses in her flight forests and mountain tracks on Dicte, with the deadly reed fast in her flesh (4.68–73).

The simile is anticipated (by the three metaphors mentioned) and the clear echoes help to tie the image of the wounded deer more closely to the actual picture of Dido. The episode of the hunt (129–59) after this vivid simile, is clearly a literal echo of the image in the simile; the fleeing deer appear again, and Aeneas is compared with the archer Apollo. . . . Dido is the real victim of the hunt, and her death, which was dimly foreshadowed in the simile of the deer, is now directly prophesied by the poet: *ille dies primus leti primusque malorum/causa fuit* (169–70). Finally, her metaphorical wound has its literal parallel, her actual wound, in the close of the book, and the verbal echoes make the repetition of the image plain.

When the simile recurs in the twelfth book, it is expanded, and the element of pursuit is more marked. Aeneas himself has been wounded beforehand and is unable to catch Turnus as they circle the battlefield five times. Also, in the fourth book's simile the deer was caught off guard and the shepherd wounded her from afar without knowing it; but in the twelfth book's simile both pursuer and pursued are fully aware and terrifyingly close, although the wound is actually not inflicted until later. The main point of the second simile is that Turnus is trapped no matter where he runs and that Aeneas is untiring in pursuit:

> inclusum veluti si quando flumine nactus
> cervum aut puniceae saeptum formidine pennae
> venator cursu canis et latratibus instat;
> ille autem insidiis et ripa territus alta
> mille fugit refugitque vias, at vividus Umber
> haeret hians, iam iamque tenet similisque tenenti
> increpuit malis morsuque elusus inani est.

Aeneas was like a hound at a time when, knowing that he has a stag entrapped by a river or hemmed in by dread of the redfeather scares, he presses on him, running and barking; the stag darts to and fro a thousand ways, in fear of ambush and the river's high bank; but the untiring Umbrian hound hangs onto him, mouth wide open, and at every moment about to grip, snapping his jaws as if he already had him, but biting nothing and eluded still.

(12.749–55)

The contrast between the two similes suggests how easily and inadvertently Aeneas wounded the unsuspecting Dido against his will, but how difficult it proves for him to inflict the fervently intended wound upon the mightier Turnus. Three times already, at the close of previous books, Turnus has escaped confrontation with Aeneas: first, by leaping into the Tiber from the walls of the Trojan camp (9.812–18); second, by drifting out to sea in pursuit of the wraith of Aeneas wrought by Juno to remove Turnus from the field when the tide of battle turns against him (10.633–58); third, by returning to the city walls upon hearing of Camilla's death just a moment before Aeneas enters the forest pass where Turnus planned to ambush him (11.896–915).

Turnus' second escape is particularly interesting, for in the tenth book Turnus himself pursues unavailingly what he thinks to be a terrified Aeneas but which is actually Aeneas' "nervous wraith in flight": *trepida fugientis imago* (10.656). The pursuit is compared to a dream with flitting shapes which delude perception (10.639–42). Also, the last line of the twelfth book's deer simile (12.755) is foreshadowed, though in reverse circumstances, by Turnus' "drinking deep of a confused and delusive hope": *animo spem turbidus hausit inanem* (10.648). The remembrance of this dream-like pursuit, in the real pursuit at the end of the poem, once again brings Dido into the context of the twelfth book. For the echo not only recalls Turnus' own attempt at suicide in the tenth book once he realized with shame and despair that he had been tricked into flight from battle, but the echo also recalls Dido's own frenzied roving in the fourth book through the streets of Carthage seeking a lost Aeneas.

These images of a besieged city and of fire, of wounding and of pursuit, are not only spread out through the whole of the fourth and twelfth books but also suggest many other literal scenes in the poem. But of the three parallel similes mentioned (wound, bird, and nightmare), the two latter pictures of the bird of ill omen and of the nightmare are unique, applied only to the death scenes of Dido and Turnus. For this reason they are especially startling when they occur and memorable in combination. Toward the close of each book, Dido and Turnus are seemingly possessed by demon-powers, profoundly bewildered in their agony of loss and failure, and hardly conscious of what they say or do. The shadows of confusion and bitter sorrow close in upon them, and their mood is externalized by accompanying pictures of lament and derangement.

In the fourth book, both pictures occur together in a single simile, shortly after Dido's last appeal to the unmoved Aeneas; his "fixity of mind" (*mens immota* [449]) is contrasted to her own increasing "derangement of mind": *demens* (469). She sees with horror the fate starkly confronting her; her only prayer is now for death, since life has become unbearable. As if to steel her will to fulfill her design and to part from the light of day, she lays offerings on the altars. The holy waters turn black before her eyes, and the wine she pours in libation is changed by some sinister transformation into blood.

When she enters her palace chapel at nightfall, she imagines herself to hear cries as though of her former husband Sychaeus calling to her; and then comes the lonely owl's deathly lamentation as well as the nightmare of a furious Aeneas pursuing her and driving her wild with fear:

> hinc exaudiri voces et verba vocantis
> visa viri, nox cum terras obscura teneret,

solaque culminibus ferali carmine bubo
saepe queri et longas in fletum ducere voces;
multaque praeterea vatum praedicta priorum
terribili monitu horrificant. Agit ipse furentem
in somnis ferus Aeneas, semperque relinqui
sola sibi, semper longam incomitata videtur
ire viam et Tyrios deserta quaerere terra.

Now from this chapel when night held the world in darkness she thought that she distinctly heard cries, as of her husband calling to her; and often on a rooftop a lonely owl would sound her deathly lamentation, drawing out her notes into a long wail; then many presages of ancient seers shocked her to panic by their dread warnings. She would have nightmares of a furious Aeneas pursuing her and driving her wild with fear, or of being left utterly alone and traveling companionless a long road, searching for Tyrian friends in a deserted land.

(4.460–68)

After dreaming of Aeneas' pursuit while she flees in frenzied terror, a strange reversal of her waking desire, Dido again fancies herself left utterly alone (relinqui, sola, incomitata, deserta) while forever and ever (semper, semper) she roams an endless path in search of her lost people. Her nightmare makes Aeneas vividly present at her death though absent in the flesh. Also, the later double echo of Dido's nightmare in the twelfth book—both in Aeneas' real pursuit of Turnus and in another simile of nightmare at the very moment of Turnus' death at Aeneas' hands—makes all three characters vividly present as the poem closes. This account of Dido's terrifying dream ends by comparing her to Pentheus and Orestes, both pursued by Furies; the passage is notable as the only direct reference in the epic to stage representations, in this case the Bacchae of Euripides and the Eumenides of Aeschylus.

In Euripides, Pentheus the king of Thebes is shown driven mad for opposing the worship of Bacchus, the form of his madness consisting in seeing double, two suns and two cities of Thebes, and the Furies advancing in ranks (469–70). In Aeschylus, Agamemnon's tormented son Orestes is shown seeking to escape his mother armed with firebrands and black snakes, while the Furies await him at the threshold to continue the pursuit (471–73). The cumulative effect of this entire scene in the chapel is one of intense terror, rendered doubly horrifying by strange sounds amidst absolute solitude as well as by the eerie fusion of real and imaginary elements.

In the twelfth book, both similes, the wailing owl and the nightmare, occur separately at the beginning and at the end of the duel's second part. As we saw, the closing duel falls into two equal parts, divided by the interlude on Olympus. The first part opens with Turnus' return to the city.

Just as Anna's account of Aeneas' immovable resolve at Carthage brought on Dido's confusion of spirit, so Saces' account of Aeneas' determined charge of Latium's walls strikes Turnus "silent with bewilderment at the picture of manifold calamity": *obstipuit varia confusus imagine rerum* (12.665).

As he bursts through the battle's center and rushes toward the city, two brief similes foreshadow the outcome of the duel. Turnus is compared to a huge boulder dislodged from the side of a mountain and crashing "headlong down from the crest" (*de vertice praeceps* [684]); while Aeneas is compared to the mountain itself "joyously lifting" its snow-covered head to the sky: *laetitia exsultans* (700). Meeting on a level stretch of ground, both heroes charge like two bulls, while the "herdsmen" in alarm draw back and stand silent in dread. When the sword Turnus is using shatters into fragments against the magic shield of Aeneas, Turnus flees in panic, circling in aimless curves over the battlefield. His own sword, the magic sword of Vulcan, has been left behind with his charioteer Metiscus when Turnus rushed from the altar in characteristic headlong haste to enter the general fighting.

While Aeneas, unable to catch up with Turnus, labors to wrench his spear from a tree stump, Turnus in his flight upbraids the Latins and demands his own familiar sword. Juturna, who had assumed the shape of Metiscus and therefore has the sword, gives it back to Turnus. Venus reciprocates by tearing Aeneas' spear from the deep root. The first encounter thus ends with both champions facing each other again, their weapons and spirits restored. When the dialogue of reconciliation on Olympus has concluded, the second and final part of the duel begins. Jupiter summons the fury Megaera, one of the "daughters of unseasonable night" (*nox intempesta tulit* [846]), and sends her earthward as an omen of death, to confound Turnus and paralyze his energies. She sweeps down, like an arrow sped hissing on its way "to dart through the shadows unseen" (*incognita transilit umbras* [859]), like a poisoned "arrow for which there is no healing": *telum immedicabile* (858). The image recalls the fourth book's simile of the wounded deer, and also the metaphors of Dido's heart secretly poisoned by Cupid's darts. It offers as well a significant contrast to Aeneas' wound miraculously healed shortly before.

When the fury reaches the battlefield, she shrinks into the form of an owl, eerily screeching and circling again and again around the head and face of Turnus, beating his shield aside with her wings:

> Talis se sata Nocte tulit terrasque petivit.
> Postquam acies videt Iliacas atque agmina Turni,
> alitis in parvae subitam collecta figuram,

quae quondam in bustis aut culminibus desertis
nocte sedens serum canit importuna per umbras;
hanc versa in faciem Turni se pestis ob ora
fertque refertque sonans clipeumque everberat alis.
Illi membra novus solvit formidine torpor,
arrectaeque horrore comae et vox faucibus haesit.

So darted the daughter of Night as she made her way to earth. When she saw the Trojan lines and the army of Turnus, at once she shrank to the form of that small bird which in the night perches on tombstones or deserted rooftops and eerily sings her late song among the shadows. Changed into this shape, the demon noisily passing and passing again flew into the face of Turnus and beat his shield aside with her wings. Every limb of Turnus went limp, numbed by a strange dread. His hair stiffened in horror; his voice was clogged in his throat.

(12.860–68)

The earlier *nox intempesta*, the dead of night when time stops and no man can use it, is echoed in the owl's unfavorable and oppressive hooting (*importuna per umbras*), an eerie sound from the night full of awe and melancholy, surrounding Turnus at midday, as before it surrounded Dido at midnight, with the atmosphere of solitude and death: *quondam in bustis aut culminibus desertis*. The flight of the bird around his head also recalls numerous other passages in the twelfth book of circular twisting and weaving, connected with the notion of unavailing pursuit and deep perplexity. Finally, the "pallor of imminent death" upon the countenance of Dido as she mounted the pyre (*pallida morte futura* [4.644]) is echoed by the strange torpor which numbs the limbs of Turnus as he faces Aeneas' quivering spear. The last line of the simile above (868) is a verbal repetition from the fourth book (4.280). It was used first to describe Aeneas' shock after the first appearance of Mercury, and is used here of Turnus as he beholds the specter of Megaera.

Both divine spirits are messengers sent directly from Jupiter; and both bring death, Mercury's command resulting indirectly in Dido's suicide, Megaera's presence directly presaging Turnus' death. Both the Olympian interlude and the descent of Megaera take only an instant in the time of the battle, between the restoration of both heroes' weapons and Aeneas' immediate move toward Turnus to bring him within range of his spear. We may regard the heavenly and earthly scenes as simultaneous, or regard the simultaneity itself as an indication that divine forces operate unbound by the world of time. Juturna has recognized in the bird of ill omen the final "imperious command" of Jupiter (*iussa superba* [877]) and has sorrowfully left Turnus, hiding once more in the water's depths both herself and her divine power to aid him. Left utterly alone, his strange numbness (novus torpor [867]) is quickly increased, growing into a "paralyzing fear and trembling at the spear-point's imminence": cunctaturque metu letumque instare tremescit (12.916).

Since Turnus' sword, magical though it may be, proves useless against the spear of Aeneas, Turnus snatches up a huge stone with impetuous haste and is about to hurl it at Aeneas, raising himself to greater height for the action and running at high speed. But he has no sense of running or moving, or lifting his hands, or giving any impulse to the stone. His knees give way, his blood seems to freeze, and the stone which he casts whirls across empty space and falls short of Aeneas. Turnus' utter helplessness and solitude are very movingly expressed by the dream simile, the last simile in the poem and one of the finest, which accompanies his final effort:

> ac velut in somnis, oculos ubi languida pressit
> nocte quies, nequiquam avidos extendere cursus
> velle videmur et in mediis conatibus aegri
> succidimus—non lingua valet, non corpore notae
> sufficiunt vires, nec vox aut verba sequuntur:
> Sic Turno, quacumque viam virtute petivit,
> successum dea dira negat.

As sometimes in our sleeping, when at night a languor of stillness lies heavy on our eyes, we dream that we strive desperately to run ever onwards, and we fail, and sink down fainting at the very moment of our greatest effort; our tongue is strengthless, the body's powers will give no normal response, and neither words nor even voice will come; so was it with Turnus, for wherever he exerted his valor to find an opening, the weird goddess denied him success.

(12.908–14)

The elements of darkness and pursuit, of helplessness and desertion, are shared in common with Dido's nightmare. But the chief difference and the most terrifying aspect of the simile applied to Turnus is its absolute soundlessness, as though the world had already vanished from around him and he were enveloped in a deathly silence, unable even to make any sound himself. Through his mind whirl many "shifting fancies" (sensus varii [915]) and he can find no place of refuge nor any strength to press home an attack on Aeneas, nor can he anywhere see his chariot or his sister at the reins. Aeneas' whistling spear flies at him as strongly as a storm cloud "charged with ghastly death": exitium dirum hasta ferens (924).

Turnus sinks to the ground with his knees bent under him, his thigh pierced. Aeneas rejects his plea for mercy (ulterius ne tende odiis [938]) and

buries his sword full in Turnus' breast. Already numbed in flight and met-
aphorically paralyzed just a moment before, Turnus' limbs relax in the chill
of death:

> hoc dicens ferrum adverso sub pectore condit
> fervidus. Ast illi solvuntur frigore membra
> vitaque cum gemitu fugit indignata sub umbras.

> Saying this and boiling with rage, Aeneas buried [condit] his blade full in
> Turnus' breast; his limbs relaxed and chilled, and his life fled moaning
> and resentful to the shades.

> (12.950–52)

The prevalent imagery at the close of both tragedies, of Dido and
of Turnus, implies not only physical destruction—besieged city, fire, wounding. It implies also a more radical destruction of purpose and a profoundly
disturbing confusion of spirit—birds of ill omen, paralysis of mind and will,
dream-pursuits, aimless circles. All of this is in sharp contrast to the brightness and wonder and hope of the eighth book, which culminates Aeneas'
visionary awareness of the future. His dreams, in the middle panel especially, present an ultimate convergence of past and future in a vast process
of reconciliation; but the two great tragedies built into the structure of the
epic bring Aeneas' *pietas* into conflict first in the opening panel with the
personal affections of Dido and then in the closing panel with the patriotic
valor of Turnus, and they both fall as sacrifices to the progress of the Roman
cause. Professor William C. Green comments:

> Aeneas is rewarded for his devotion by severe hardships and anguish of
> heart. He is granted a unique and splendid vision, but it is only a vision
> after all, and he is never fully certain of the truth of things. He moves
> resolutely through the obscure issues of life, discerning a distant goal and
> approximating it by slow steps, but feeling the weight of sorrow all the
> way, and intensely preoccupied with perplexing choices.

In the end as in the beginning, both Carthage and Latium (and the
continuing memory of Troy) furnish images and actions of frustration and
hopelessness. The bright Arcadia of the eighth book concluding the visionary middle panel shows Aeneas in a wonderland filled with tenuous
hope and free of tragic loss. But the whole narrative, as it opened with the
mysterious portents of Troy's fall and the traumatic flight into exile, also
ends in an atmosphere strongly resembling a nightmare, a labyrinthine
maze of dream and reality interfused and of success and failure inextricably
mingled. The design of the epic thus encloses the vision of glory with a
fusion on either side of violence and the unknown.

The *Aeneid* consistently exhibits persons and events in antithetical contrast with one another, implying tragic contradictions beneath the surface. The poem's final word in any matter is never a "dogmatic thesis" but always a "balancing of possibilities," and it bears clearly the imprint throughout of Virgil's divided mind. The central hero can understand only in part, even though he must act as if he had full understanding; and his adventure is a tale of success but also of essential unhappiness, because the fruits of victory seem to become dust and ashes in the act of achievement.

The final slaying of Turnus contains an ambiguity found in all the other major events of the epic. It will always be possible to say that for Aeneas to have spared Turnus might have been a betrayal of his mission for which everything else had been endured, or that his taking of Turnus' life was an act of stark revenge culminating a series of disasters to friend and foe alike. The poem's context leaves the event in a mingled balance of good and evil which eludes our moral judgment or any single psychological response. Again, it might seem that Aeneas could have accomplished his mission with less disaster to others if he were more sensitive to individual feelings and unspoken private desires; but the question remains whether his task could have been carried through at all without his unswerving commitment and his refusal to consider feelings and desires opposed to that task. Responsible for the past and dedicated to the future, Aeneas like every man bears the burden of both in memory and in desire, as well as the harrowing fusion of both in present action, and the mystery of the unknown surrounding all. His achievements are forever qualified by the remembrance of injury and imperfection; he shares emotionally in every loss and failure of contrary purpose, and must endure the awareness as the price and the very form of his glory.

It would be equally wrong to consider the *Aeneid* either an unqualified hymn to glory or a bitter attack on the worth of its achievement; the poem is neither propaganda nor renunciation. The glory is radically qualified throughout, yet the reiterated censure of it is intensely sympathetic and regretful. This unique fusion of triumph and regret is accomplished predominantly through the form of the work, the total pattern of its parts which in breathing together contain and dispense a sense of life unique to the poet of Rome.

Because the elements of panegyric are skillfully incorporated into the pervasive tragic design, with each of the two moods by repeated contrast making its opposite all the more explicit, the poet in effect neither praises nor condemns what he vividly portrays. The problems of human action are perceptively and artfully posed in the structure and sense of the whole epic, but final judgment is suspended. The *Aeneid* reveals, as William Green says:

> Virgil's preference for the concrete story that suggests rather than states the truth, that adumbrates the direction where the truth may lie, that like a parable or a myth expresses values rather than facts, that constantly leaves room for both sides of a case to linger in the mind.

In the light of all we have said, there are two last quotations from the center of the poem which may focus what this study has tried to convey and which the reader will need to reflect upon. The first phrase occurs just before the climax of the dream in the sixth book, when Aeneas has encountered the spirit of his father in the underworld and Anchises is about to reveal the glorious vision of the Roman future. As the two stand by Lethe's river, Aeneas first asks who the countless souls are crowding its banks, and Anchises answers that they are those destined to live in the body a second time once Lethe's waters of oblivion have removed all memory of their past lives. At this point, only an instant before the longest and most forceful vision of earthly glory unfolds, Aeneas cries out in unbelief that the dead should ever wish to return to the world of suffering and live through it all again. His cry ends in the question "Why this appalling love of the anguished for the light?" (6.721): *Quae lucis miseris tam dira cupido?*

The union of the vision and the cry forces us to consider neither glory nor despair alone but the truth their fusion evokes; and this tension of opposites is the poem's most characteristic feature. The epic as a whole proclaims nothing strictly, yet it allows everything to coincide in the power of its design, which resonates invisible but radiant through the words that bring it into being. Captured within the explanatory design there lies latent the mood of a universal melancholy at the contradictions of life—a deep and comprehensive sadness that man can act only to destroy, that no perception is sure and no purpose guaranteed, that the loveliest qualities of existence are the most fragile and evanescent, that glory is a path of evil, that everything living is touched with death. A revelation almost intolerable outside the solemn sweetness of his verse, this somber sense of human life rests in the structure of Virgil's poem like a sleeping beauty waiting to be disclosed, emerging in answer to concern. Hazardous to awaken and haunting to endure but long desired and true, the Virgilian vision irradiates his poem "like a light wind or most like a fleeting dream" (6.702): *par levibus ventis volucrique simillima somno.*

W. R. JOHNSON

The Worlds Virgil Lived In

He err'd not, for by this the heavnly Bands
Down from a Skie of Jasper lighted now
In Paradise, and on a Hill made halt,
A Glorious Apparition, had not doubt
And carnal fear that day dimm'd Adams eye.

— MILTON

Great writers are never the products of the times they live in, though they often seem so because they reflect— indirectly but brilliantly—the events, the common attitudes, hopes, and fears of their contemporaries. But they do not merely react to events or passions or "doctrines of the times" as purely popular writers do; they also react against events and contemporary attitudes and use these critical re- actions to shape something permanent and true out of the ephemeral. All these true truisms mean here is that the term "the Augustan Age" identifies a propaganda device that was very successful and is now a handy but somewhat deceptive category for people who are engaged in writing or lecturing about the poetry or the art or the political events or social patterns that existed within a certain span of time. The only world that Virgil lived in was the poetic one he created out of the various dying and evolving worlds that he inhabited with his contemporaries. In this chapter I shall examine some of the raw materials that these partial worlds offered Virgil when he began to fashion, and as he kept fashioning, his epic; in looking at these raw materials I have two aims.

First, I think it is important to qualify the idea that Virgil is an Augustan poet. Whatever its connections with the Ara Pacis, which it partly inspired, it would be more nearly correct to say that the *Aeneid* created the Augustan Age than to say that the Augustan Age produced, in any way, the *Aeneid*. It was the passionate concern and the imagination of Virgil that supplied an intellectual coherence to a period of time that would otherwise have lacked it, and of the few contemporaries of Virgil who cared about that coherence, Augustus took from it only what interested him. It was the mind and heart of Virgil that brought intellectual and aesthetic order to the confused and anxious times in which he lived.

Second, since in many of the configurations it presents, Virgil's epic is about degenerations and renewals; since in at least one of its aspects it ponders the tragic failure of classical humanism to confront its own weaknesses and the new dangers that threaten it from without, it seems useful for a reading of the poem to emphasize that Virgil lived in an age when the shared metaphors that any society requires in order to exist were disintegrating and when, therefore, Virgil and his contemporaries were beginning to inhabit separate and divided worlds. This problem did not worry Lucretius, who had no use for this kind of metaphor or for the kind of society that required metaphors for its existence. But the tough independence of Lucretius, rare in any age, was clearly very rare in the late republic and early empire, and Virgil was worried about the disintegration of the shared metaphors and their community. The *Aeneid* records, among other things, Virgil's effort to close with and to master this worry over the divisions of a unity he believed in. And the dying and divided worlds that Virgil lived in were only renewed and unified by Virgil's hard-won ability to admit the fact of their death and division. When we talk of the Augustan Age, whether we know it or not, it is often this single act of self-discipline and courage that we have in mind.

"QUOD CREDAS": THE SOCIAL ORDER

Virgil was roughly fifteen years old when Catullus and Lucretius were engaged in creating their different poetic emigrations from the ruining city: the one turning, with something like the cultivated despair of a modern symbolist, towards an elaborate and beautiful nihilism; the other hammering out a music and a vision that could contain and express his austere loneliness and his inner freedom from fear and from society. Since it is well known that the Romans thought that society was reality, it will be seen that both of these poets, each in his own way, had invented a desperate remedy. When Virgil was just over twenty years old, the war between Caesar's men and Pompey's men began. He was twenty-six when Caesar was murdered and Cicero, in a final burst of idealism and practicality, attempted to sum up in *De Officiis* what the republic had tried to be and what it could have been and should have been. At twenty-eight he began his pastoral experiments, and he continued to work at them during a period when, it seemed, there was some hope for Rome after all. These he completed when he was thirty-three, and—when hope had begun to waver and fade again—he began what was to be his technical masterpiece, the *Georgics*, which was completed when he turned forty-one, and hope had returned again. What all this means, even perhaps for those who despise biographical criticism, is that Virgil grew to his young manhood and began and continued his poethood under the constant reality, or the constant threat, of civil war.

This brief sketch of the political situations in which Virgil disciplined his gifts and perfected his powers gives little warrant to the notion that during the twenties "the Augustan settlement was hailed with almost universal enthusiasm" or that Roman "defeatism and despair were succeeded by unbounded confidence and hope." It is true that the *Aeneid* frequently shows marks of enthusiasm and a good deal of hope and that nowhere in the poem do we confront anything that smacks of the anonymous wit's grand muttering: "omnia mutasti Saturnia saecula, Caesar, / incolumi nam te ferrea semper erunt." This ironic view of the permanence of the Augustan settlement could not be precisely formulated until long after Virgil was dead, until Ovid imagined it thoroughly because he had had the unfortunate advantage of living under the completed settlement and had begun to guess what price had been paid for it and would continue to be paid. Writing in the twenties, Virgil may well have felt varying degrees of confidence in Augustus, but even Virgil, a tragic lyricist with little satiric impulse, watched the first decade of the principate with the anxiety and foreboding that constantly inform his epic. Nor is the reason far to seek. Marvelous as Augustus clearly was, capable and even fair-minded as he often seemed (and very frequently was), not even this miracle could obliterate the century of terror. Suppose Augustus should die before the miracle was consummated? Suppose, in a way more dreadful still, he should alter his purposes? It is the clear terrible truth of civil war and the fact of uncertainty about anything in human affairs that shape this poem and stick in the mind when we put the poem aside. (But the myth demands certainty.)

The war that fills the last half of the *Aeneid* is, unequivocally, a civil war. When Allecto has completed her dirty work and is, much against her will, about to be sent back where she belongs (*invisum numen, terras caelumque levabat*), she announces her grand success in this fashion: *en perfecta tibi bello discordia tristi: / dic in amicitiam coeant et foedera iungant* (7.545–546). She refers to the fact that the Trojans and the Latins, who were fated to become one people in a great *civitas*, have had their union tainted from the outset by Juno's interference:

> verum ubi nulla datur caecum exsuperare potestas
> consilium, et saevae nutu Iunonis eunt res,
> multa deos aurasque pater testatus inanis
> "frangimur heu fatis" inquit "ferimurque procella!
> ipsi has sacrilego pendetis sanguine poenas,
> o miseri. te, Turne, nefas, te triste manebit
> supplicium votisque deos venerabere seris;
> nam mihi parta quies omnisque in limine portus
> funere felici spolior."

> But when no power is granted him to check
> their blind resolve, when all moves at the will
> of savage Juno, then—again, again—
> father Latinus calls upon the gods
> and on the empty air; he cries: "The fates
> have crushed us, we are carried by the storm.
> Unhappy men! The penalty for this
> will yet be paid with your profaning blood.
> O Turnus, vengeance, bitter punishment
> for this unholy act will wait for you;
> too late your prayers will venerate the gods.
> My rest is near, my harbor is in view;
> a happy burial is all I lose."

> (7.591–599)

Thus Latinus, ignorant of Allecto and Juno and crying out to the *empty* air, singles out Turnus for chief blame. Aeneas—ignorant of Allecto, Juturna, and Juno—will, in his desperation, blame Latinus:

> ipse inter primos dextram sub moenia tendit
> Aeneas, magnaque incusat voce Latinum,
> testaturque deos iterum se ad proelia cogi,
> bis iam Italos hostes, haec iam altera foedera rumpi.

> Aeneas
> himself is in the vanguard, stretching out
> his hand beneath the ramparts; and he shouts
> his accusations at Latinus, calls
> the gods to witness that he had been forced
> to battle; twice the Latins have become
> his enemies; twice they have broken treaties.

> (12.579–582)

Turnus will blame Juturna, out of real desperation, for he has guessed the truth:

> o soror, et dudum agnovi, cum prima per artem
> foedera turbasti teque haec in bella dedisti,
> et nunc nequiquam fallis dea, sed quis Olympo
> demissam tantos voluit te ferre labores?

> O sister, I knew you long since, both when
> you first disturbed our pact by craftiness
> and plunged into these wars; and when you tried—
> in vain—to trick me, hiding your godhead.
> But who has willed that you be sent from high
> Olympus to endure such trials?
>
> (12.632–635)

Yes, Turnus, Latinus, and Juturna are all, in a sense, to blame for the breaking of the *foedera* and for the appearance of *discordia*, but behind the violence, confusions, and misunderstandings that open the second part of the poem with Book 7 and close it with Book 12, *saevae nutu Iunonis eunt res*, even though as Juno herself admits with splendid, chilling accuracy as she dismisses Allecto:

> te super aetherias errare licentius auras
> haut pater ille velit, summi regnator Olympi;
> cede locis; ego, si qua super fortuna laborum est,
> ipsa regam.

> The lord of high
> Olympus will not let you wander free
> about the upper air. Be gone from here.
> I can attend to all that now remains.
>
> (7.557–560)

But if Jupiter objects to Allecto as *agent provocateur*, what does he think of what his wife is about to do?

> nec minus interea extremam Saturnia bello
> imponit regina manum.

> ilicet infandum cuncti contra omina bellum,
> contra fata deum, perverso numine poscunt.

> tum regina deum caelo delapsa morantis
> inpulit ipsa manu portas et cardine verso
> belli ferratos rumpit Saturnia postes.

> Meanwhile the royal daughter of Saturn gives
> a final touch to war.

At once, despite the signs and oracles
of gods, through some perverted power all
ask for unholy war.

                Then the queen of gods,
when she had glided from the heavens, forced
the slow gates; on their turning hinges Saturn's
daughter burst the iron doors of war.
             (7.572–573, 583–584, 620–622)

Virgil's brilliant reshaping of Ennius' verse (Saturnia replaces Discordia)
and the theologically perverse, almost Gnostic oxymoron (*contra fata deum
perverso numine*) strongly emphasize that what is happening in Book 7 and
what will soon happen in Book 12 means, inevitably, the corruption of the
city. For Juno to become Discordia, for her *numen* to become *perversum*,
this represents a condition in the life of the city and a tendency in human
affairs that finds no solution whatever in the poem. The poem may indeed
point beyond itself to solutions (clearly it points to the need for solutions),
and, to the extent that it does, it may be said to show some degree of hope
or even of confidence. But if Juno does not win in this poem (and it is not
clear that she does not), she does not lose either. And if she does not lose,
the dark forces of social corruption have not been dissipated and the realities
of human savagery and selfishness remain.

Yet out of a century of civil war, of social corruption, savagery, and
selfishness, come these bare, clumsy truths: *disce, puer, virtutem ex me ver-
umque laborem, / fortunam ex aliis* (12.435–436); *quaecumque est fortuna,
mea est: me verius unum / pro vobis foedus luere et decernere ferro* (12.694–
695). In this view, *virtus, labor verus,* and this attitude to *fortuna* are seen
as adequate instruments of political integrity because they must be. Given
the times Virgil lived in and his other materials, this is sublime. Many
readers of the *Aeneid* who talk of its greatness may think they have in mind
the triumphal marches of Books 6 and 8 (a few, of course, really know
what they like and deserve what they get), but what in fact has stayed with
them is the stubborn, humble wisdom of *disce, puer* and *quaecumque est
fortuna,* which is magnificent and sublime because it can chasten our common and erroneous notions of what magnificence and sublimity are. In its
social allegories the *Aeneid* makes clear that the greatness of a *civitas* has
nothing to do with glory and grandeur and has everything to do with taking
responsibility. Very few poets have dared to imagine the evils of a *civitas*
that will not accept responsibility, and no poet has imagined them more
closely or more successfully than has Virgil. To sentimentalize and trivialize
his achievement by appeals to the Augustan settlement or to Christianity

and classical culture is to defame his artistry. Augustus or no, the social world Virgil lived in was tragically divided between the corrupt and ruined freedom of its past and the corrupt security of its new, unfamiliar Hellenistic future. It is the nature, causes, and consequences of this kind of division that Virgil's social *praxis* bids us ponder.

"QUO TENDAS": THE METAPHYSICAL ORDER

Even had the Augustan settlement been as clear to its creator and to its poet as it has seemed in other times, the world view or world views of Virgil and his original readers would obviate the kind and the degree of stability and clarity that many readers have read into Virgil's intentions and into his final design. Behind this reading of the poem, both from the angle of its politics and from the angle of its "philosophy," there lies the belief that Virgil's Rome, like Cicero's, is grounded in and nourished by Platonic and Stoic intimations of order. Yet if, as I suggest, the genuine intellectual and rational strength of this period in Rome is to be found in Lucretius, and if the failure and debility of the Platonism and the Stoicism of late republican Rome are to be found in Cicero's courageous, but on the whole unsuccessful, attempts to rationalize the vanishing political order by appeals to the failing philosophical systems of the past, then it may be no disservice to Virgil and no misreading of his poem to suggest that one of Virgil's problems in writing his epic was that the philosophical, ethical, and religious unities that had survived even into the recent past were precisely what he did not have to build on. Vestiges of the old unities remain, it is true, and Cicero uses them as best he can in constructing his own magnificent and desperate synthesis, even as Augustus uses both Cicero and some of the forms and contents of the vanishing and the vanished republic to construct his new political unity. But the work of Cicero is the summing up of a world that has almost disappeared at the time of its writing, and the work of Augustus is the planning and the seeding of a world that will not come to its great flowering, as Gibbon rightly insists, until almost a century after Augustus' death. In terms of his spiritual and philosophical materials, then, as in terms of his political materials, Virgil is dealing with fragments of the past and dreams of things to come. Many poets—maybe most good poets—have the same problem or a similar problem, but most poets who attempt a foundation epic or who write poems in which they seek to justify their culture or to gather to unity the components of their culture have something more nearly like a fixed tradition to work with than Virgil had. And particularly if we suppose that Virgil's chief aim was to justify Rome's manifest destiny, we might expect that he would need the foundation of a sound theodicy. As we have seen in our examination of Jupiter's last appearance in the poem, Virgil seems to go out of his way to demonstrate the perils and confusion of the religious traditions from which such a theodicy might be fashioned.

One measure of the perils and confusion of that tradition is to be found in the failure of Augustus to complete the religious and moral reforms that he deemed necessary for the success of his entire *renovatio*. And in this regard it is worth emphasizing the connections that obtain between Augustus' political goals and methods on the one hand and the waning of Graeco-Roman rationalism and the rise of superstition and the mystery religions on the other. Though Augustus himself wanted no part of the mystery religions and though he fought the growth of superstition, thinking of himself (correctly enough) as a conservative Roman gentleman, the world that he and Virgil lived in and the political artifact that he was busy shaping had in fact lost all but the final letter of rational Graeco-Roman religion. This ruin of traditional religion Virgil uses with fine effect in designing his story of cosmic unreason and of human efforts to combat that unreason. It would be foolish to suggest that there are not sometimes unironic echoes of the old Olympian rationalism joined with authentic echoes of Plato, Zeno, and indigenous Roman spirituality, but these memories of old spiritual wisdoms jostle with, and are often overwhelmed by, the recurrence of the new antirationalism as well as by the genuine mystical yearnings that arose in Rome and throughout the empire at the time when Augustus was at work on his settlement and Virgil was at work on his poem.

Paradoxically enough, Cybele appears as an Olympianized deity in the *Aeneid,* and there may be some degree of irony—whether intentional or not we need not try to decide here—in Virgil's ascribing to the Asiatic goddess a benevolence and a providence that would normally belong to the Olympians. That the goddess from Aeneas' homeland should be, with his mother, his protectress is natural enough, but the comparative impotence and remoteness of the Olympians in this poem (Juno is the great exception) contrast strikingly with Cybele's compassion and power. Yet it is not in Cybele that we see adumbrations of the new religious sensibility and proofs of the disintegration of the old sensibility. It is rather in two quite different modes of apprehending the divine, both of which contrast sharply with the tradition that Augustus was determined to restore. The first mode we find in the Neopythagorean moods (it is too much to call them doctrines or beliefs) that we find in Book 6 and that have been Platonized and Stoicized by Virgil's critics with little success. The second mode consists of the chthonian and daemonic elements that appear both in Book 6 and (frequently) throughout the last six books of the poem. To this second mode Virgil often adds an Etruscan coloring, for with the revival "of interest in astrology and the Eastern cults, men turned also to the lore of Etruria; the more so since this might be considered more respectable: anomalously, Etruscan customs now appear to have been regarded as romanized and part of Italic tradition, in contrast to the wilder beliefs that were reaching Rome from the East."

The heyday of Orientalism is a long way off when Virgil is writing the *Aeneid*, but what Auerbach calls "the darkening of the atmosphere of life" has already begun in Virgil's lifetime, and his poem reflects these beginnings and uses them. I am not suggesting that Virgil himself was swept away by this riptide of the Zeitgeist, and I am not trying to play *post hoc propter hoc*. Rather, I am emphasizing, because it seems not to have been sufficiently emphasized in this regard, that much of what Virgil has to work with in the way of "doctrines of the times" involves dark emotionalism or water-color mysticism, both of which are hostile to Lucretian affirmation of man's liberty and of the intelligibility of the world he lives in; to Cicero's (and Augustus') affirmation of the *res publica*; to Plato's or to Zeno's ways of saying, "And all shall be well and all shall be well and all manner of thing shall be well"; in short, to every shade and variety of classical rationalism and classical humanism. This is the new world where figures as different as Isis, Cybele, Nigidius Figulus, and Posidonius may feel at home. It is with these figures that the future lies, and at least some of the things they stand for (both good and bad) are present in the *Aeneid*, however inchoately, for the first time in a major ancient mimesis. The *Aeneid* is not an irrational or an antirational work, but it combats irrationality in ways that are new in antiquity because by Virgil's time unreason has assumed new faces and new strength while reason has lost much of its real strength.

We have examined some of these losses, particularly as they appear in Book 12, [previously]. We now turn to the description of Allecto in Book 7. Juno hails her at 331 in this fashion: *hunc mihi da proprium, virgo sata Nocte, laborem*. One cannot always tell what the writer of literary epic intends with his formulas, but it seems not unreasonable to suppose that *sata Nocte* was intended to resonate to the verse in Book 12 (860) which describes the flight of the Dira: *talis se sata Nocte tulit terrasque petivit*. These figures, Allecto and the Dira, frame the action of the second half of the *Aeneid*; both are creatures of darkness that are connected with irrational and utterly incomprehensible works of destruction, and both are, whatever their specific models might be, Virgil's reimaginations of nightmarish beings that Greek rationalism had utterly excluded from its normal modes of conceiving the human world. Both are Furies, but in their behavior they show not only the dark violence of hellish powers but also the gratuitous sadism that marks a special kind of hell. Evil for them is good; they look not to a deliberate and voluntary rejection of good for a sanction for their acts, since an almost mechanical perversion of good is its own sanction. In short, for Allecto and the Dira (though not, of course, for Jupiter and not quite for Juno) evil is not a means to an end, it is an end in itself; it is therefore, by definition, unintelligible. But this unintelligibility is not horrifying as Allecto and the Dira see it (or, in the case of the Dira, as we are made to see it, for we see her with the corrupt objectivity with which she sees herself): for them it is a delight and a glory. In other words, we are passing from the world of Graeco-Roman rationalism into the worlds of Seneca's tragedies, of Lucan, of Apuleius, and of barbaric Christianity.

> exim Gorgoneis Allecto infecta venenis
> principio Latium et Laurentis tecta tyranni
> celsa petit tacitumque obsedit limen Amatae,
> quam super adventu Teucrum Turnique hymenaeis
> femineae ardentem curaeque iraeque coquebant.
> huic dea caeruleis unum de crinibus anguem
> conicit inque sinum praecordia ad intima subdit,
> quo furibunda domum monstro permisceat omnem.
> ille inter vestes et levia corpora lapsus
> volvitur attactu nullo fallitque furentem,
> viperream spirans animam; fit tortile collo
> aurum ingens coluber, fit longae taenia vittae
> innectitque comas et membris lubricus errat.
> ac dum prima lues udo sublapsa veneno
> pertemptat sensus atque ossibus implicat ignem
> necdum animus toto percepit pectore flammam,
> mollius et solito matrum de more locuta,
> multa super nata lacrimans Phrygiisque hymenaeis. . . .

> At once Allecto, steeped in Gorgon poison,
> makes first for Latium and the high palace
> of the Laurentian chieftain. There she sits
> before the silent threshold of the queen,
> Amata, who is kindled by a woman's
> anxieties and anger, seething over
> the Trojans' coming, Turnus' thwarted wedding.
> Then from her blue-gray hair the goddess cast
> a snake deep in Amata's secret breast,
> that, maddened by the monster, she might set
> at odds all of her household. And the serpent
> glides on, between the queen's smooth breasts and dress,

and winds its way unnoticed; by deceit
it breathes its viper breath into her frenzy.
The giant snake becomes a twisted necklace
of gold, a long headband to bind her hair,
and slithers down her limbs. And while its first
infection, penetrating with damp poison,
has gripped her senses and entwined her bones
in fire, before her soul has felt the force
of flame throughout her breast, Amata speaks
softly, as is the way of mothers, weeping
over her daughter and the Phrygian wedding.
                                    (7.341–358)

The passage is extraordinary for its macabre beauty and for the description
of how a human soul is sapped of its reason and robbed of its power of
choice that glimmers under that beauty. There is no objection to someone's
supposing that this is a picture of Amata's psyche before she does what she
does and says what she says (that is clearly the sense of *quam super adventu
. . . coquebant*), but I point out that this is not the sort of thing that goes
on in *Iliad* I when Athena stops Achilles from killing Agamemnon; it is
more like the sort of thing that goes on when Cupid poisons Dido's mind
and heart in *Aeneid* I: the effect is wholly psychological but the cause is
supernatural, evil, and invisible (*attactu nullo*). These deliberate confusions
of supernatural cause presented as physical cause that issues in psychological
turmoil and impairment of volition are elaborated in Allecto's attack on
Turnus, for she appears to him in a dream; in his dream he ridicules her
and she hurls a torch into his body:

> sic effata facem iuveni coniecit et atro
> lumine fumantes fixit sub pectore taedas.
> olli somnum ingens rumpit pavor, ossaque et artus
> perfundit toto proruptus corpore sudor.
> arma amens fremit, arma toro tectisque requirit;
> saevit amor ferri et scelerata insania belli,
> ira super. . . .

And saying this, she cast a torch at Turnus,
fixing the firebrand within his breast,
and there it smoked with murky light. Great fear
shatters his sleep, sweat bursts from all his body
and bathes his bones and limbs. Insane, he raves
for arms, he searches bed and halls for weapons.
Lust for the sword and war's damnable madness
are raging in him and—above all—anger. . . .
                                    (7.456–462)

Is the torch less real than the snake because Turnus dreams and Amata wakes? Are the torch and the snake less real than the poison of Cupid? No, Cupid and Allecto are no more states of mind or symbols of states of mind than the Dira of Book 12 is a state of mind. All of these agents of evil become states of mind for those whose minds and volitions they have perverted; but they nevertheless remain realities that exist in the space and the time of the poem which they inhabit together with the human figures.

> postquam acies videt Iliacas atque agmina Turni,
> alitis in parvae subitam collecta figuram,
> quae quondam in bustis aut culminibus desertis
> nocte sedens serum canit importuna per umbras,
> hanc versa in faciem Turni se pestis ob ora
> fertque refertque sonans clipeumque everberat alis.
> illi membra novus solvit formidine torpor
> arrectaeque horrore comae et vox faucibus haesit.

> As soon as she can see the Trojan
> ranks and the troops of Turnus, suddenly
> she shrinks into the shape of that small bird
> which sometimes sits by night on tombs and lonely
> rooftops, where it chants late, among the shadows,
> its song of evil omen; so transformed,
> the foul one howls before the face of Turnus,
> flies back and forth; her wings beat at his shield.
> Strange stiffness, terror, took the limbs of Turnus;
> his hair stood up; his jaws held fast his voice.
>
> (12.861–868)

As the dreadful thing beats at the face of Turnus, his terror gathers into itself all the terrors that have preceded it: the unseen horror is at last physically present, and the daughter of darkness has become visible. This sickening apotheosis of hell gains some of its subtle horror from the sur-realistic catachresis, *subitam figuram* (note also the fine oxymoron, *atro lumine,* in the previous passage), but its special success derives from the emphasis on a peculiarly sinister quality that all the ministers of evil in the poem share and that surpasses even the brilliant imaginations of evil and madness that we find in Greek tragic choruses. What Turnus meets face to face, what evokes in him nightmarish impotence and despair, is not a traditional bogey cleverly magnified; it is rather a wild, vindictive negation of goodness, an active, gloating privation of goodness and being.

　　If I suggest that much of this strange, new vision of evil came from Etruria, I am not suggesting that the Iris of Book 4 exists because Virgil saw Vanth in the François tomb or that the snakes and torches of Allecto were inspired by the death demons we know from Etruscan tombs. Nor did Virgil need to see the Orcus tomb to imagine Allecto or the Dira. I am not even suggesting that this Etruscan coloring in the *Aeneid* is present there because Virgil grew up in Mantua, though I do not think it is a waste of time to speculate on this possibility. The Etruscan revival, combined with the growth of the mystery religions and the rise of Neopythagoreanism, was useful to Virgil because it provided him with poetic materials for his imagination of a darkening world. The ministers of darkness (Iris in Book 4 and Cupid in Book 1, as well as Allecto, the Dira, and Juno herself) are not new creations in the sense that they have no models in Greek mimesis, but they are new in their reveling in evil, their pleasure in the mindless destruction (which is what I am calling their Etruscan coloring), and, more important, they are new in their ability to dominate the *muthos* of a poem and to threaten to dominate the *praxis* of a poem. The primacy and triumph of evil are intolerable thoughts in the classical moments of Graeco-Roman culture, so intolerable that the least hint of mere dualism is combated ferociously. In Virgil's poem, for the first time, the possibility that hell can triumph is found to be worth pondering. As political integrities are seen in this poem not as actualities but as potentialities to be realized only with desperate effort against terrible odds, so the primacy of goodness and truth is seen as vulnerable to dreadful and incomprehensible hazards. I do not say that this is what Virgil and his audience believed or felt most of the time; I only suggest that this intimation of the possible failure of rational order and rational freedom in the universe, in human history, and in individual existence is clearly part of the materials of Virgil's poem, and, in my reading of the poem, this intimation of the danger to rational order in the universe and rational freedom in human lives comes near to being the central *praxis* of his poem.

In shaping this material, in closing with evil as it presents itself in human history and in the lives of men, Virgil no more affirms the triumph of unreason and *ira* in the universe and in history than he affirms their defeat. It is from its capacity for approaching metaphysical and political despair without quite despairing that the *Aeneid* wins through to its extraordinary courage and power; it is because the poem knows how "to grieve and not to grieve" that it leaves us disturbed and unsolaced without leaving us frozen in wan hope. Virgil proffers us a desperate, patient strength we can believe in because he gives us no calm and not much hope:

> obstipuit varia confusus imagine rerum
> Turnus et obtutu tacito stetit; aestuat ingens
> uno in corde pudor mixtoque insania luctu

et furiis agitatus amor et conscia virtus.
ut primum discussae umbrae et lux reddita menti. . . .

Confused by all these shifting images
of ruin, Turnus stood astounded, staring
and silent. In his deepest heart there surge
tremendous shame and madness mixed with sorrow
and love whipped on by frenzy and a courage
aware of its own worth. As soon as shadows
were scattered and his mind saw light again. . . .

(12.665–669)

These seem to me among the most precise, the most compassionate, and the most tragic verses in the entire poem. They sum up what Virgil knows best about us and what he is best able to imagine about what he knows. I doubt that any other poet could have combined these elements—our real weakness and our real strength—with such sympathy, such dispassion, and such power. At this moment, on the edge of defeat and despair, an affirmation of coherence and *virtus* is possible because Virgil has completed his imagination of what we have to fear and what we have to fight against that fear with. The *Aeneid,* I have tried to suggest, is polycentric, and every reader will find the center that suits him or her. For what it is worth, this is mine.

"QUOD AGAS": THE MORAL ORDER

. . . then he realized that it was the pot itself that caused the evil, and he realized too that anything that entered into the pot, however wholesome it might be, must be destroyed when it was poured in because of this innate evil. He saw that this was so partly because the pot was chipped and leaked, so that it could never, by any strategem, be filled, and he saw that it was partly so because it tainted everything that was poured into it, caused everything it contained to acquire a foul taste.

(*Lucretius* 6.17–23)

Flawed in his own nature, flawed no less in the works of his mind, heart, and hands—that is man as seen by Epicurus if he remains unpurged by strictly rational truths. Though not unparalleled in Graeco-Roman thought, this denial that human beings can will or reason their way to happiness and justice in society by using natural gifts that have been disciplined by tradition shows a radical departure from the norms of classical humanism in its rejection not only of the ideal of responsible and purposeful action in society but also of the concept of an eternal, rational order that defines

and guides human action in its beginnings and its ends. If there is indeed
a problem with Virgil's poem, it is only the problem that he received as
his donnée and struggled with, heroically, for a decade: the conflict between
the Epicurean analysis of the problems of evil (an analysis which Virgil
seems, for the most part, to have accepted) and his ambivalent faith in
the idea of salvation in and through history. Had Virgil been less convinced
by the Epicurean diagnosis of human suffering, and had he been more
vividly impressed by the possibilities of the rebirth and renewal of societies
and by the meaning of history, perhaps he might have been able to reconcile
the Epicurean *summum bonum* with the more conventional, classical *summa
bona*. But Virgil, to his honor, but not to his peace of mind, could not
reconcile these opposing sanctuaries, and he remained, to the end of his
poethood, a haunted wanderer.

For the Epicurean temperament, the social order, which is a kind
of perversion of friendship, can do little good but can do and invite endless
harm. Since the Epicurean ideal is freedom from ignorance for the individual, the body politic only serves to nourish what it feeds upon—fear of
catastrophe, dependence upon changing circumstance—in short, painful,
destructive illusions about things as they are and men's proper good. An
Epicurean can manage, without deluding himself, to find and safeguard the
garden that is his because, very strictly speaking, it does not matter in what
city his garden may be; he is, by definition, a fierce and proud internal
émigré. And in planting and tending his garden, he relegates the city to
what he regards as its proper and actual place—outside, on the margins of
reality, among the other necessary and unnecessary illusions. In the garden
the problems of evil can be handled because the *vitia* are seen as at once
natural and within us, that is to say, they are capable of remedy. They do
not have a life of their own, they are not mysterious dangers lurking outside
the walls of the garden, waiting, hoping to destroy. Lucretius had written
a great poem, in a sense an epic poem, about the fight of the human spirit
to liberate itself from the illusion that illusions are real; Virgil's reading of
that poem was probably the most important thing in his life as a poet (to
call that reading an event would be misleading since it is clear that the
reading was habitual and unending). Our problem, then, was Virgil's. Why
should a man who read *De rerum natura* so passionately and who absorbed
it so thoroughly undertake to write a poem that is not merely about what
happens in history but is also about the vindication of the meaning of
history in general and the meaning of the City in particular (in Epicurean
terms, about how illusion is vindicated by illusion)? Why should an

Epicurean attempt to write not merely a foundation epic but *the* Foundation Epic (imagine, if you will, a Shaker who "believed in the green light" at work on the Great American Novel)?

These questions admit of no exact answer, but they invite specu-lation. Suppose Virgil's heart was divided. Suppose he read and reread his Lucretius as a religious atheist might peruse his Saint Paul—desperate, faithful in his disbelief, hoping, at some moment, for the illumination, because the fears that were being so uncannily catalogued were, precisely, his own fears, and almost believing that he might discover the fears were, as the writer kept insisting, groundless? But suppose that, unpersuaded that the objects of his dread were unreal, he kept turning toward a belief in a divinely rational design wherein the small evils, though real, were part of a pattern, were christened by truth and justice, were gathered into the large goodness, invisible yet ineffably secure. If the stern freedoms of Epicurus could not save, then perhaps the rational cosmos and the renewed city, their microcosm, might win what a single human being had not strength to win—freedom from evil and fear, freedom for goodness and joy.

Basing my arguments on these speculations, I would suggest (it is no more than suggestion, for I do not pretend to be dealing with facts) that the disintegrations of the world he lived in, which were not really balanced by the uncertain political restorations of that world, caused Virgil to despair of the good myths of order and reason and to seek both comfort and strength in the disciplines of Epicurus. But, for whatever reasons, the wisdom of Epicurus could not solace the intensity of Virgil's dread, and he returned to the good myths (and the bad myths) of the Cosmos and the City. And continuing in this vacillation and indecision, he wrote a great epic which succeeds partly because its author has the honesty to admit not only the intensity and durability of his fears but also the depths of his weakness and indecision. It is, I submit, the nakedness, the purity of his initial pity for himself that persuades us to believe in its transformation into compassion for us.

Having accepted his donnée—the pull toward embracing Epicurean freedom and the counterpull toward justifying the rational cosmos and its *civitas*—Virgil discovered in shaping his poem the tragic paradoxes that give the *Aeneid* its particular texture, resonance, and range. The evils that Lucretius focuses on in the passage quoted above: the negative evil, which is a privation or absence of good; and the positive evil, which is flawed action proceeding from mistaken perceptions and judgments, must, in an epic poem, be hypostatized into actions performed by characters. First as symbols in a fiction, then, disastrously, as false entities in a myth, the darkness within becomes the darkness without. When objectified in this way, the natural weaknesses and natural ignorance of Aeneas, Dido, and Turnus become Juno and her ministers: on the social level, *discordia;* on the moral level, *violentia* and *ira;* on the metaphysical level, a blind momentum towards destruction and nothingness, evil for the sake of evil. All of this is unacceptable in an Epicurean poem because what was, before the mythologizing, merely a tendency and a possibility has become a fact, has become almost an unalterable law of denatured nature. Illusions, evil illusions, the privation of and the desire for the annihilation of being have become first realities, then reality itself. And in a Stoic or Platonic or Aristotelian poem, any of which might be, in varying degrees, tolerant of such allegory at the outset, this hypostatization of evil would be no more acceptable than it is in the Epicurean epic: the metaphors must remain convenient metaphors. But for Virgil they do not and cannot. Since he is prevented by his grasp of Epicurus and by the tragic history of his country from giving full allegiance to the concept of the rational cosmos, reified evil refuses to be subordinated to the grand and rational design, insists on its own way, rushes off into the deeper darkness, bearing with it the meaning of history and the dream of rational freedom. Thus in the *Aeneid* there grows a constant impulse toward awful dualism that mocks the splendid unities of classical humanism, with its belief in an intelligible universe and in purposeful human activity inside that universe. The metaphors for evil have become, here below, the truths.

In his fear, in his vast Epicurean sensitivity to pain and suffering, Virgil nevertheless turned from the calm, austere garden back to the world where unreasoning power is a reality that must somehow be persuaded or suffered and where pain must be inflicted or endured. The garden was impossible because he could not teach himself not to hear the screams and riot outside. Yet when he ventured out to help, he found that he had neither the toughness nor the stamina to withstand the onslaughts of reality even for himself, much less to hearten his fellow sufferers or to restrain the monsters or tame them. It is this extraordinary sensitivity to pain that will not permit him to ignore suffering and that will not permit him to condone it by explaining it away. So the darkness that he had sought to evade first in the garden and then in the city moved against him. Terrified though he was, he stood firm to report what he saw, and, as the poem bears witness, the depth of his terror is the index to the greatness of his courage.

An Epicurean hero, excruciatingly responsive to pain, moves through a world where *hou an kratēi archein* (Thucydides 5. 105.2) is law, where sick fantasies seem on the verge of becoming essential realities, and where men's natural limitations become so magnified that their virtues seem in danger of being transformed into the opposing vices. The same Epicurean hero, his freedom and reason perfected in Stoic obedience to the commands of good patriotism and holy destiny, moves in a world where freedom and reason lose their significance as justice and truth, which are their proper agents, glimmer fainter and dissolve in vengeance and deception. Aeneas is an extraordinarily good man, but in the world where he is fated to suffer and to act, goodness is (or is perhaps) not enough, nor is reason, nor is freedom. Courage, in a sense, is almost enough, and Virgil's poem is not about winning battles but about losing them and learning how to lose them. At a moment in time when the possibility of rational freedom seemed, to a sensitive observer, jeopardized and its uses uncertain, Virgil summoned up the strength to imagine us in our utter vulnerability and desolation, and, refusing the old impossible consolations that were being newly counterfeited, he affirmed our moral strength by insisting on our moral weakness and on the real evils that threaten the goodness we might grow towards if we could resist the belief that we have won through, that the worst was past, that evil was outside us and was real in the way that good is real. New "sensemaking," in Kermode's phrase, required of Virgil that he shape a new formulation of heroism. If Virgil's imagination had not been steeled with Lucretian discipline, his compassion might have dwindled into Gray's delicate and false antithesis:

> To each his suff'rings: all are men,
> Condemn'd alike to groan,
> The tender for another's pain;
> Th'unfeeling for his own.

And had his imagination not been suffused with a Ciceronian humanism that Christians may easily be forgiven for mistaking for their *caritas*, his patriotism and ambition might have persuaded him to be content with frigid reworkings of a misremembered, misunderstood Homeric grandeur.

No poet, not Dante himself, has imagined the disintegration of justice and truth with such precision and such power, and for this reason no poet, not Homer himself, has shown how precious and how fragile are the formation and equilibrium of man's integrity of spirit. The multiple allegories of Virgil reveal in their shifting configurations the reality of goodness and the unspeakable nonbeing of evil. The poet no more condemns us to the darkness than he promises us the light. But he shows us, in unforgettable pictures, what the darkness means, which is, as the mystics tell us, a way of showing the shadows of light. To minimize the intensity of Virgil's imagination of darkness is, in effect, to reject his imagination of *to kalon*. Or, to put it another way, Virgil's poetry can let us ponder for ourselves what society, justice, and being mean because it has closed with and faced what their absence is and means.

His times doubtless taught him a great deal about what these absences were and meant, but, good Epicurean that he was, he had probably learned his hardest and best lessons about absence and darkness from the Epicurean discipline of self-scrutiny. *Et c'est assez, pour le poète, d'être la mauvaise conscience de son temps.* Yes and no. Aeneas, Dido, and Turnus are in us as they were in Virgil. It is because he discovered and revealed the perennial shape of what truly destroys us—not because he accurately reflects the grandeurs and miseries of a crucial and dynamic age (as he does), not because he croons us gentle lullabies of culture reborn (as he does not)—that we continue to trust him to guide us through the dim mazes of our arrogance and fear.

MICHAEL C. J. PUTNAM

Aeneas and the Metamorphosis of Lausus

I shot him dead because—
Because he was my foe,
Just so: my foe of course he was;
That's clear enough; although. . . .

— THOMAS HARDY, "The Man He Killed" (1902)

My essay will review some aspects of the relationship between *pietas* and the use of force in the *Aeneid*. The intimate cooperation between piety and power regularly defines Rome and her founding hero. Ilioneus' sketch to Dido of his absent leader is an early example (1.544–5):

> rex erat Aeneas nobis, quo iustior alter
> nec pietate fuit, nec bello maior et armis.

> Our king was Aeneas. No other was
> more righteous in piety nor more
> powerful in war and arms.

Dido herself bitterly demonstrates this collocation in her final soliloquy, where *dextra* proves equally related to Aeneas' strength at arms and to his faithless breaking of a compact (4.597–99):

From *Arethusa* 1, vol. 14 (1981). Copyright © 1981 by the Department of Classics, State University of New York at Buffalo.

> . . . en dextra fidesque,
> quem secum patrios aiunt portare penatis,
> quem subiisse umeris confectum aetate parentem!

. . . behold the right hand and the pledge of him who they say carried with him the gods of his fatherland, who supported on his shoulders a father undone with age.

The Sibyl puts the conjunction summarily to Charon, presenting her companion as (6.403):

> Troius Aeneas, pietate insignis et armis.

> Trojan Aeneas, outstanding for piety and arms.

Ilioneus, now introducing Aeneas to Latinus, can boast of his king's *dextram potentem* and allude again to *fides* and *arma*.

But, as the epic progresses and words are replaced more regularly by deeds and definitions by exemplifications, this mating of abstract duty to gods, family and patriotic mission with the physical means towards its validation becomes a more ambiguous union, shading into the use of force for questionable goals, often for the gratification of private feelings rather than the fulfillment of idealistic, public purposes. I would like to examine in detail one striking instance of Aeneas in power drawn from the tenth book, the death-scene of Lausus, and then follow out parallel passages, ending with a brief look at Aeneas' final confrontation with Turnus.

We have learned from the seventh book of Lausus' personal beauty and of his prowess at taming horses and harrowing wild beasts, but from the start we are prejudiced against his father Mezentius, the *contemptor divum* with a bent for the macabre torturing of his victims. Yet in the tenth book the human, private image diverges from the public. Son remains faithful to father, and in a striking manifestation of *pietas* shields Mezentius from the onslaught of Aeneas—*genitor nati parma protectus* (10.800). The reprieve is short-lived. The titular hero soon buries his sword in the side of the youth, as he himself is centered in the language, *per medium Aeneas iuvenem* (816).

At this moment, when the reader is drawn to Lausus, protecting his father and wearing a tunic woven for him by his mother, Virgil seizes the occasion for an irony pointed against Aeneas. Before he wounds Mezentius and initiates the dissolution of one of the more poignant parent-child relationships in the epic, Aeneas is given his standard epithet *pius* (783), and as he prepares to wound Lausus mortally the poet has him shout (811–12):

quo moriture ruis maioraque viribus audes?
fallit te incautum pietas tua.

Whither do you rush, about to die, and dare things greater than your
strength? Your piety deceives you in your folly.

Aeneas ironically interprets in negative terms the abstract that had always
been his, symbolized in his rescue of his father and son from Troy and in
his visit to Anchises in the underworld. It becomes an impediment, making
Lausus vulnerable to his opponent's *saevae irae* (813), and killing him.
Virgil reverses our expectations by having Aeneas grimly see himself as an
incorporation of a *pietas* that destroys in a particularly vicious manner
because it kills the embodiment of a *pietas* that saves. And, as at the death
of Turnus which concludes the epic, Aeneas takes no responsibility. What
his maddened words would have the immediate—and distant—hearer believe is that not Aeneas but *pietas*, and his antagonist's *pietas* at that,
performed the deed. If Lausus had been *cautus,* the hero implies, he would
not have practised *pietas* and would have escaped death.

The final *tua* (812) therefore serves a double purpose. It shows
Aeneas shifting the cause for Lausus' death onto Lausus' own practise of
Aeneas' virtue. But it also reveals a half-conscious awareness that he himself
is blameworthy, while the reader is left wondering about the depth of
Aeneas' commitment to *pietas* elsewhere. How often, we ask, does Aeneas
adhere to or reject *pietas* for subjective, even self-serving, reasons?

For Aeneas to impute Lausus' defeat not to himself but to *pietas*
smacks of self-deception, fabricated to ward off the full implications of his
words and action. At moments of rage *pietas* and *arma* do not easily blend.
In the case of Lausus' death each destroys. Aeneas' arms, working out a
continued desire for vengeance, do the actual deed, but Aeneas' abstraction,
as practised by Lausus and explained by Aeneas, abets the negative impulse.
Meanwhile the reader's disposition changes from understanding for Aeneas,
about the sometimes violent task of establishing Rome, to compassion for
his victims. Though Mezentius despises the gods, publicly abrogating an
important form of *pietas*, he gains at the end a measure of our sympathy.
When it comes to the practise of virtue in the heat of war his son feels
and displays both *amor* and *pietas*, while *pius* Aeneas performs the greatest
act of *impietas* by killing first the son who protects, then his wounded father.
His deeds in battle elicit our appreciation of Lausus, whose affection for
Mezentius makes the latter less despicable, but our respect is undermined
for Aeneas who is brutalized by an inability to respond sympathetically to
his own supposedly characteristic virtue in the operations of others. In

moments of rage the merely physical controls his life, to suggest more similarity with than distinction from Mezentius himself.

Then occurs one of the most beautiful and moving moments in the epic. After lines of unremitting fury, culminating in the death of Lausus, we have a moment of quiet, as Aeneas contemplates the features of his victim (821–24):

> At vero ut vultum vidit morientis et ora,
> ora modis Anchisiades pallentia miris,
> ingemuit miserans graviter dextramque tetendit,
> et mentem patriae subiit pietatis imago.

But when the son of Anchises saw the face and features of the dying man, the features pale in marvelous ways, he groaned deeply from pity and stretched out his right hand, and the picture of paternal piety entered his mind.

Epic diachronism yields to lyric depth and intensity. We enter a complex verbal world where reiteration of words, assonance and alliteration force the reader to hear sound echo in sound, and where such interweaving and repetition linguistically mimic Aeneas' own pause to look, and look again, as the poet slows action to a stop. *Vultum vidit, modis miris, morientis* and *pallentia* form unifying sound clusters, but it is the repetition of *ora* at the end of line 821 and the beginning of line 822 that especially causes the reader to follow Aeneas' own mental progress and momentarily choose contemplation over action, explanation over heedless, continued doing. Line 822 adds nothing to plot, much to atmosphere. It is a golden line, brilliantly centered around *Anchisiades* which stands out, furthermore, as the longest word in lines 821–2 and the only one that lacks melodic intimacy with any of its neighbors.

As we savor this calming panel breaking the onrush of narrative, we watch, first, the metamorphosis of Lausus from living to dead, from body to spirit, from physical being to disembodied emblem. Virgil would have us think of those *simulacra modis pallentia miris* from among whom, Lucretius tells us, the ghost of Homer arose to enlighten Ennius. In the first *georgic* Virgil draws on the same phrase to describe those images that appeared among the disquieting portents accompanying the death of Julius Caesar. Venus, in *Aeneid* 1, tells of the apparition in dreams to Dido of her unburied husband, *ora modis attollens pallida miris* (354), raising his face pale in marvelous ways. As we join Aeneas in beholding Lausus' color paling and life giving place to death, we turn from surface to substance and examine through Aeneas' eyes the change in Lausus from literal to figurative. He alters from palpable enemy, to be killed both by and even at the expense of the hero's prime virtue, to a wraith that is symbol of that virtue, *patriae pietatis imago*, the personification of piety toward one's father. As war's wildness is momentarily subdued by thought, Aeneas appears to see beyond what his previous intensity had not allowed into human motivations that should be, but have not always been, a part of his thinking during his bout of killing. Contemplation and madness, *pietas* and slaughter would seem incompatible entities.

Pause in epic thrust for a moment of lyric intensity is thus a metaphor for the differentiation between history's relentless progress—the teleology of a brilliant Roman destiny personified in the conduct of its founding father—and the personal suffering this progress causes. The tale of Mezentius operates on both levels at once. Virgil imputes to Mezentius alone what seems to have been a common pattern of Etruscan behavior. But by stressing the public odiousness of Mezentius' former conduct he makes more remarkable the private devotion of Lausus, faithful to his father even to the sharing of exile. Moreover, through his son's sacrifice the *contemptor divum* elicits a vivid demonstration of *pietas* which in turn forces *pius* Aeneas to become a killer of the pious. Larger abstract notions of slaying barbarous enemies to rid the world of the primitive and the bestial are constantly questioned by Virgil when focussed against the realities of human emotions, and the pause, Aeneas' and the reader's, from linear action at Lausus' death is one of the most poignant examples in the epic.

The transformation of Lausus is also the transformation of Aeneas. By imitating him, Aeneas for a moment becomes Lausus' double. The phrase *patriae pietatis imago* is equally his. The Aeneas who buried his sword into the body of Lausus has become *Anchisiades*, perceiving in Lausus' saving conduct an emblem of his own behavior toward his father. He no longer stands alone but becomes part of a relationship of son to father, particular son to particular father. Although he will soon proclaim, with a renewal of callousness, that Lausus' consolation is his fall "by the right hand of mighty Aeneas" (*Aeneae magni dextra* 830), that right hand is at present stretched forward in a gesture not of violence but of pity, perhaps even of supplication. Pity now becomes the chief component of this late learning. Aeneas is *miserans* as he begins to speak, his initial apostrophe to Lausus is *miserande puer* (825), and he defines the youth's death as *miseram* (829).

There is another vehicle by which Aeneas not only commiserates but verbally becomes Lausus, just as he suddenly remembers his own sonship. At the moment in the previous duel when Lausus rescues his father, Aeneas has just wounded Mezentius with his spear and, "happy (*laetus*) at

the sight of Etruscan blood," has drawn his sword for the kill. This is Lausus'
reaction to the sight (789–90):

> ingemuit cari graviter genitoris amore,
> ut vidit, Lausus, lacrimaeque per ora volutae. . . .

As he looked Lausus groaned deeply from love of his dear father, and
tears rolled down his face. . . .

The phrases *ingemuit graviter* and *ut vidit* recur in close proximity at the
moment of Lausus' death, attached now to Aeneas, as he and we notice
the youth's features, deathly pale instead of tear-stricken. For Aeneas, after
his mortal deed, to react in the same way as Lausus about the saving of his
father, is for the poet to fuse the two characters and to have Aeneas, in
the hiatus before he turns to kill Mezentius, share Lausus' emotion to the
point of linguistically merging with him as well.

That the conjunction is brief does not detract from its power, but
the reader is prepared by Aeneas' prior deeds in the book not only for the
mood to be evanescent but to learn once again that such thoughts do not
influence his actions. One previous example from book 10, which will turn
our attention to earlier books of the epic, must suffice to illustrate Aeneas'
inattention to *pietas* in the heat of combat. In his bloodlust after the death
of Pallas he first secures eight victims to be offered alive as sacrifice on the
young hero's pyre. After that he slays Magus who is a suppliant (523),
grasping Aeneas' knees. Magus' initial words are well chosen to affect the
reader, though they do not deter Aeneas who twists their tone (524–5):

> per patrios manis et spes surgentis Iuli
> te precor, hanc animam serves gnatoque patrique . . .

I beseech you by the shades of your father and the hope of growing Iulus,
save this life for a son and for a father . . .

Magus' plea is a pastiche contrived from book 6. His first line recalls Palinurus' prayer to Aeneas to lead him across the Styx (364):

> per genitorem oro, per spes surgentis Iuli. . . .

I pray you by your father, by the hope of growing Iulus. . . .

The helmsman's request appeals to the gestures, if not the emotions, of
pietas (370):

> da dextram misero et tecum me tolle per undas. . . .

Give your right hand to me in my misery and carry me with you through
the waves. . . .

Before Aeneas can reply, the Sibyl forbids any intervention.

The second line of Magus' speech reaches further back in book 6 to an earlier prayer, of Aeneas to the Sibyl. His request is briefly put (108–9):

> . . . ire ad conspectum cari genitoris et ora
> contingat. . . .

> . . . may I be allowed to make my way to the sight and face of my dear father. . . .

And his plea follows readily (116–7):

> . . . gnatique patrisque
> alma, precor, miserere. . . .

> . . . kindly one, I beseech you, pity son and father. . . .

In the press of battle he denies the power in Magus' words that he had expected to be able to bring to bear himself, in proposing to the Sibyl his strange, pietistic adventure. In common with Lausus he shares love of a dear parent, but forgets its validity when passion has mastered him. In book 6, where Aeneas is a *supplex* (115) and the tangible efforts to carry out his mission have not brought the moral dilemma of the final books, he is introduced by the Sybil to Charon as *tantae pietatis imago* (405). He incorporates in himself what he will see in Lausus after he has killed him, and rage has momentarily retreated before understanding and commiseration. When father and son do meet (679–702), it is again the gesturing of hands and facial expressions which are the manifestations that, in Anchises' words, *vicit iter durum pietas* (688). Anchises stretched forth both palms, weeping, and Aeneas attempts in vain to clasp hands with his father, as he too weeps. There is a shared emphasis on the features of each, the *ora* through which both demonstrate *pietas*, by which Lausus also showed his love for Mezentius and in which Aeneas too saw a symbol of piety.

Pietas, therefore, reveals itself regularly by facial and verbal gestures of supplication and affection. It is not incompatible with *arma* in a general definition of the Roman achievement that combines force with human understanding. Yet it remains unreconcilable with the maddened and the irrational, especially when the weapons of war are involved. This we know from the beginning of the epic. The first we hear of Aeneas, his sufferings in war and conveyance of gods to Latium—*pietas* and *arma* combined—are contrasted to the *saevae memorem Iunonis iram* (1.4–6). Immediately thereafter the hero who appears *insignem pietate* (10) is caught between an emotional queen of the gods (*dolens regina deum* 9) and the narrator's amazed questioning that *tantae irae* (11) could persist among the immortals. The contrast remains alive throughout the book and the epic. At lines 251–3, for example, Venus juxtaposes the anger of unnamed Juno and the *pietatis honos* that is due Aeneas for his fidelity. The contrast is summarized in the first simile of the epic. Juno has given her resentments full play and stirred up Aeolus and his winds against the Trojans. Neptune senses the confusion and rightly imputes it to *Iunonis irae* (130). Virgil compares his calming presence amid wildness untrammeled to a man *pietate gravem ac meritis* (151) who soothes a ferocious mob to whom fury lends arms (*furor arma ministrat* 150).

In the first book Aeneas is buffeted by the elemental nature of Juno and her creatures, with little power to resist. During the bitter night of Troy's fall, the subject of book 2, Aeneas can take a more active, if un-productive role. We therefore watch with interest the relationship between Aeneas' first acts of piety and his recourse to arms, and how the polarity between enlightenment of mind and dark lack of understanding often shapes this relationship. Here too *imagines* play an important role in helping Aeneas clarify the obscure, penetrate behind the facades of motivation and action, and, finally, move away from bouts of futile violence toward an acceptance of a future symbolized in the professions of *pietas*.

The first "image" in book 2 is Aeneas' dream of Hector (270–1):

> in somnis, ecce, ante oculos maestissimus Hector
> visus adesse mihi. . . .

> In dreams, behold, most pitiful Hector seemed
> to stand before my eyes. . . .

The sleeping hero cannot yet appreciate the meaning of Hector's wounds, which would be to remember his mutilation by Achilles. Hector's speech, therefore, has a twofold importance. It forces the reality of his loss on Aeneas and forewarns that his tragedy anticipates the general suffering of Troy's demise. Hector then pronounces the futility of reliance on arms and succinctly predicts to Aeneas his future, suggesting his first act of *pietas* (293–4):

> sacra suosque tibi commendat Troia penates:
> hos cape fatorum comites. . . .

> Troy commits to you her holy objects and her household gods; seize them
> as comrades of your fortune. . . .

The vision of Hector allows Aeneas to face the truth of both present and future. At the same time Hector's wraith, by thrusting fillets, Vesta and the everlasting fire into his hands, proclaims Aeneas as protector of Troy's gods in transition.

It is a part that wakened Aeneas is not prepared to accept. For a moment he seems aloof from the *furentibus Austris* that fan the flames and akin to a shepherd who comprehends a stream's rampage only through a distant echo. Yet, forgetful of Hector's revelation and command, he plunges irrationally into arms (314):

> arma amens capio; nec sat rationis in armis. . . .

> In madness I seize arms; nor is there sufficient reason in arms. . . .

In his own words, *furor* and *ira* drive his mind headlong (316). The first "image" has proved wasted on Aeneas who takes up arms not in defense of *pietas* but under the sponsorship of the unthinking use of force that so often stands in its way.

The next revelation to Aeneas comes after the central episode of the book, the forcing of Priam's palace and the decapitation of the old king. Aeneas seems only a voyeur of this impious sequence of events as Pyrrhus kills first Polites before the eyes of his parents, then Priam himself. He makes no attempt to intervene or avenge the double murder, perhaps because he is meant to appreciate that the death of its aged leader betokens the downfall of Troy. After the appearance of Hector *armorum horror* (301) had increased to the point that it had wakened the sleeping hero. Now it surrounds him (559–63):

> At me tum primum saevus circumstetit horror.
> obstipui; subiit cari genitoris imago,
> ut regem aequaevum crudeli vulnere vidi
> vitam exhalantem, subiit deserta Creusa
> et direpta domus et parvi casus Iuli.

But then first dreadful horror surrounded me. I stood amazed; the vision of my dear father stood before me when I saw the king, his age mate, breathing forth his life from a cruel wound, deserted Creusa came before me, my plundered house and the fate of little Iulus.

Yet instead of rushing thoughtlessly into war Aeneas now allows the vision to develop a deeper significance. The hero responds to the sight of *pietas* affronted by becoming possessed with *pietas* of his own. It is no wonder that the description and especially the phrase *subiit cari genitoris imago* reverberate in the remainder of the epic. Anchises appears again a *cari genitoris* as Aeneas requests the Sibyl to visit his father in Hades (6.108), and the phrase *subiit imago*, as we have seen, initiates Aeneas' realization that in Lausus he had killed an emblem of *pietas*, forced to die "because of love for his dear father" (*cari genitoris amore* 10.789), and had himself become a deadly, not saving, manifestation of the same presumed virtue.

Yet, instead of implementing his new insight, Aeneas again yields to impetuosity and contemplates the killing of Helen. Anger, not the spirit of filial duty, rules his thoughts (575–6):

> . . . subit ira cadentem
> ulcisci patriam et sceleratas sumere poenas.

> . . . anger overcomes me to avenge my fallen fatherland and to extract punishment for crimes.

As he admits, before he has a chance to turn words into deeds, *furiata mente ferebar* (2.588). He is the passive victim of insanity rather than the active pursuer of a more noble, less tangible, goal. What changes his mind is another vision (589–91):

> cum mihi se, non ante oculis tam clara, videndam
> obtulit et pura per noctem in luce refulsit
> alma parens. . . .

> when my kindly mother offered herself to my sight, never before so clear to my vision, and gleamed in pure radiance through the night. . . .

With the appearance of Venus both the hero's parents replace Helen as the primary objects of his thinking. Her first words demand such recollection (594–8):

> nate, quis indomitas tantus dolor excitat iras?
> quid furis? aut quonam nostri tibi cura recessit?
> non prius aspicies ubi fessum aetate parentem
> liqueris Anchisen, superet coniunxne Creusa
> Ascaniusque puer? . . .

> My son, what great resentment arouses your uncontrollable anger? Why are you raging? Or whither has your care for us gone? Will you not first see where you left your father Anchises spent with age, whether your wife Creusa and the boy Ascanius survive? . . .

Useless vengeance against the past is replaced by renewed allegiance to family ties, which means allegiance to continuity and, ultimately, acceptance of future destiny. The abstractions which polarize around this change are standard, with one exception. The resentment, anger and rage that press Aeneas toward the unheroic urge to kill a woman, are countered now by an appeal to *pietas* defined specifically by the word *cura*. It is *nostri cura*, "care for us," love of Venus, that should have motivated Aeneas' deeds.

As will be the case when he is exposed to the deeper significance of Lausus' death, Venus' potency has the other extraordinary but complementary effect of allowing Aeneas, in pondering a course of action, to see beyond the superficial and observe larger forces at work upon humankind. *Tyndaridis facies invisa Lacaenae*, the (ironically) hateful features of Helen, had, according to Venus, impelled Aeneas to an equally superficial, negative waste of energy. Venus now dramatically unclouds her son's vision to allow him to look beyond appearance and watch *divum inclementia* at work. This is Virgil's only use of the abstraction in the *Aeneid*, and it gives emphasis to an occasion where Aeneas can note the force of divine unforgiveness at work, in Juno, *saevissima* and *furens*, in Athena, equally *saeva*, and in the father of the gods himself, urging on his colleagues. Presumably Aeneas, and we, at moments where we must scrutinize the symbolic meaning of events, would associate *inclementia* with ferocity, and *clementia* with restraint.

The last "vision" occurs at the end of the book. Aeneas returns to his father's house and persuades him, with the help of a series of positive omens, to leave Troy. In the process of retreat, as Aeneas carries out his first great act of *pietas*, shouldering his father and grasping Iulus by the hand, Creusa is lost and Aeneas, *amens*, returns in quest. Her sudden appearance to him parallels the previous epiphanies of Hector and Venus (772–3):

> infelix simulacrum atque ipsius umbra Creusae
> visa mihi ante oculos et nota maior imago.

The sad ghost and shade of Creusa herself appeared before my eyes and a vision larger than her wont.

Its potential is not dissimilar. Like Venus, Creusa chides Aeneas for his indulgence in *insano dolori* (776). Then, expanding on the example of Hector, she reveals to Aeneas the *res laetae* of the future, a kingdom and royal wife. Her last words, however, center on a love that is intimate with *pietas: nati serva communis amorem* (789). As she disappears, and Aeneas attempts to hold her, Virgil uses three lines that he will repeat exactly in book 6 as son greets father (792–4):

> ter conatus ibi collo dare bracchia circum;
> ter frustra comprensa manus effugit imago,
> par levibus ventis volucrique simillima somno.

Three times there I attempted to throw my arms about her neck; three times the vision, embraced in vain, fled my hands, kin to light winds and very like a swift dream.

Each figure is a crucial *imago* in Aeneas' life, a ghost that foretells the future after a period of insecurity and search. Each exemplifies a melancholic aspect of the life of the hero, unable to embrace those dear to him, forced away from Dido for whom he does care, and allotted at the end of the epic a *coniunx* thrust on him by fate. Yet each also is a creative influence in disparate ways—Creusa, by calming his final act of *dolor* in book 2 with a look at the future, Anchises by expanding that future in a delusive vista where arms and piety, clemency and power seem to abide in harmony.

Hence in book 2 as a whole we regularly find emotionality opposed to reason, especially when directed toward long-range goals. Such moments of irrationality are often centered on immediate gratification, understandable however mortally misguided. Heedless action finds its counterpoise in the words of Hector, Panthus, Venus and Creusa, and the thoughts and insights they arouse. The hero's display of aimless chauvinism that follows his dream of Hector is not defended within his narration, and his rationalization for killing Helen, argued in a soliloquy he quotes himself delivering a moment before he almost performs the deed, Aeneas himself qualifies as the product of a maddened mind (*furiata mente*).

It is inevitable that discussion of such polarities must focus on the finale of the poem as Aeneas ponders the situation of the now suppliant Turnus, and then slays him. How is Aeneas to see him, and how, as he weighs alternatives, will whatever analysis he makes of his victim sway him, as he hesitates? Their differentiation (as well as commonality) is made explicit by the poet's concentration on the eyes and right hands of each hero, preceding and following Turnus' last words. Before he speaks we watch Turnus (12.930–1)—

> ille humilis supplex oculos dextramque precantem
> protendens. . . .

He, a suppliant, with eyes humbled, and stretching forth his right hand in prayer . . .—

and after, our attention focusses on the hero in power (938–9):

> . . . stetit acer in armis
> Aeneas volvens oculos dextramque repressit. . . .

> . . . Aeneas stood fierce in arms, rolling his
> eyes, and restrained his right hand. . . .

The eyes of Turnus are humbled, of Aeneas revolving in thought, as victoriously he plots out the possibilities before him. When Turnus states that the Ausonians have seen him, conquered, stretch forth his hands (*victum tendere palmas* 936), he merely reinforces the contrast between his gesture of supplication and Aeneas' posture of strength his right hand momentarily restrained.

The gesture of supplication is one that Aeneas would have understood. He had seen his father twice use it, first, as Troy falls, in asking Jupiter to confirm the omen of fire on Iulus' head (*palmas tetendit* 2.688), second while greeting Aeneas in the Underworld (*palmas tetendit* 6.685), when last he saw him. He had employed it himself to Jupiter in prayer to save the burning ships (*tendere palmas* 5.686), and watched it in the suppliant Liger in book 10 (*tendebat palmas* 596–7). The reader remembers it from the hero's initial appearance in the epic, awed by the prospect of death from nature and preparing to address those who die (to him) more heroically at Troy (1.92–4):

> extemplo Aeneae solvuntur frigore membra;
> ingemit et duplicis tendens ad sidera palmas
> talia voce refert. . . .

Suddenly Aeneas' limbs were undone with cold; he groans and, stretching both hands toward the stars, speaks thus aloud. . . .

Line 92 closely resembles the description of Turnus, frightened by the Dira sent by Jupiter to ensure his final defeat (12.867):

> Illi membra novus solvit formidine torpor. . . .

A strange numbness undoes his limbs in fear. . . .

This spectacle is complemented shortly later by the prospect of Turnus incapable of movement (*gelidus concrevit frigore sanguis* 905), and imitated most clearly in the next to last line of the poem as Turnus dies (951):

> . . . ast illi solvuntur frigore membra.

> . . . but his limbs were undone with cold.

Matters have come full circle. Aeneas, once helpless before the elements, has now become the elemental power, abetted by Jupiter and his Dira, before which Turnus must pray in supplication and which finally destroys him. But the closest parallel between the two is suggested by the previous words of Turnus (12.932–4):

> . . . miseri te si qua parentis
> tangere cura potest, oro (fuit et tibi talis
> Anchises genitor) Dauni miserere senectae. . . .

> . . . if any care of a sad father can touch you,
> I beseech you (Anchises was also such a father
> to you), pity the old age of Daunus. . . .

Virgil has graphically sketched Turnus' aging and debilitation in the lines that lead up to the final duel. (Our growing sympathy for prideful Turnus now suffering humiliation is not unlike our response to savage Mezentius at the moment his vulnerability is shielded by his loving son.) Suddenly, therefore, we find his prototype not in wounded Hector but in Priam whose first, dramatic words to Achilles, as he comes to ransom his son's body, remind him of his father Peleus (*Il.* 24.486–7):

> Achilles like to the gods, remember your father, whose years are like mine,
> on the grievous threshold of old age. . . .

They would also serve to recall to Aeneas his own vivid display of *pietas*, searching out his father in the underworld, and, as we have observed, his preliminary position as suppliant, craving pity from the Sibyl (6.115–7):

> quin ut te supplex peterem et tua limina adirem,
> idem orans mandata dabat. gnatique patrisque,
> alma, precor, miserere. . . .

> Nay he also in prayer gave me commands that as a suppliant I seek you out and approach your threshold. I pray, kindly one, pity both son and father. . . .

First introduced in the epic as a new Achilles, Turnus becomes now not only Priam before Achilles but also Aeneas before the Sibyl. He should appear to his victor as a figure of Aeneas himself, as he appeals to an *imago* Aeneas should well remember. Instead of following the pattern of book 10 where he saw Lausus as an emblem of *pietas* only after he has killed him (and only then does he become *Anchisiades*), Aeneas has a chance to be affected by words, ideas and memories, to pity before rather than after a deed, even to spare, combining force with generosity, not madness. He could show that he also has absorbed what the reader has learned from the conclusion of book 10.

The phrase *parentis cura* and its association with two fathers, Anchises and Daunus, should also cast Aeneas' thoughts back to the past. The reader associates the phrase with Aeneas' love for Ascanius (1.646) and, as Andromache reminisces, with Ascanius' for his lost mother (3.341). Aeneas might hear again Venus' question after he has nearly killed Helen:

> . . . aut quonam nostri tibi cura recessit? non prius aspicies ubi fessum
> aetate parentem liqueris Anchisen. . . . ?

Remembrance of both parents, the *cura parentum* for which *pietas* should provide the motivation, contrasts with the *dolor, ira* and *furor* that, in Venus' words, Aeneas had just displayed by his desire for vengeance against

Helen. It is not, however, Turnus as image of *pietas* or even as representative of Aeneas himself that moves the hero to act at the epic's end. Turnus' words do in fact cause him to delay, to experience a moment of detachment which means at least the possibility of *clementia*, of words taking precedence over deeds. What impels Aeneas to kill is the sight of Pallas' baldrick worn by Turnus. It serves as a *saevi monimenta doloris* (945) which drives Aeneas mad, *furiis accensus et ira/terribilis* (946–7). It is not *pietas*, and the moderation both Venus and Anchises see in its practise, but *ira* that holds the hero in thrall as he embarks on his final action. The clarity of broadened vision that Aeneas is allowed in book 2, when he beholds divine *inclementia* about its devastating work, and that is offered to him so brilliantly as action pauses for the double figuration of Lausus' death, is once again, and for the last time, obscured.

W. R. JOHNSON

The Broken World:
Virgil and His Augustus

And so it was I entered the broken world
To trace the visionary company of love . . .

:—HART CRANE

Among the many splendors of the *Georgics*, the opening of Book 3 is touched with special splendor and special wit (10–18):

> I shall first lead, if the time be granted me,
> The Muses to my home from Aonian heights,
> Shall give my Mantua the Hebrew palm,
> And on the level green shall cause to rise
> A marble temple where great Mincius winds
> His lazy paths amid the tender reeds.
> At the temple's core will Caesar's shrine be set—
> For him, I shall, in Tyrian splendor, steer
> Beside the river's course the victor's car.

Just previous to these verses, Virgil has said an ironic farewell to Callimachus and to Alexandria, and what follows these verses is a commitment to epic— to the epic he perhaps has begun to sketch in his mind even as this passage, which is among the *Georgics'* finishing touches, is being written. Yet if Virgil here lays claim to and temporarily puts on the robes of both Hesiod

From *Arethusa* 1, vol. 14 (1981). Copyright © 1981 by the Department of Classics, State University of New York at Buffalo.

and Pindar, the entire proem of Book 3 remains Callimachean. Virgil *is* Hesiod and Pindar here (for in a sense, these borrowed voices are genuinely his while he borrows them), but Virgil has also become the Roman Alexander. In describing the doors of the new temples of poetry that is partly his and partly Augustus', Virgil emphasizes the magnitude of Augustus' triumphs, even as he acknowledges and celebrates his debt to Callimachus with the flawless refinements of this passage, its elaborate yet controlled fantasy, its playful magnificence. This moment mirrors, after all, the world restored, the world made new, and decorum requires something extravagant yet carefully polished—what Virgil needs here and invents is a unique *maniera* that will rival and surpass that of Callimachus and of the Ptolemies. There are other passages in the *Georgics*—the opening of Book 1 and the close of Book 4—in which this wit, this ambition, and this exultation are in evidence; but this is the grand affirmation of Virgil's triumph and of Augustus' in the *Georgics* or elsewhere in his poetry.

What is this glittering jubilation doing in a poem about cows and hogs, about grapes and bees and manure? Well, if one is determined to versify manuals about agriculture, an occasional piece of *jeu d'esprit* is surely not amiss—particularly when one is writing not for peasants but for one's literary friends and for one's leading statesman. As a matter of fact, there is considerable dissonance in the *Georgics;* between matter and manner, between intellectual, aesthetic convictions and emotional needs, between the past on the one hand and the present and the future on the other. But when we read the poem—that is, when we hear it rather than analyze it— these dissonances vanish into varied harmonies, into supreme polyphony. The *Georgics* is Virgil's masterpiece, not only technically but also emotionally and intellectually. In the *Eclogues,* the balance between artistic choices (Callimachus) and moral imagination (*Romanitas,* the fact of Rome) seems adequate perhaps, but it is not: because "suave beauty" hides, but cannot transform or even counter, anxiety and moral uncertainty. In the *Aeneid* the extreme discrepancy between artistic method and ethical dilemma returns and widens and produces a heartbreaking, disconsolate poem that is too big for poetry, that cannot be constrained by the limits of art and explodes its frame. But in the *Georgics,* these conflicts and the many voices that ponder and try to mediate among them are under sure control and achieve the equilibrium that they crave. Why should this be so? How does Virgil manage in the *Georgics* to blend darkness and light, anxiety and calm, lamentation and victory-song into this brilliant concord? Before I try to answer this question, let me define what I take to be the core of the conflicts in Virgil's poetry, the sand for his pearls.

First, there is Callimachus himself and the Callimachean Roman tradition that Virgil inherits from the generation of Catullus and shares with other great poets of his own age. As Clausen has suggested, there is a peculiar, inescapable collision between Callimachean poetics and Roman worldview. Every major Roman poet from Catullus through Ovid felt this collision within himself, responded to it, and shaped his art because of it and by means of it. The world Callimachus wrote in encouraged artistic distance and mandarin indifference to questions of politics, ethics, and spirituality. Such poetry could be wholeheartedly about culture and peaceful abundance, about leisured refinements of sensibility, could finally concern itself with poetry itself, because, in the aftermath of Alexander's reordering of the Greek world, there was, in a very real sense, nothing much else to write about except one's gratitude for peace, one's exquisite isolation, one's sense of poetry and of the fading past; because, in the Birdcage of the Muses, art replaces life, life which has vanished or become too boring or too complex, too frightening or too trivial. This charming *sprezzatura* seems to have looked very promising to the generation of Catullus; it offered, at first, an alternate lifestyle to all the baffled and sad young men who found their city collapsing about them just as they came to manhood. If the world is frightening or if it is a frightening illusion, what better cure for one's malaise than the cult of worthless beauty, than fables of doomed and dazzling love? Their elders had told them foolish lies about society, about *virtus* and *industria*, and those lies had harmed their minds and hearts. What better way to undo this damage—insofar as it could be undone—than to find shelter in lovely illusions that one shapes for oneself and for one's companions in busy melancholy?

But the past was not so easily got rid of. Catullus voyages to the artificial paradise of Callimachus—and finds himself adding a strange final stanza to his translation of Sappho; and finds himself writing poems about Attis and Ariadne, stranded dreamers who had abandoned reality (*ego mei pars*, I, part of myself, 63.69); and finds himself saying in 68 (68a: 15–18; trs. Whigham):

> Often enough
>   when a man's toga first sat on my shoulders
> I chose love & the Muses
>   in the onset of youth
> in the tart mixture of Venus
>   seeming sweet. . . .

Then on to thoughts of his brother's death (and perhaps of his own), of ruined love and of failed poetry. . . . The aesthetics of Callimachus imply, indeed demand, a renunciation of ethical and political concerns. This is a renunciation that no Roman Callimachean, not even Catullus, and not even Lucretius, could finally be quite easy with. For Virgil, this renunciation was a haunting difficulty that he never quite solved (the other Roman Callimacheans, in their various ways, came near to solutions).

Next there is Virgil's Epicureanism: another evasion of the failed past and of the confusing present, another kind of withdrawal and distancing (or so it may have seemed to him when he was young). Although Virgil's particular Epicurean circle seems to have been very partial to Julius Caesar, the fact remains that the followers of Epicurus, no less than those of Callimachus, tended to scorn or at least to indifference where politics was concerned (*Georgics* 2.490–498):

> Blest is he who has looked on things as they are,
> Who has trampled under him fear and pitiless fate
> And the roar of hungry hell. And happy, too,
> That man who discerns the truth of rural gods,
> Of Pan and old Silvanus and the Nymphs;
> Him the people's favor cannot bend,
> Nor royal splendors fright, no civil war,
> Nor barbarous armies massing in the North,
> Nor Rome's own force nor kingdoms soon to fail.

There is here a peculiar, effective fusion of the Epicurean and the farmer. The *Cecropius hortulus* has become the Italian farm: in both one finds the good, hidden life, self-sufficiency, independence, calm. Both the man of Epicurus and the farmer pay no heed to the frightening absurdities of Roman politics (501–502). Those whose minds are fixed on eternity, whether that of the atoms and the void, of the constant flowerings of the infinite worlds, or that of the rhythm of being, the season's qualities, the permanence of *iustissima tellus* (the most just earth, 460), cannot and will not allow their minds and hearts to be drawn into, to be devoured by, the illusory ephemera of life in the great world. To the end of his life, Virgil tries to reconcile irreconcilable visions—on the one hand, the integrity of the individual, his commitment to, his faith in, his own sanity and moral responsibility, a disciplined calm that is neither selfish nor solipsistic; on the other, the claims of *res publica,* to which *virtus* devotes itself, and the absolute value and meaning of community as Cicero defines it in the closing sections of the *de officiis* I. In his intellectual and spiritual life, the tension between these discordant visions give Virgil's poetry its unique, tragic purity. In the *Georgics* these visions find, momentarily, a possible, an ideal harmony. In the *Aeneid* they will not. In that poem the conflict between the calm of the garden and the action and violence of history will be magnified and dramatized lyrically in great and broken poetry.

Last and not least of the conflicts in Virgil's poetics is the one that always rages for him between the genre that he chooses and his extraordinary lyric genius. Here, I define the lyric sensibility as one which is primarily concerned with the mimesis of emotion (finding metaphors for emotions) and which has little interest in ideas and their conflicts (as in drama) or in the conflicts, the structures and dynamics of society (as in epic). Here again, as in his Callimacheanism and Epicureanism, Virgil's essential concern is with distance from life (as the great world understands it); here also his focus is on the individual consciousness, on its grandeurs and corruptions, its strength and vulnerability. This conflict creates not only extraordinary beauty but also violence and dissonance when Virgil writes pastorals; when he comes to write epic, it shatters this genre and transforms it. Only when he was writing lyrical didactic, when the model is Hesiod and the subject farming, the life of man in nature, only in the *Georgics* is this lyrical conflict truly resolved.

I return now to my original question. Why is it that in the *Georgics* the usual contradictions and oppositions of Virgil's poetry are gathered into luminous harmonies? Why is it that here, and not really elsewhere, the figure of Augustus becomes part of lyrical harmonics, is itself a principal instrument of those harmonies? There is, so far as I can tell, no easy answer to this mystery. We don't know, for instance, why Virgil chose to write a long lyric poem on farming (for it is no more likely that Maecenas really suggested or ordered this poem than it is that Pollio suggested the *Eclogues* or that Augustus suggested or ordered the *Aeneid*), but the appearance of Varro's book on farming, if not the major part of Virgil's *donnée*, was quite important to the poem's shaping, both to its spirit and to the answerable forms that Virgil found for its spirit.

Still, at a purely literary level, two things matter here. First, the theme of farming and the themes that it generates are perfectly suited to the lyric sensibility. Praise of nature and labor, the passage of time and the change of seasons, the mysteries of birth, growth, and death, the stars and their weather—all of these things belong to lyric poetry and all of them offer the metaphors for emotions that were Virgil's central concern as a poet. Second, at the period when the *Georgics* was being composed, Callimachean modernism had clearly triumphed, and Virgil was writing for an audience that understood what he was doing and that appreciated both the difficulty of his task and the skill that accounts for his success in performing his task. We may speak here of a coterie or of several independent coteries, but one might better speak of something wider and stronger that a coterie—one might speak of a movement, provided we understand that literary and intellectual movements are freer and more intricate, less disciplined and less doctrinaire than handbooks come to make them seem. We get some sense—dim, to be sure, but sufficient—of what this movement was and meant and who belonged to it from Horace's *Satire* 1.10. The ethos that this crucial poem sketches is the one in which Virgil wrote the *Georgics*: plenty of support from discerning friends; a clear sense of the maturing and deepening of his powers; perfect material and perfect conditions for composition. Any writer's dream was, for seven years or so, Virgil's reality. While this ideal situation was real, all conflicts could find their proper harmonies. Callimachus, Epicurus, the lyric modes, and the Roman farmer could, whatever their seeming dissonances, for all their apparent oppositions, be gathered into the difficult, the necessary coherence.

But there is a final element in this perfection, this almost impossible perfection of circumstances, and it is perhaps the most important of them all: it is Augustus, or, as he was then, Octavian. Both for what he was and did and tried to do and also for what he came to symbolize in Virgil's mind, in his poetry, Octavian is the center of Virgil's extraordinary freedom to do what he wants and needs to do in the *Georgics*. The thirties in Rome were, of course, uncertain, sometimes even chaotic; but, after decades of bloodshed and terror, there seemed finally some reason for hope, some good chance that peace and reason could be salvages from the ruined past. And, to Virgil and to others in the movement to which he belonged, the chief hope clearly lay with Octavian. Among the members of the movement that Horace's poem catches in amber three are particularly interesting and important because they are no less political than they are literary: Pollio Maecenas, and Messalla, who along with the unnamed Gallus, mediate between the world of poetry and the world of politics. Their presence in both worlds, their unification of these worlds, helped make possible the vitality of Virgil's imagination of *salus*, of the new world's *sōtēr*. This imagination of the world restored, this praise of regeneration, which was hesitantly begun in the *Eclogues* (when there was cause for hesitancy), reaches its perfection in the *Georgics*. This unity is secured by the triumph of Callimachus, by the encouragement of Pollio, Gallus, Maecenas, and Messalla, and by the passion and the abundant freedom that Virgil found and earned when he meditated on Italy's past and Italy's future, as he recaptured the essence of Roman culture, its pure faith in *industria* and in *virtus*, its reliance on the soil and on those who tend it. At the center of this complex yet simple vision of *Romanitas* is Octavian, in whom the figure of Alexander and the figure of Cato, the shapes of the good future and of the good past, are fused.

Then, something began to happen, and the harmony and the world were broken. Exactly what is was and when, slowly, imperceptibly, it happened, we don't know and probably never shall. Even before the *Georgics* was completed, Pollio had made the grand refusal, had declined to participate in the crusade against the East, and had affirmed his independence, his own *virtus*. And then, a few years later, Maecenas also found himself in conflict, against his will, with the symbol of order and safety, with its incarnation, its reality. So, by the time that Virgil was struggling in earnest to find the core of his epic representation of his vision of Italy's *salus*, his mediators were disappearing, and his lyrical epic began to be about something more than Italy's need for regeneration and salvation.

I don't mean that Virgil had changed his mind about Augustus, or that he had come to dislike him or to hate him (in truth, we know nothing whatever of Virgil's personal feelings about Augustus, and even if we did, that knowledge would belong, not to the study and enjoyment of poetry, but to "serious gossip"). Virgil's mind had not changed, but Augustus and his world had changed. This alteration was, so it now seems, both necessary and inevitable. The world *could* be made new—but only at the price of relinquishing the past. And the future belonged not only to Italy and her tough, independent farmers but also to the civilized world in which *virtus*, except in the Emperor, was no longer needed. Virgil saw that and fought to imagine it, by concentrating on *Fatum*, by pondering the destiny of the world and Rome's place in it. But this task of imagination brought new tensions and new conflicts. The figure of Cato and the figure of Alexander would no longer endure coinherence. It is the figure of Cato that vanished to make room for the figure of Alexander, and the virtuous farmer gave way to the virtuous Prince.

Augustus, then, still remains, in the *Aeneid*, the symbol of hope for *salus*, but the world has become wider, more problematic, more mysterious than it had been in the *Georgics*. It is not merely Italian hopes that must be answered now; it is also the hopes of all humankind that must be answered. Something has been won, but something has been lost. The hopes are grander and wider, but so are the dangers and the uncertainties. The metaphor for *salus* still shines, but often now it is clouded over with darker visions. We begin to wonder what price has in fact been paid for safety, we are no longer sure what battles have been lost or what battles have been won. Perhaps hopes for salvation and renewal were not quite real; perhaps they were hungerings after splendid but hopeless ideals; perhaps they were only illusions. . . .

We sometimes forget that Virgil died just at the end of the first quarter of Augustus' reign, that for Virgil, Augustus was not so much the achievement of Italy's *salus* and the world's as he was a symbol for its possible attainment, an image of our needs and our hopes. We forget this because, though Virgil died with his uncertainties about *salus* and its symbol, about his final poem, Augustus, in all sincerity and with great bravery and intelligence, tried to live out the ideal destiny that his profoundest poet had imagined for him, tried to become the reality of which Virgil had made him the radiant and troubled symbol.

GORDON WILLIAMS

Ideas and the Epic Poet

During the last half-century two totally opposed views about the relationship of the *Aeneid* to the times on which it was written have come to be current: on the one hand, it is seen as a clear case of propaganda for Augustan ideology; on the other, it is interpreted as a point of view hostile to Augustus and all he stood for. Here are some characteristic quotations:

(*a*) The character of the epic hero is neither splendid nor striking. That was not intended. The perpetual guidance lavished upon the hero is likewise repugnant to romantic notions. Aeneas is an instrument of heaven, a slave to duty. "Sum pius Aeneas," as he stamps himself at once. Throughout all hazards of his high mission, Aeneas is sober, steadfast and tenacious: there can be no respite for him, no repose, no union of heart and policy with an alien queen. Italy is his goal—"hic amor, haec patria est." And so Aeneas follows his mission, sacrificing all emotion to *pietas*, firm in resolution but sombre and a little weary. The poem is not an allegory; but no contemporary could fail to detect in Aeneas a foreshadowing of Augustus. [Syme (1939), pp. 462–63]

(*b*) But there is of course a broader problem that we have hardly touched upon so far in this book. That is the justification of Virgil's "ideological" viewpoint, the extent to which his poetry may not be vitiated by Augustan "propaganda," if indeed we can use so unkind a term without question-begging. First of all, it seems quite plain that Virgil was himself a convinced Augustan. He was clearly inspired by his theme: he believed in his own "ideology." He really saw in Augustus the type of man who

From *Technique and Ideas in the "Aeneid."* Copyright © 1983 by Yale University. Yale University Press. Translations by the author.

could bring peace out of fratricidal war, order from anarchy, self-control from selfish passion, in a sense, an "age of gold" from an age of iron. [Otis (1963), p. 389]

(c) Virgil seems to say here [in the final scene], if we judge correctly, that Aeneas—and through him Augustus—can never fulfill in fact the ideal conditions of empire, where force and freedom must be fused into a fortunate amalgam. [Putnam (1965), pp. xiii–xiv]

(d) The purpose of the *Aeneid* is clear enough. The poem commemorates a great victory, the battle of Actium, which came soon to symbolize the end of decades of bloody civil war.

(e) The ideal contemporary reader we postulated earlier would take it for granted that somehow or other, Aeneas was Augustus.

(f) If the Aeneas of Book 4 suggests Julius Caesar or Mark Antony, the Aeneas of Book 12 points plainly to Augustus; and the portrait is hardly a flattering one. [Quinn (1969), pp. 22; 54; 253]

(g) The thought of this intelligent, sensitive, reflective poet, at the height of his powers and in the maturity of his later years, subscribing to a limited political program as the basis of his epic—surely that is artificial and mind-boggling. It is also degrading. [Di Cesare (1974), pp. viii–ix]

From propaganda for Augustus to propaganda against Augustus is an easy step for the attitudes expressed by these quotations (and many, many more examples of both points of view could be adduced). Both extremes require several strategies of interpretation: for instance, a literal and partial reading of the poem, and a conviction that an ideology is either being expressed or attacked (by another ideology, of course). The inadequacy of seeing Aeneas as "an instrument of heaven" or of interpreting the poem as a commemoration of the battle of Actium can be demonstrated, and one purpose of this book has been to attempt that demonstration. It is perhaps harder to demonstrate the violence that is done to the text of the *Aeneid* by excavating some kind of "ideology" out of it.

The attempt, however, should start from a distinction between ideas and ideology. It is simple enough to list the major elements in the ideology of Augustus (as we can detect it in the pronouncements of his *res gestae*). But what ideas are expressed in the *Aeneid*? It is easy to sense that many complex ideas are there expressed, but indirectly and in such a way that they bear no clear relevance to Augustan ideology. Again the criteria by which an ideology is judged are expedience, usefulness, practicability, effectiveness, and so on. Ideas, on the other hand, are powerful sources of poetic energy and emotion, neither of which has the slightest relevance to ideology, and their quality is judged by their capacity to generate that combination of intellectual and emotional power. In short, there are many ideas in the *Aeneid* and no ideology.

A further strategy of interpretation is needed even by those who proclaim that the *Aeneid* is not an allegory. This is to regard Aeneas as in some way symbolic of Augustus; another way of formulating this thesis is to say that Aeneas is a forerunner of, or that he foreshadows, Augustus. But either formulation involves an unwelcome consequence. For if Aeneas is to be symbol for, or even to foreshadow, Augustus, then the time-span of the *Aeneid* is in some way symbolic of the time-span of Roman history as a whole down to, and including, the age of Augustus. But the poet has made every effort to show that point of view decisively mistaken. For the major indexes that relate the immediate field of the *Aeneid* to Roman history as a whole and to the age of Augustus in particular all have a peculiar feature: they are so designed as to suggest a continuum of history that is in the most important ways Roman, extending from the late twelfth century B.C. to the time of the poem's composition. The first of them (Juppiter's prophecy at 1.257–96) is actually designed to constitute an exemplary chronological framework that establishes the time of Aeneas as an integral part of Rome's earliest origins.

What generates poetical excitement in the *Aeneid*—and no doubt did so in its poet—is that sense of the magical and inspiring story of the origins of a state which was destined in the poet's time to include under its rule almost all of the known world. Antiquity in general may have been unencumbered by anything like the modern "idea of progress" (though there has recently been argument against this idea), but Romans viewed their own state as evolving gradually over a very long period of time and thus, in this(as in other respects) quite different from other ancient states that sprang into existence, like Athene, full-grown from the head of Zeus. The idea is well formulated by Cicero in words he puts into the mouth of Scipio Africanus the younger. Scipio is telling how much he learned from the great Cato (*de republica* 2.2):

> is dicere solebat ob hanc causam praestare nostrae civitatis statum ceteris civitatibus, quod in illis singuli fuissent fere quorum suam quisque rem publicam constituisset legibus atque institutis suis, ut Cretum Minos, Lacedaemoniorum Lycurgus, Atheniensium, quae persaepe commutata esset, tum Theseus tum Draco tum Solo tum Clisthenes tum multi alii, postremo exsanguen iam et iacentem doctus vir Phalereus sustentasset Demetrius, nostra autem res publica non unius esset ingenio sed multorum, nec una hominis vita sed aliquot constituta saeculis et aetatibus.

He used to declare that the constitution of our state was superior to all other states for the reason that in them it was virtually one man in each case who had founded the state on his own laws and institutions, as Minos did for Crete, Lycurgus for Sparta, for Athens (whose constitution had often been changed) at one time Theseus, then Dracon, then Solon, then Cleisthenes, then many others, finally when it was bloodless and prostrate that scholarly man, Demetrius or Phalerum, had revived it. But our state had been founded not by the genius of one man but of many, nor in one man's lifetime but over several centuries and the ages of many men. . . .

Then Scipio undertakes to "demonstrate our state to you both at its birth and in its years of growth and when it became adult and firm and strong" (de republica 2.3). The metaphor of the gradual growth of a human being is used to express the concept.

Scipio, however, starts with Romulus in the eighth century. When Virgil does is to start the whole process with Aeneas, and the nature of Aeneas' contribution is made clear in the speech of Juppiter in Book 1. It is not just the settling of the Trojans in Italy, but (1.264) *moresque viris et moenia ponet* "he shall found a way of life and fortifications for them." The contribution of behaviour is at least as important as that of the physical buildings designed to protect the state. The concept is used by Anchises to define the nature of Roman civilization (6.852): *pacique imponere morem* "to impose a settled way of life on peace." The poetical interest of Aeneas lies in the vision of a man who is a Homeric hero yet is also a primitive colonizer and possesses elements of behaviour, of morals, of values that mark him out from all his surroundings as a proto-Roman. In many ways, then, Aeneas is a man of the twelfth century, and in certain situations of stress where other standards cannot be applied, he is shown to revert to the pattern of behaviour of a Homeric hero. That is why he is void of interest if one regards him as a symbol of Augustus or even as a forerunner of him (except in the most literal and limited way). The poetical excitement of Aeneas lies in the concept and creation of an individual who belongs to one world but has visions of another that are so far in advance of his time that he cannot help but be torn between them. Augustus—together with all good Romans at all times—has inherited a moral tradition from the past that is specifically Roman; the index of the shield at the end of Book 8 is designed to bring out that aspect of the tradition. It is exactly those qualities, expressed in the valuation placed on *pax, fides, libertas, pietas,* and *virtus,* that are to be seen, at times dimly, in the character of Aeneas and also, to some extent, in that of Evander and his people. But the *mores* established by Aeneas are not Trojan; that is guaranteed by

Jupiter's promise to Juno (12.834). They are phenomena of the frontier spirit of a man who has to rely on himself, discover his own values, and invent a system of behaviour that responds to the situation in which he finds himself. But they are also related to what is best in Italian values, even if this does not come through explicitly in the action of the *Aeneid*, since there the Italians are enemies of the Trojans. In fact, those *mores* come closest to what is suggested about the Italian age of Saturn, though more by Evander (8.314–36) than by Latinus (7.202–04). After that age there was a decline, the leading characteristics of which were war and greed (8.326–27). It is to the prelapsarian state of Italy that the ideal and some-what instinctive *mores* of Aeneas and of Evander are related.

Somewhere at the basis of all ideology, at whatever remove, are ideas, though they lose blood and life when translated into an ideological programme. Consequently, it is possible to abstract ideas from the *Aeneid* and assert that they are relevant to the ideology of Augustus; and then to take the further step of claiming that the *Aeneid* supports the political programme of Augustus. But this is as much a travesty of a subtle and complex text as to assert the opposite: that the ideas of the *Aeneid* are conceived in such a way as to throw doubt on any hopes invested in Augustus, if not to attack his ideology directly. It is, in fact, very hard to say what the ideas of the *Aeneid* are, and some violence and over-simpli-fication are done to the text just by attempting to do so. The reason for this is that the ideas are inherent, unstated; they emerge from the changing patterns of the narrative as underlying assumptions that possess all the more power for not being formulated. But the apprehension of these ideas is an important source of emotional power in the text.

For instance, the value of peace becomes an insistent note in the second half of the *Aeneid*. It becomes clear in the portrait of idyllic peace in Italy during the reign of Latinus in the first half of Book 7. This is, in fact, an irony, since the reality is far from peaceful, as will become evident, and the ideal of peace is more convincingly exhibited among Evander and his people. The ideal is given powerful expression by Aeneas when the Italian embassy comes to ask a truce for burial of the dead (11.108–11):

> quaenam vos tanto fortuna indigna, Latini,
> implicuit bello, qui nos fugiatis amicos?
> pacem me exanimis et Martis sorte peremptis
> oratis? equidem et vivis concedere vellem.

What stroke of undeserved ill-fortune, Latins, enmeshed you in such a war that you shun our friendship? Do you ask me for peace on behalf of the dead and those cut down by the chance of war? I should for myself certainly have wanted to grant it to the living also.

A different view is suggested by Turnus at the climax of his contemptuously angry speech to Allecto disguised as an old temple-attendant (7.444):

> bella viri pacemque gerent quis bella gerenda

War and peace will be conducted by men whose business it is to conduct war.

Here peace is subordinated to war in the main clause by the use of *gerere*, a verb meaning "to wage" and naturally associated with *bellum*; in the subordinate clause peace is omitted altogether. The sentence, by its structure, portrays a man who lives for war. That will be a major element in the portrait of Turnus; it is the opposite with Aeneas. That constant sense of peace as the essential condition for the ideal life colours the tragedy of Books 7–12 and underlies the frustration of Aeneas.

But this peace is not the peace of Augustan ideology, the *parta victoriis pax* (*res gestae* 13). Peace in the poet's sense is an absolute value. Its nature, paradoxically, emerges most clearly in another leading idea of the poem, hatred of war. For war destroys the values of peace. That idea is poignantly expressed in the first death of the Italian war when the poet speaks an epitaph over Galaesus, killed (7.536) while he was trying to mediate for peace. It comes out in the constant pity of the poet, expressed in descriptions of horrible deaths and in the recurring epitaphs and apostrophes. War transforms character, so that Aeneas reverts to the type of Homeric hero, speaking in a loathsome way for instance, to Tarquitus (10.557–60):

> istic nunc, metuende, iace. non te optima mater
> condet humi patrioque onerabit membra sepulcro:
> alitibus linquere feris, aut gurgite mersum
> unda feret piscesque impasti vulnera lambent.

Now lie there dead, frightening man. Your fine mother will not lay in the earth or weigh down your limbs with an ancestral tomb. You will be left for wild birds, or the wave will carry you sunk in its tide and ravenous fishes will lick your wounds.

The words are a combination of what Odysseus says to Socus (*Iliad* 11.450–55 "ravenous birds") and Achilles to Lycaon (21.122–35 "fishes"). Even the attractive Pallas, whose noble speech to his followers precedes his *aristeia* (10.369–78), is then shown perpetrating horrors (380–425) before he is himself slain.

War is seen to be almost an absolute evil—but not quite, because the poet recognises that there are times when a man has no choice but to fight, as Aeneas must, after doing all that he can to prevent war. In the same way, it seems to be suggested, Augustus had no possible option but to fight Antony and Cleopatra at Actium (8.678–713). The ideal society is free from war, and so the climax to Juppiter's great speech shows war eliminated by Augustus (1.293–96). But there the poet is clearly thinking mainly of civil war, and it is above all at this kind of war that his hatred is directed; for that reason the Italian war is portrayed as a sort of civil war. There is some tenuous connexion with Augustan ideology and the ceremony of closing the gate of Janus; it was closed three times by Augustus—in 29 B.C., in 25 B.C., and on one later, unknown occasion (*res gestae* 13)—and the multiple closures indicate its propaganda value. But it is only a tenuous connexion, and a far more Augustan attitude is shown in sentiments such as those of Horace in *Odes* 3.2, lauding war against foreigners as the gymnasium of patriotism.

Another idea of the epic is the value placed on tradition, or *mos* and *mores*, on the concept of settled custom. But of its nature tradition cannot be established and maintained by one man. There must be like-minded successors. Aeneas is shown in the poem establishing a way of life that depends on a series of values virtually unknown to the heroic world. The tradition is handed on to his son, who is to imitate him (12.435–40), and so on. It is to that sense of a settled tradition broken by civil war that Augustus appealed when he wrote, early in his *res gestae* (8.5): "by new laws passed on my proposal I brought back many exemplary practices of our ancestors that were perishing in our time and I myself have handed on to posterity for imitation exemplary practices in many fields." But because no man is exempt from death such a tradition can be unexpectedly broken; the paradigmatic case of this in the *Aeneid* is the dirge performed over the dead Marcellus, designated successor to Augustus. The sense not only of the inevitability of death but also of its unpredictability is one source of the considerable tone of pessimism that pervades the epic. In consequence, all human planning is frail and every tradition uncertain. The more confident Roman, and still more Augustan, attitude is put into the mouth of Anchises (6.852) *pacique imponere morem* "to impose on peace a settled way of life." That attitude is explicitly stated; the other, left to be inferred, is more powerful.

Similarly left to be inferred is another idea basic to the epic: it concerns the problem of human free will versus necessity. Is the writer of quotation (*a*) [at the beginning of this essay] right in talking about "the perpetual guidance lavished upon the hero" and Aeneas as "an instrument of heaven"? The poet uses the gods as a figure by which the problem of free will can be accommodated. But what emerges from the epic is that men are conscious of their freedom of will at the moment of action; it is only the privileged poet who has the vantage point capable of seeing a pattern in history and of understanding that what did happen could not have happened otherwise. The problem, in fact, is not a problem: there are just two points of view that cannot coincide. The noble speech of Pallas to his followers has just been mentioned; it is a fine expression of the dilemma (10.369–78):

> quo fugitis, socii? per vos et fortia facta,
> per ducis Euandri nomen devictaque bella
> spemque meam, patriae quae nunc subit aemula laudi,
> fidite ne pedibus. ferro rumpenda per hostis
> est via. qua globus ille virum densissimus urget,
> hac vos et Pallanta ducem patria alta reposcit.
> numina nulla premunt, mortali urgemur ab hoste
> mortales; totidem nobis animaeque manusque.
> ecce maris magna claudit nos obice pontus,
> deest iam terra fugae: pelagus Troiamne petemus?

Where are you running away to, my friends? ⟨I beseech⟩ you by the brave deeds, by the name of our leader Evander and the wars won by him and by hope that now arises to rival my father's fame, do not put your trust in your feet. A path must be hacked through the enemy by steel. Where the press of men thrusts there most densely, through there does your glorious country demand you and your leader Pallas back. No divine powers oppress us; we are mortals oppressed by a mortal enemy: we have the same number both of souls and of hands as they. See! the tide imprisons us with the great barrier of the ocean, there is no land left for running away: is it the sea we are to make for, or Troy?

The Homeric analogue to this, the speech of Ajax to his troops as the Trojans reach the Greek ships (Iliad 15.733–41), makes no mention of gods. The poet of the Aeneid uses the gods in the following narrative, but Pallas knows nothing of that. What emerges clearly here is the isolation of man, his total self-dependence, his responsibility for his own acts and their consequences. There are no gods to help or hinder; they are a poetic device for expressing the hindsight of history.

Another powerful idea operative throughout is that moral judgments have no necessary claim to absolute right or wrong (see chapter 8). Here again the gap between the temporality of the narrative and that of the composition operates. For in the twelfth century the poet represents both sides as thinking in their own terms and each judging itself to be justified; in the age of Augustus can he look back and see that two totally incompatible sets of criteria were operating, between which judgment could only be made, if at all, on a third set of terms unknown to the actors, and so, from their point of view, arbitrarily. The poet withholds judgment, and his integrity has the effect not only of generating emotion but also of making a reader see such moral dilemmas as a feature not of one time or place but of the human condition as such. The technique—it is close to what Keats called "negative capability" (defined as "capable of being in uncertainties, mysteries, doubts, without any irritable reaching after fact and reason")—creates a depth and range that is beyond the easy certainties of other poets.

There is a further aspect to moral ambiguity that has not yet been touched on. For there is a distinct contradiction, though it remains always implicit and unobtrusive, between the poet's hatred of war and the laudation of Augustus as a conqueror. It is always a voice other than the poet's that pronounces the laudation: at 1.289–96 it is Juppiter; at 6.791–800 it is Anchises; and at 8.722–28 it is the workmanship of Vulcan. In the first of these statements, Augustus will wage the war to end all wars, but the emphasis here is heavily on the cessation of civil war; in the second, the laudation is of extension of the empire as such and the fear with which Augustus is already regarded in the twelfth century by potential enemies; in the final passage, it is laudation of his sheer conquest of peoples from all over the world. The principle is voiced by Anchises (6.851–53): Rome's arts are those of government, the imposition of law and custom, clemency to the humbled, and the crushing of the arrogant by war. The poet recognises two standards in somewhat the same way as he recognises that fame is due to Pallas for the slaughter of enemies at the same time as he grieves over his death (10.507–09). There is a moral ambiguity between the valuation of peace (and hatred of war) and admiration for the greatness of Rome. For ultimately, greatness is owed to, and to some extent measured by, military power. The fame of Greece derives from the arts of peace; they are the poet's arts, and so he dissociates himself from the expression of what he nevertheless recognises to be fact of life by using voices other than his own. The two points of view cannot be reconciled; they can only be expressed and judged on their own terms. This is the essence of moral ambiguity—and of poetic integrity.

This dichotomy of irreconcilable points of view can also be regarded as measuring the gap between the two secondary fields of the epic: the field of Roman history and the age of Augustus on the one hand, and on the other, the field of the human condition in a hostile universe. The general ideas that lie at the basis of the epic are related to the latter field. It is to be noticed that these ideas are inherent; they are never expressed as such and can only be distantly apprehended by the reader. The themes that focus on Augustus, on the other hand, are stated explicitly. They have a relationship to the major elements of Augustan ideology, but, because of the way in which the poet puts those themes in the mouth of privileged persons (gods and Anchises), he dissociates himself from direct implication in their expression. An interesting exception to this can be seen in Book 8. For Evander, when he conducts Aeneas about the site of future Rome, gives expression to a way of life that was certainly idealised in the age of Augustus—the life of simple virtue in natural surroundings (8.337–69). Here the poet deliberately enters the text in his own voice to point the contrast with contemporary Rome (348–50) and 360–61). This is a theme that lies at the roots of the *Georgics*, and it seems likely that the ideas that underlay certain aspects of Augustan moral reform excited the poet's sympathetic imagination in a way that military greatness and political goals did not. Hence, at this point the two fields of the human condition and the age of Augustus intersect.

The association of the primary field of the poem with that aspect of the secondary field which is the age of Augustus suggests that one of the poet's basic concepts was this: the ideals of human existence that can be poetically shown to have been implicit in the first beginnings of the Roman state in the twelfth century are only now, at last in the age of Augustus, coming to be realised. The proposition is optative. It is no propaganda for a particular regime but a poetical vision, disappointed and betrayed in reality, yet the hallmark not only of an age (and shared by other poets of the time) but also of the historical vision of a great poet.

However, it is questionable whether this exactly is the final impression left on the reader. It seems, rather, as if the poet used the twelfth century to some extent to redress the present and in Aeneas, contrary to what most commentators now assert, created a figure closer to the ideal in one important respect than any contemporary Roman could be. For Aeneas at no point shows interest in the kind of fame that is acquired by military prowess. Quite the opposite: he does everything possible to avoid war and shows every sign of sharing the poet's hatred of it. The *pax Augusta* was recommended on no such grounds; patriotism and conquest were as closely linked as in Horace *Odes* 3.2. Anchises puts the Augustan point of view not only in (6.853) *debellare superbos* but in his stated purpose in the review of Roman heroes (6.718, 806–07, and 889)—to inflame Aeneas with pride in the fame to come from Roman military superiority. There is no sign that anything of the kind played any part in Aeneas' motivation. He can revert to being a Homeric hero when frustrated in his better plans, but his real soul is laid bare more surely in the account of the Greek destruction of Troy or in his tears elicited by the Trojan scenes on Dido's temple (1.459–65)—tears quite different from the dramatic tears of Odysseus when he hears the ballad of Demodocus (*Odyssey* 8.83–95), which were the Homeric model for the poet—when he says (1.461–62):

> sunt hic etiam sua praemia laudi;
> sunt lacrimae rerum et mentem mortalia tangunt.

Even here great deeds receive their rewards, there are tears for what happens and mortal sufferings touch the heart.

This is a fine index to the secondary field not of Roman history but of the human condition, and it is true that Aeneas in relation to all he takes a part in is linked as often to that aspect of the age of Augustus. It is as though, in spite of apparent optimism about the age of Augustus, the poet's natural pessimism was so great that in the end human achievement, its significance and certainly its permanence, is called into question, especially in the face of the fact of death. Aeneas wondering how the blessed dead could ever want to come to life again is a synecdoche for the poem's judgment on man and his universe. Such indexes again and again enforce a judgment that measures ideals not by the terms of Rome's national self-interest and self-esteem but by the requirements of the human condition itself.

If this is true, then it helps to support the answer given to the other general problem faced by this book: to choose between two rival readings of the *Aeneid*. The conclusion clearly suggested by this examination of the epic is that the world of Aeneas is to be viewed as a part of the real world of human experience, and that the poet is not giving a direct account of the constitution of the universe when he uses the concepts of Fate and the gods; on the contrary, those concepts are figurally active (mainly in a metaphorical mode) in the narrative and are to be distinguished from authorially guaranteed beliefs. The poet does not express beliefs directly, but instead a sense of deep pessimism is conveyed about the capacity of human beings to attain ideals in a universe that is essentially hostile. The hope that is constantly expressed in the formulation of such ideals is pitifully vulnerable to the very nature of the human condition.

K. W. GRANSDEN

The Funeral of Pallas

Book XI is the only book of the
Aeneid to open with a dawn-formula. The mood of this opening is in strong
contrast to the deliberately controlled savagery of the end of X, the defiant
death-speech of Mezentius and the remarkable cluster of violent and ag-
gressive words in the final lines:

> "*hostis amare*, quid *increpitas mortemque minaris?*
> nullum in *caede nefas*, nec sic ad *proelia* ueni,
> nec tecum meus haec pepigit mihi foedera Lausus
> unum hoc per si qua est uictis uenia *hostibus* oro:
> corpus humo patiare tegi. scio *acerba* meorum
> circumstare *odia*: hunc oro, defende *furorem*
> et me consortem nati concede sepulcro."
> haec loquitur, *iuguloque* haud inscius accipit *ensem*
> *undantique animam diffundit in arma cruore.*

> "My bitterest foe, why do you have to crack death-threats at me?
> I wouldn't have gone to war if I'd scruples about killing.
> And when you killed my son there were no concessions,
> But if there are such, for the defeated, then I ask only this:
> Let my body be buried deep. I know my own people's hatred
> Is waiting on every side. Protect me from their fury
> And let my son and me share the same sepulchre."
> He spoke; and deliberately offered his throat to the sword
> And drained his soul out on a stream of blood.

Hated even by his own men, redeemed only by his love for his son, Mezentius dies. It is as though in his arrogance he deliberately shares with his

---

From *Virgil's Iliad: An Essay on Epic*. Copyright © 1984 by Cambridge University Press.

killer the responsibility for his own death. Now "the monstrous anger of the guns" gives place to a solemn ritual, the burial of the dead, which takes up two days of a twelve-day truce. On the third day (11.210) there is a war council of the Latins, occupying the central section of the book, whose structure follows the usual triadic pattern. This third day, which ends with the end of the book, sees the renewal of battle: the final section is dominated by the *aristeia* of Camilla.

Thus book XI offers a great variety of tone and incident. The opening is dark and majestic, with a drum-like, leaden reception of the word *maestus* ("gloomy," "sombre"), a form of which is found eleven times in the book (nine times in the other three war-books, IX, X, XII, put together, and fourteen times in books I–VIII). The central section is a rhetorical debate in which Turnus and a new character, Drances, play large parts, while the final section is varied and relieved by the presence of Camilla, the first part played in the poem by a woman since the "Bacchic" scenes in VII.

The last three books of the *Aeneid* are the most complex in structure and the richest in variety of mood and incident. They make enormous demands on the reader's concentration. It is the reader who must relate the divisions of the narrative to each other and gradually construct as complete a meaning as possible for the whole. Meanwhile, the reader will become increasingly aware not only of a narrator who links the various parts of the poem, but also of an "implied author" who becomes, in the last three books, a more and more considerable and indeed dominant element in the poem's "meaning." The more use Virgil makes of Homer's *Iliad,* the more the modern reader is driven back to that source and the more he has to make an assessment of Virgil's dependence on, and divergence from, his model. It is like having to read two epics at once.

The breaks and intervals between books, and between triads in each book, become charged with greater significance as the reading proceeds. We have already noticed the gap between the end of IX, Turnus carried *laetus* back to his own troops, and the grand opening of X

panditur interea domus omnipotentis Olympi

And now the gates of omnipotent heaven are opened

in which Jupiter proclaims his refusal to take sides. Throughout book X the implied author was never far away, directing the reader to the shifting fortunes of the narrative, making him ask what divine indifference means in terms of human misery—does it differ much from divine interference? Jupiter's lofty statement

rex Iuppiter omnibus idem.
fata uiam inuenient.

King Jupiter is the same for all men.
Fate will find the way.

is separated by paragraphs of violence and death from 10.758–9, where

the gods in Jupiter's house feel pity for the pointless anger
Of either side, and for all the efforts of men.

In that passage, antithesis follows antithesis, and the repetitions and pair-
ings of words comment on the action narrated, indeed do more than comment; they make of it a rhetorical representation which brings the narrative
to a virtual standstill and stalemate. Both sides attack, both are winning,
both are losing, neither will yield. Juno watches on one side, Venus on
the other, and in the middle of the conflict a pale Fury out of hell keeps
the war going. Just so, at the battle of Actium on Vulcan-Virgil's vatic
shield, we have seen and Aeneas has seen, the gods ranged on either side,
with the war-god raging indiscriminately at the heart of the conflict, Civil
Strife, Bellona and the Furies at his side.

A conflict which neither side can win for a long time, a war of
attrition, is a *donnée* of Homer's *Iliad*, and accounts to a considerable degree
for the psychological tensions so brilliantly drawn in the first two books of
the *Iliad*, the quarrel between Achilles and Agamemnon and the latter's
weak and ill-judged testing of the troops. Virgil's Iliad lasts only a few days,
yet in this brief time he includes this aspect of the Trojan war, its sense
of stalemate, frustration, and tension. In Homer's *Iliad* there is no final end
to the war, though the death of Hector, the Trojans' only real champion,
acts as a symbolic prefiguration of that end. But Hector's death is not the
end of Homer's narrative. In book xxiv Achilles gives back Hector's body
to Priam, a personal decision made not (as Achilles characteristically insists)
in response to Priam's supplication ("I myself am minded to give him back
to you") but in conformity to the expressed concern of Apollo ("Achilles
has destroyed pity") and the will of Zeus, who refuses to interfere directly
but sends Thetis to plead with her son: a symmetry which mirrors the
situation in book i. This gesture of reconciliation ends the story of the
wrath of Achilles in a mood of love and pity but is far from prefiguring—
indeed its tone and mood contradict—the end of Troy as we see it in *Aeneid*
ii, when the Greeks (now without Achilles) showed no pity to their conquered foes. This is why an epic about the wrath of Achilles "means" to
every reader something much more complete and all-embracing than the

proclaimed subject might suggest. The motif of the eventual fall of Troy, repeated prophetically several times in the poem, helps to create in the reader a sense of a larger meaning which demands a response to the total context of the Trojan war, from its remote first cause through the sacrifice of Iphigeneia, the quarrel with Agamemnon, the deaths of Patroclus and Hector, and so down to the coming of the Amazon, the death of Achilles, the wooden horse, and the sack of the city.

In the *Aeneid* the death of Turnus and the end of the war in Latium are the same. But they are not the end of the whole story or of the significance of the *Aeneid*. Through various prophetic passages the poet brings into the narrative events which lie beyond the heroic age, events which Aeneas, gazing on the Shield, delights in as pictures, while ignorant of their meaning. In a curious way, this too has become prophetic: for Virgil's implied Augustan reader, those events whose meaning Aeneas could not understand were his own history, but the modern reader will identify with Aeneas, delighting in images whose historical meaning he may not be able to reconstruct. Yet he must take his unfamiliarity with Roman history into his reading of the *Aeneid;* as he may also, perhaps, have to take his unfamiliarity with the Bible into his reading of *Paradise Lost.* "An epic," said Pound, "is a poem containing history," and by history we may also understand legends, myths and traditional tales as well as "what happened in the past." The modern reader may bring to his reading of secondary epic ignorance of the past, so that, indeed, the epic becomes all that he knows of the past: the *Aeneid* will contain for him, as it did for many in the times when Greek culture was forgotten, the whole of the *Iliad* and the fall of Troy and the subsequent *nostoi.* It will also contain the triumph of Augustus.

But "meaning" for a reader of literary epic does not stop with knowledge of facts, legends and Homer. For the reader of the second half of the *Aeneid*—and that reader will additionally achieve a retrospective sense of books I–VI different from any he would have gained had the second half not been attempted—what may now come across most intensely is the poet himself, not the epic narrator of a Romanised Homeric conflict, but the commentator and moraliser on a spectacle of misery, carnage and "impartial" disaster for both sides. A heroic poem expressing hatred of war is not wholly surprising: many passages in the *Iliad* express an intense and possibly traditional nostalgia for peace as it was before the Achaians came, while others depict the waste and madness of war. But in the *Aeneid* such sentiments dominate and colour the entire narrative. The presence and sensibilities of the empathising poet emerge more and more strongly as the reader encompasses the closing books of the epic.

Indeed, by the end of x, the reader's own sense of the war-narrative as a rhetoric of violent images has become more intense and more restless. After the deaths of Nisus and Euryalus in ix, have come the deaths of Pallas, Lausus, Mezentius; the last word of x is blood, the last image that of blood spurting from Mezentius's throat over his armour, the last speech that of Mezentius, proud, bitter, contemptuous, ready for Aeneas's sword, asking only, as Hector had once asked, for safe burial: the whole scene forms, in terms of epic narrative, a scene from an imaginary theatre of cruelty and of the absurd. Aeneas does not answer Mezentius in the violent and characteristically rejective fashion in which Achilles had answered Hector. He gives, indeed, no answer, and the book ends abruptly, as does xii, with an act of almost ritualised bloodshed.

From that ending of x to the dawn which opens xi the reader has to bridge an eloquent gap or blank in the narrative. Indeed, the first line of xi

Oceanum interea surgens Aurora reliquit

with the echo of *interea* from 10.1, *Panditur interea . . .* , serves a similar kind of narrative bridge-function. Aeneas, as this day dawns, though troubled by Pallas's death, his thoughts wholly on the dead and the need for burial (*sociis dare tempus humandi* in line 2), does first his duty as a Roman: he gives thanks to the gods for victory as the new day starts. We may recall the beginning of book viii when after a troubled night Aeneas faces the rising sun and prays to the river-god Tiberinus for protection, before he goes upstream to Pallanteum. Aeneas *imperator* has become Aeneas *pontifex*, *pius* Aeneas, as he is again, supremely, in the final book. The narrative now slows down to the rhythm of a funeral cortège, as we settle to a deeply felt slow movement in the symphony, a long-drawn-out, solemn funeral march.

The opening of xi is both a continuation of, and a break from, the end of x. We paused in our reading as the blood of Mezentius flowed from his throat. The new day comes up with the new book, a coincidence found nowhere else in the poem, and we at once entered the troubled mind of Aeneas. We see Aeneas carry out the construction of a trophy, a practice current in the armies of Virgil's own day, a Romanisation of epic warfare, which also has an epic grandeur appropriate to a bronze-age warrior. With barbarous and grim splendour a huge oak lopped of its branches is decked in the armour of Mezentius, *contemptor diuum* in life but in death subject to the proper rites imposed by his conqueror and antithesis, *pius* Aeneas. Aeneas then reviews the military situation and gives a brief *hortatio*:

"This is a great achievement, men; be of good courage,
For what still waits. Here are the spoils of war, a proud king's
Weapons. Mezentius is in my hands now. Here he is.
Now to march on Latinus and his citadel . . .
Meanwhile let us commit the unburied bodies of our comrades
To earth, the only honour of the underworld.
Go," he said, "and to those noble souls who with their blood
Have won for us this land, pay the last tributes
Of honour, and to Evander's town of mourning let Pallas
Be sent home, for the black day of death
Which took him, found him not without courage."

The narrative moves away now from the dead Mezentius, the primitive and crude trophy, to the long intense description of the funeral of Pallas, a passage displaying all the techniques of the literature of pathos. We follow the narrative, and the cortège, through Aeneas's eyes; his immense sense of desolation which we experience, his sense of Evander's loss. It is Aeneas who superintends the placing of the body on the bier, and he who pronounces, in the second paragraph of book XI, the funeral oration.

This speech is one of the focal points of the entire poem, around which some of its central moral and emotional attitudes are organised. Through it the reader may direct his sense of the narrative away from the grand heroic gestures of the epic of action, the necessities by which things happen and by which they are as they are, towards that which was not to be, towards the intuition of loss and pain. Like all great literature, the *Aeneid* frequently enacts the things which were not enacted, says the things which were not said, whereby the reader constructs an alternative world in which "If only Pallas had not died" (but he had to) becomes "Pallas did not have to die." and then (momentarily) "imagine a world in which he did not die." For a while, one of the poem's most important characters still lives in that other world—Evander does not yet know of his son's death. The rhetoric of *consolatio* becomes in terms of the narrative a means by which the reader may construct a meaning for the entire poem which depends on negation, not affirmation. The key words of Aeneas's speech are words of negation, disappointment, loss, failure, an ironic awareness of the gap between heroic boast and human destiny: *non haec, spe . . . inani, exanimum, nil iam caelestibus ullis debentem, uano . . . honore*, and the ubiquitous *maesti, maestum, maesto, maestus, maesta*, the declension of sorrow.

Aeneas begins his oration with words in which the implied reader secures another secondary epic allusion to Homer. In *Iliad* XVIII Achilles laments Patroclus:

Ah me. It was an empty word I cast forth on that day when in his halls
    I tried to comfort the hero Menoitios.
I told him I would bring back his son in glory to Opous . . .

Aeneas addresses Pallas as *miserande puer,* words he heard his father use, in the Elysian fields, about another young hero who died before he was "put on," whose premature death, indeed, is foretold even before he is born, thus deepening the sense of mortality which underlies Virgil's use of the idea of reincarnation. The words *miserande puer* belong to Marcellus, but also to Nisus and Euryalus and now to Pallas and so to every young man of whom these characters are types.

O young man, most pitiable, did Fortune grudge you
To me, though she came smiling? You were not to see
Us in our kingdom, nor to your father ride home victorious.
No. This was not the promise I gave Evander your father at our going
When he embraced me and charged me and charged me to begin an
    empire
But told me in fear of dangerous foes and a tough war.
And oh, perhaps even now, led on by hope's fool's light,
He is saying his prayers and piling with offerings his altar,
And here we are, and his son lifeless with nothing left
Of obligation to any god, and so with empty pomp,
Comrades in sorrow, we bring him home.
Ah so unlucky, soon to see this bitter death.
Is this our homecoming, our long awaited triumph?
Was this my grand assurance? Oh Evander, at least you shall not
See him defeated by the wounds of shame, nor pray
A father's prayer for death because your son has saved
His life but not his honour. But oh, how great
A rock, how great a refuge, is lost to you,
My son, and to Italy.

Achilles, after mentioning his vain promise to Patroclus's father, does not refer again to Menoitios; instead, he foretells his own death at Troy and makes a pledge to kill Hector. It is characteristic of Virgil to sustain a single large and universal image of pathos; to invite us to feel, not only with Aeneas but through Aeneas with Evander. Aeneas, having been a surrogate father to Pallas, speaks as a father and for a father, a father as yet ignorant, like Andromache, in *Iliad* XXII, who hadn't yet heard the news and was preparing Hector's warm bath for his return from the battle, "while he," says the poet, "fat from warm baths was cut down by Pallas Athene at the hands of Achilles." The pathos of this famous piece of dramatic irony is transformed by Virgil into a different scene: the ignorance is the same, but an intensely Roman act of prayer and *pietas* replaces the domestic task; Aeneas puts words of awareness and tragic grief proleptically into Evander's mouth just as Homer invites his audience to feel with Andromache in those terrible last moments of ignorance before she learns the news. In *Aeneid* XI when Evander hears the news and goes out to meet the cortège, his own words are made by the poet to begin with an echo of Aeneas's

> non haec, o Palla, dederas promissa parenti

> This was not the promise you made your father, Pallas

cf. Aeneas:

> non haec Euandro de te promissa parenti
> discedens dederam . . .

> This was not the promise I gave Evander your father about you
> At our going . . .

Then the reader anticipates Evander's grief, carries his sense of the poem's unfolding meaning beyond Evander's immediate unawareness, to realise the full significance of this protracted episode. Moreover, Aeneas's speech gives the reader a further chance to link the meaning of the narrative across the break between books X and XI, for while it is true, as we saw, that X ends in violence and blood, the dying hero Mezentius, *contemptor diuum*, has already put into the poem an intensely moving version of a father's sense of agony at his son's death. He feels a kind of guilt in survival, at having not yet gone from the light—"but I am going;" and he turns to address his horse Rhaebus, in another marvellous transformation of Homer, in words which are peculiarly Virgilian in their pathos:

> Rhaebus, we have lived a long time, if anything
> Mortal can be said to live long . . .

Even the proud, now vanquished foe, second only to Turnus among the Latin chiefs, whose symbolic figure, a lopped trunk decked with arms, stands as the first gaunt image of book XI, even Mezentius has in the author's direction of the narrative close of book X made a contribution proleptically to the long perspectives of pathos through which the reader of book XI must now pass. Evander, too, expresses the by now familiar Virgilian sentiment of "contempt for the light." And he expresses a further sentiment which links his speech back to the opening image of XI:

> You too would now be standing, a huge trunk on the field,
> If your ages and strengths had been equally matched,
> Turnus.

The death of Mezentius, his lopped image, must stand for the time being for the death of Turnus, Pallas's slayer; yet Mezentius is not wholly disjunct from the pathos of Pallas's funeral and Evander's and Aeneas's grief; his own lament for his son is, as it were, held over from book x and allowed to permeate the reader's sense of the unfolding of the brief, tragically charged Virgilian Iliad. Pallas's death now makes Turnus's confrontation with Aeneas certain; the Iliadic structure, and the sentiment, require it; the reader expects no other end. Only the death of Camilla is to be encompassed; otherwise, the rest of the poem is dominated by Turnus.

Aeneas's last words of ritual despatch over Pallas are among the briefest and most eloquent of all his speeches.

> nos alias hinc ad lacrimas eadem horrida belli
> fata uocant: salue aeternum mihi, maxime Palla,
> aeternumque uale.

> We from this place to other tears by war's same dreadful doom
> Are called. For ever and for ever, noblest Pallas,
> Hail and farewell.

These formulaic words echo both Achilles' farewell to Patroclus in *Iliad* 23.19 and Catullus's words over his brother's tomb (101.10). Thus ends the first part of book xi. The majestic funeral tone, the repetition of *maestus*, continues to dominate the passage which follows, until Evander and his dead son face each other and the dreadful reality is brought home to the reader, who now reads through Evander. As the funeral cortège winds its way towards Evander and that final outburst of grief, *maestam incendunt clamoribus urbem*, other Iliadic themes are being interwoven into the narrative. The funeral of Pallas signals a twelve-day truce for the general burial of the dead. The Iliadic models are the truce after the fight between Ajax and Hector in book vii together with the truce granted at the very end of the *Iliad* by Achilles. Neither of these models corresponds exactly in structure to that in *Aeneid* xi. Aeneas plays the Achillean role of truce-granter, but he has not yet killed his Hector, and the moral argument is that of the implied author. Aeneas replies to the request of the Latin ambassadors in carefully chosen, emphatically rhetorical words which require the reader to consider not merely epic precedent but also moral justice.

> Do you ask me for peace for the dead?
> Indeed I should have wished to extend it also to the living.
> I only came here because fate said it was my place.
> I have no quarrel with your people. It was your king who
> Rejected my guest-friendship, preferring Turnus and war.

The point is taken up, speciously, by Drances, a Latin leader who hates Turnus and flatters Aeneas with rhetorical flourishes:

> O great in fame, greater in action,
> Hero of Troy, with what praise shall I lift you to the sky?
> Shall I start with your moral scruples or your military prowess?

Drances now goes on to say that he will try to persuade Latinus to resume his alliance with Aeneas and repudiate Turnus. In the debate which follows, Drances comes out as an opponent of war, but he does not thereby emerge as trustworthy or admirable, any more than Belial does when he counsels peace in the debate in Pandemonium. Drances' praise of Aeneas is a re-working of a familiar formula, almost a cliché of his character, equal in renown for *pietas* and for prowess, an epic vaunt used by Aeneas himself, for example, at 1.544; here the smooth flattery might suggest a sneer if Drances did not hate Turnus so much.

It is sometimes said that early in XI Virgil is at pains to reinstate Aeneas in the reader's eyes after showing him, in book X, subject like other men to *furor* in the extreme and catastrophic situation of battle. Williams goes so far as to speak of Aeneas being here in his normal frame of mind after the frenzy he showed in X, but the reader's memory is not so short that he can forget. It is the reader's task to make sense of inconsistencies in behaviour, if this is what they are, and of the gaps between books and episodes. If there are judgements to be made, the reader must make these too, and change them as he reads. One might read the poem, to give an extreme instance, in such a way as to place most emphasis on the battle scenes ("this is what Aeneas really enjoys, all the time he has been con-trolling himself, now all his *furor* is released"): the exemplary story of Hercules and Cacus in VIII, in which the saviour hero showed *furor* against his enemy, then becomes paradigmatic of the entire epic. One might reduce such passages as Aeneas's speech to Drances and the other Latin represen-tatives about the truce (11.108–19) to propagandist rhetoric on the part of the Augustan author, inserted to ensure that the founder of the *gens Iulia* has clean hands. One might read the hero's frequent protestations— "I would not have come here if fate had not sent me," etc.—as mere self-justification, no more convincing than his words to Dido ("It is fate, not my own will, that took me from you"); Dido's silence in the underworld may then express the reader's own lack of conviction about the validity of "this" Aeneas.

It is probably not surprising that some critics, faced with a work as complex as the *Aeneid*, should seek to simplify it. This is partly the result of the poem's having been too long a school book. The modern reader is too seldom able to manipulate the multiplicity of viewpoints it contains, the shifting of the narrative from narrator to hero to other characters, the continually changing perspectives, the variety of pace and tone, the way the episodes can stand alone and must yet relate to each other, the gaps between passages and between books, the elaborate time-structure which takes the reader backwards and forwards around a "now" which is both Virgil's Augustan present and the reader's own time, the "now" when he reads: the fact that so much of the poem is written in the historic present facilitates this synchronic structure. The episode being read will always seem to draw into itself all the perspectives of the whole epic. All this makes the *Aeneid* a very modern piece of fictional narrative, which can only be properly understood if the reader is aware of his own role and responsibility: to make sense of the poem from all its parts and from the interstices between them. Any judgement we pause to make, struck by the force of a particular scene, and the apparent contradictions which (in a naive reading) this judgement seems to set up, must be seen as partial, true perhaps, but for the time being. Any judgement which decides that Aeneas the apologist, the statesman, the man of *pietas* is "normal" and Aeneas the frenzied is abnormal has in a sense fallen victim to a propagandist or "ennobling" interpretation of the poem, in which the battle-scenes are distasteful reminders of the unpalatable realities of *imperium*. War is uncivilised, and a "civilised" poet cannot really "mean" what he writes about war: true, but the poet's discourse on the insanity of war (shared by his whole generation, sick of *discordia*), operates within a narrative in which war becomes a grand rhetorical topos. We must not so etiolate Virgil as to remove from him all zest for heroic narrative. I believe, too, that for Virgil the *Iliad* remained a great masterpiece; in attempting a recension of it in terms of his own nation's legendary past, he did not intend a repudiation. Whether its object is to sack a city or to found one, war remains insane; he that wills the end must will the means. And the greatness of the end, the positive act of founding a city as distinct from the negative act of destroying one, does not automatically glorify the means. For the modern (as distinct from the implied Augustan) reader, even the end, *urbs condita*, is now subject to the ironies of history: "Alaric has avenged Turnus."

After Evander's farewell to Pallas, the scene changes back to the battlefield and the sombre burial of the dead. A new day dawns at line 182, marking the end of one of the shortest narrative days in the poem (182 lines). The funeral cortège has taken, as it would have had to do, a whole day to wind its way back to Pallanteum. The day now dawning is ushered in with a characteristically Virgilian and deeply appropriate version of a familiar topos:

> Aurora interea miseris mortalibus almam
> extulerat lucem referens opera atque labores.

> And now dawn to miserable mortals her kindly
> Light had revealed, bringing back toil and labour.

Behind the panoply and rhetoric of the funeral and of the war council about to take place, the life of man is all the time as wretched as it was in *Iliad* xvii, when all heroic grandeur was reduced to zero in the meditative words of Zeus to an immortal horse. Here the epexegesis, *opera atque labores*, extends and reinforces the sense of mortal man's unending tasks. The new light shows up the desolate spectacle of the battlefield, the building of pyres, the ritual of the Trojan cremations, the lamentations until nightfall. Two days are allotted to the burial; after describing the Trojan rites the poet turns to the Latins, and depicts their mourning in slow spondaic measure:

> tunc undique uasti
> certatim crebris conlucent ignibus agri.

> And all around the devastated fields
> Are lit by fitful and conflicting fires.

The women of Latium in particular are already in profound reaction against the war:

> dirum exsecrantur bellum Turnique hymenaeos;
> ipsum armis ipsumque iubent decernere ferro.

> They curse the dreadful war and Turnus's marriage contract.
> Him they bid fight, let him decide the war with his sword.

They will recall now, with (and for) the reader, how they let Amata, fury-driven, lead them into a Bacchic frenzy, crying vengeance in the name of that same marriage contract. Soon now we shall see them file repentant into Athene's temple.

The long first section of *Aeneid* xi ends at last at line 224, having reached its climax in the passage showing the grief-stricken "city of most wealthy Latinus," *praediuitis urbe Latini,* the unusual adjective powerful with irony. The language is highly wrought, with elaborate alliterative patterns (the repeated "c" at lines 207–9, for instance), the repeated verb *maerentes, maerentem* (root of *maestus*) emphasising the extent of a shared and protracted grief, *longi luctus.* The entire passage is modelled on the lamentation for Hector and funeral truce in *Iliad* xxiv (with the earlier and structurally less significant truce in *Iliad* VII) yet, as so often in the last part of the *Aeneid,* Virgil moves further from the tone and spirit of the *Iliad.* In structure and thematic focus, his *Iliad* is modelled on Homer's, with a Patrocleia and with careful assimilations of the deaths of Sarpedon and Euphorbos. But each action in the *Aeneid* generates an immense charge of emotional discourse which slows the reader down in a way he is not slowed down in the *Iliad* even by the funeral of Patroclus or of Hector. The normal pace of reading the *Iliad* is fast; even the passages of extended pathos and sensibility do not decelerate this pace noticeably. The normal pace of the *Aeneid* is slow; the heavier hexameter, the longer descriptions, the proportion of feeling to action, all contribute to this. The interaction in the *Aeneid* between events and responses is an extreme and fascinating example of expressionism.

The miserable mortals on whom another day of toil and labour dawns become specifically the *miseri Latini . . . matres miseraeque nurus,* the miserable mothers, brides and sisters of dead warriors; Homer's formula "wretched mortals" is not now a piece of traditional gnomic wisdom, the proper response of man to his mortality, but a sense of the intolerable burden which living and action place on human sensibility. The pressure to end this war, after only a few days is already overwhelming, for it is more than a story-book war. It is for the implied reader a paradigm of historical civil war. In the *Iliad,* after nearly ten years, an attempt to end the war by single combat between Paris and Menelaus is aborted by divine intervention. The only heroes who "must" die in order to produce the narrative of the wrath of Achilles, are Patroclus and Hector. No other important heroes die in the poem. In the *Aeneid,* Aeneas must get rid of all his rivals as surely, and with as firm a basis in historical necessity, as Octavian had to.

The quarrel over Helen is not the "real" theme of the *Iliad.* Virgil not only wrote the wrath theme out of his Iliad. He assimilated the motif of the rape of Helen into his Patrocleia and his version of the Achilles Hector confrontation. In the *Iliad,* we see Helen not so much as a *casus belli* but as its chief and most self-aware victim. As an element in the narrative, she belongs with the effects not the causes of war. Though in no way blamed by the Trojans, she knows how the poet will project her into the future. She foresees the Iliad.

In the *Aeneid,* Turnus sees Aeneas in Iliadic terms as Paris to Menelaus, an effeminate oriental seducer, the dancing-master and chorus-boy of Hector's and Priam's taunts against the hero whom Aphrodite loved and rescued from Menelaus's spear. But the motif of the marriage-contract is a true *casus belli* in the *Aeneid* since whoever marries Lavinia succeeds to the throne of Latium. Helen's recovery carries no territorial guarantee to her rescuers, whose aim is plunder and destruction, not empire. The Trojan war is vendetta and the saving of "face." It is not through Paris or Menelaus or the bumbling Agamemnon, but through the story of Achilles, Patroclus and Hector, that Homer brings tragic intensity and meaning to the ten-year siege. For Virgil, the "cause" of his *Iliad*, the silent and all but invisible Lavinia, seems mere pretext. The Latin war must be fought so as paradigmatically to lay the foundations for that past on which Virgil's Rome is constructed. The ultimate cause of the war is to be found in history itself.

The inevitable finality of Troy's fall, from which the *Aeneid*, and the Roman foundation legend, takes its beginning, lies far beyond the end of Homer's *Iliad*, yet that end is included in the poem by Homer, in the famous prophetic words of Agamemnon and Hector:

> For I know well this thing in my heart and mind:
> the day will come when holy Ilium shall be destroyed
> and Priam and the people of Priam of the good ash spear.

For Virgil that inescapable "cause," now past, reverberates through the narrative as part of the effect of the Italian Iliad: the winning of the gods back to the city of *pietas* which they seemed once to have abandoned— back to the new Troy, Rome.

> uenit summa dies et ineluctabile tempus
> Dardaniae. fuimus Troes, fuit Ilium et ingens
> gloria Teucrorum; ferus omnia Iuppiter Argos
> transtulit.

> The last day and inevitable time has come
> To Ilium. We are past, Troy is past, and our mighty
> Glory. So cruelly Jupiter has taken all
> Over to the enemy.

At the end of the *Aeneid*, the last stage of the working out of destiny through the will of Jupiter does indeed involve the final disappearance of Troy; the Trojans, who throughout their wanderings and throughout the poem, have striven to keep alive their traditions and identity, must now surrender them: the grim words of Panthus, recalled by Aeneas to Dido, come true at last. With Turnus's death the ghosts of Hector and Priam are finally laid to rest, and the very name of Troy, sounding out like a musical figure for the last time at 12.828 (the last word spoken in the epic by Juno) vanishes for ever. If Jupiter changed sides and deserted Troy, Juno now changes sides herself to become a tutelary deity of the Roman people and one of the divine guardians of the Capitol. This is the magnitude of the finality which the Virgilian Iliad sets out to achieve. Not only Homer's Troy, but in a sense Homer's *Iliad* is subsumed in the *Aeneid*, to such an extent that for a long time it usurped its model as the supreme epic of heroic warfare. The rediscovery of the original *Iliad* in the Renaissance and in the centuries which followed, had the effect of putting the *Aeneid* back into the transforming intertextual relation to the *Iliad* which Virgil had always assumed and intended.

Chronology

B.C. 70   Publius Vergilius Maro born on October 5, near Mantua.

c.60–54   Virgil is educated in Cremona. After he finishes studies in 54, Virgil goes to Milan. During this time, the First Trium-virate (Caesar, Pompey and Crassus) is formed, and Caesar beings his Gallic wars.

53   Virgil moves to Rome, to begin legal training.

49   Having turned from his study of the law, Virgil is probably living and writing poetry in an Epicurean society in Cumae. Caesar crosses the Rubicon, thus initiating civil war against Pompey (Crassus has already been killed).

44   The Ides of March—Caesar assassinated on the steps of the Capitol, thus fomenting further civil war, this time between the Second Triumvirate (Octavian, Antony and Lepidus) and Brutus and Cassius, Caesar's killers.

42   Defeat of Brutus and Cassius at the Battle of Philippi.

41   Virgil begins work on *Ecolgues*. Further civil war—Antony against Octavian.

38   Virgil completes *Eclogues* and begins *Georgics*.

37   Virgil publishes *Eclogues*.

31   Having completed *Georgics*, Virgil begins to work on the *Aeneid*. Battle of Actium—Octavian defeats Antony and Cleopatra.

29   Virgil publishes *Georgics*.

27   Octavian now known under the title of Augustus.

23   Marcellus, nephew to Augustus, dies; reference to him in *Aeneid*, Book VI.

19   Virgil sails to Greece to revise *Aeneid*, which he thinks will take about three years. Augustus urges him to return to Italy, which he does, falling ill on the voyage. On his deathbed in Brindisi, Virgil insists that the manuscript of the *Aeneid* be burned after his death, as it is incomplete. He dies in Brindisi on September 21. Augustus overrules Virgil's request; and the *Aeneid* is published after only minimal revision by Virgil's executors.

Contributors

HAROLD BLOOM, Sterling Professor of the Humanities at Yale University, is the author of *The Anxiety of Influence, Poetry and Repression* and other volumes of literary criticism. His forthcoming study, *Freud: Transference and Authority*, attempts a full-scale reading of all of Freud's major writings. A MacArthur Prize Fellow, he is the general editor of *The Chelsea House Library of Literary Criticism*.

E. R. CURTIUS was the most eminent modern European critic of the entire tradition of Western literature from Homer through Goethe. His books include *European Literature and the Latin Middle Ages* and *Essays in European Literature*.

BRUNO SNELL is one of the major European scholars of classical literature. His book *The Discovery of the Mind* is a comprehensive study of the tradition that goes from Homer through Virgil.

ADAM PARRY was Professor of Classics at Yale. His tragic early death prevented a full harvest of his gifts, but his essays on Greek and Latin poetry, and his edition of the writings of his father, Milman Parry, are lasting contributions.

THOMAS GREENE is the Frederick Clifford Ford Professor of English and Comparative Literature at Yale University. His books include *The Light in Troy, The Descent from Heaven* and a study of Rabelais.

KENNETH QUINN is the author of *Virgil's "Aeneid": A Critical Description* and *Catullus, Poems: A Commentary*.

DOUGLAS J. STEWART is Professor of Classics at Brandeis University and the author of *The Disguised Guest: Rank, Role and Identity in the "Odyssey."*

J. WILLIAM HUNT teaches in the Department of Modern and Classical Languages at the University of Notre Dame. He is the author of *Forms of Glory: Structure and Sense in Virgil's "Aeneid."*

W. R. JOHNSON teaches in the Department of Classics at Cornell University, and is the author of *Darkness Visible: A Study of Vergil's "Aeneid."*

MICHAEL C. J. PUTNAM teaches at Brown University and is the author of *The Poetry of the "Aeneid."*

GORDON WILLIAMS is Thomas A. Thacher Professor of Latin at Yale University. His books include *Tradition and Originality in Roman Poetry*, *Change and Decline: Roman Literature in the Early Empire* and *Figures of Thought in Roman Poetry*.

K. W. GRANSDEN teaches at the University of Warwick and is the author of *Virgil's Iliad: An Essay on Epic Narrative*.

Bibliography

Arethusa 1, vol. 14 (1981). Special Virgil issue: "Virgil: 2000 Years."

Auden, W. H. "Secondary Epic." In *W. H. Auden: Collected Poems*. Edited by Edward Mendelson. London: Faber & Faber, 1976

Auerbach, Erich. *Mimesis: The Representation of Reality in Western Literature*. New York: Doubleday and Co., 1957.

Bernario, Herbert W. "The Tenth Book of the *Aeneid*." *Transactions and Proceedings of the American Philological Association*, vol. 98 (1967):23–36.

Boyle, A. J. "A Reading of Virgil's Eclogues." *Ramus* 2, vol. 4 (1975):187–203.

Broch, Hermann. *The Death of Virgil*. Translated by Jean Starr Untermeyer. New York: Pantheon Books, 1945.

Burke, Paul F., Jr. "The Role of Mezentius in the *Aeneid*." *The Classical Journal* 3, vol. 69 (1974):202–07.

Campbell, Joseph. *The Hero with a Thousand Faces*. New York: World Publishing Co., Meridian Books, 1956.

Camps, W. A. *An Introduction to Virgil's "Aeneid."* Oxford: Oxford University Press, 1969.

Clausen, Wendell. "An Interpretation of the *Aeneid*." *Harvard Studies in Classical Philology*, vol. 68 (1964):139–47.

Commager, Steele, ed. *Virgil: A Collection of Critical Essays*. Englewood Cliffs, N.J.: Prentice-Hall, 1966.

Cruttwell, R. W. *Virgil's Mind at Work*. Oxford: Basil Blackwell & Mott, 1946.

Culler, Jonathan. "Apostrophe." *Diacritics*, vol. 7 (1977):159–69.

Di Cesare, Mario A. *The Altar and the City: A Reading of Vergil's "Aeneid."* New York: Columbia University Press, 1974.

Drew, D. L. *The Allegory of the "Aeneid."* Oxford: Basil Blackwell & Mott, 1927.

Duckworth, G. E. *Structural Patterns and Proportions in Vergil's "Aeneid."* Ann Arbor: University of Michigan Press, 1962.

———. "The Significance of Nisus and Euryalus for *Aeneid* 9–12." *American Journal of Philology*, vol. 88 (1967):129–50.

Eliot, T. S. *On Poets and Poetry*. New York: Farrar, Straus & Co., 1957.

Gransden, K. W. *Virgil's Iliad: An Essay on Epic Narrative*. Cambridge: Cambridge University Press, 1984.

Graves, Robert. "The Virgil Cult." *Virginia Quarterly Review*, vol. 38 (1962):13ff.

Greene, Thomas M. *The Descent from Heaven: A Study in Epic Continuity*. New Haven: Yale University Press, 1963.

Highet, Gilbert. *Poets in a Landscape*. London: Hamish Hamilton, 1957.

————. *The Speeches in Vergil's "Aeneid."* Princeton: Princeton University Press, 1972.

Horsfall, Nicholas. "Numanus Remulus: Ethnography and Propaganda in *Aen.* ix. 598ff." *Latomus*, vol. 30 (1978):1108–16.

Hunt, J. William. *Forms of Glory: Structure and Sense in Virgil's "Aeneid."* Carbondale: Southern Illinois University Press, 1973.

Jackson Knight, W. F. *Roman Vergil.* London: Faber & Faber, 1944.

Johnson, W. R. *Darkness Visible: A Study of Vergil's "Aeneid."* Berkeley: University of California Press, 1976.

Johnston, P. A. *Virgil's Agricultural Golden Age.* Leiden: E. J. Brill, 1980.

Lennox, Peter G. "Virgil's Night-Episode Re-examined (*Aeneid* ix. 176–449)." *Hermes*, vol. 105 (1977):331–42.

Lewis, R. W. B. "Homer and Virgil: The Double Themes." *Furioso*, vol. 5 (1950):47ff.

Little, D. A. "The Death of Turnus and the Pessimism of the *Aeneid.*" *Australian Universities Modern Language Association Journal*, vol. 33 (1970):67–76.

Lloyd, Robert B. "*Aeneid* III: A New Approach." *American Journal of Philology*, vol. 78 (1957):133–51.

Luck, Georg. "Virgil and the Mystery Religions." *American Journal of Philology* 2, vol. 94 (1973):147–66.

Mack, Sara. *Patterns of Time in Virgil.* Hamden, Conn.: Archon Books, 1978.

Mackay, L. A. "Hero and Theme in the *Aeneid.*" *Transactions and Proceedings of the American Philological Association*, vol. 94 (1963):157–66.

Mench, F. "Film Sense in the *Aeneid.*" *Arion*, vol. 8 (1969):381–97.

Montagu, John R. C., ed. *Cicero and Virgil: Studies in Honour of Harold Hunt.* Amsterdam: Adolf M. Hakkert, 1972.

Moskalew, Walter. *Formular Language and Poetic Design in the "Aeneid."* *Mnemosyne*, suppl. vol. 73 (1982). Leiden: Brill.

Nelson, Lowry, Jr. "Baudelaire and Virgil." *Comparative Literature*, vol. 13 (1961):332ff.

Nisbet, Robert. *History of the Idea of Progress.* New York: Basic Books, 1980.

Otis, Brooks. *Virgil: A Study in Civilized Poetry.* Oxford: Clarendon Press, 1963.

————. "Virgilian Narrative in the Light of its Precursors and Successors." *Studies in Philology*, vol. 73 (1976):1–28

Pavlovskis, Zoja. "Man in a Poetic Landscape: Humanization of Nature in Virgil's *Eclogues.*" *Classical Philology* 3, vol. 66 (1971):151–68.

Poschl, Viktor. *The Art of Virgil: Image and Symbol in the "Aeneid."* Translated by Gerda Seligson. Ann Arbor: University of Michigan Press, 1962.

Putnam, Michael C. J. "*Aeneid* VII and the *Aeneid.*" *American Journal of Philology* 4, vol. 91 (1970):408–30.

————. *The Poetry of the "Aeneid."* Cambridge, Mass.: Harvard University Press, 1965.

Quinn, Kenneth. *Virgil's "Aeneid": A Critical Description.* Ann Arbor: University of Michigan Press, 1968.

Reed, Nicholas. "The Gates of Sleep in *Aeneid* 6." *Classical Quarterly*, vol. 23 (1973):311–15.

Ridley, M. R. *Studies in Three Literatures*. London: J. M. Dent & Sons, 1962.

Rose, H. J. *The Eclogues of Virgil*. Berkeley and Los Angeles: University of California Press, 1942.

Segal, C. P. "*Aeternum per saecula nomen:* The Golden Bough and the Tragedy of History." Part I, *Arion* 4 (1965):617–57; Part II, *Arion* 5 (1966):34–72.

Snell, Bruno. *The Discovery of the Mind*. Cambridge, Mass.: Harvard University Press, 1953.

Sparrow, John. *Half-Lines and Repetitions in Virgil*. Oxford: Clarendon Press, 1931.

Thornton, Agathe. *The Living Universe: Gods and Men in Virgil's "Aeneid."* Dunedin: University of Otago Press, 1976.

West, David. "Multiple correspondence Similes in the *Aeneid*." *Journal of Roman Studies* 59 (1969):40–49.

West, D., and Woodman, T., eds. *Creative Imitation and Latin Literature*. Cambridge: Cambridge University Press, 1980.

Willcock, M. M. "Battle Scenes in the *Aeneid*." *Proceedings of the Cambridge Philological Society*, n.s. 29 (1983):87–99.

Williams, Gordon. *Tradition and Originality in Roman Poetry*. Oxford: Clarendon Press, 1968.

———. *Change and Decline: Roman Literature in the Early Empire*. Berkeley: University of California Press, 1978.

———. *Technique and Ideas in the "Aeneid."* New Haven: Yale University Press, 1983.

Williams, R. D. "The Purpose of the *Aeneid*." *Antichthon* 1 (1967):29–41.

———. *Virgil: Greece and Rome*. Oxford: Clarendon Press, 1967.

Williams, R. D., and Pattie, T. S. *Virgil*. London: British Library of England. A State Mutual Book, 1982.

Wilson, C. H. "Jupiter and the Fates in the *Aeneid*." *Classical Quarterly* 29 (1979):361–71.

Wilson, J. R. "Action and Emotion in Aeneas." *Greece and Rome* 16 (1969):67–75.

Acknowledgments

"Virgil in European Literature" by E. R. Curtius from *Essays on European Literature* by E. R. Curtius, copyright © 1973 by Princeton University Press. Reprinted by permission.

"Arcadia: The Discovery of a Spiritual Landscape" by Bruno Snell from *The Discovery of the Mind: The Greek Origins of European Thought* by Bruno Snell, copyright © 1953 by the President and Fellows of Harvard College. Reprinted by permission.

"The Two Voices of Virgil's *Aeneid*" by Adam Parry from *Arion* 4, vol. 2 (Winter 1963), copyright © 1963 by *Arion*. Reprinted by permission.

"The Descent from Heaven: Virgil" by Thomas Greene from *The Descent from Heaven. A Study in Epic Continuity* by Thomas Greene, copyright © 1963 by Yale University. Reprinted by permission.

"Did Virgil Fail?" by Kenneth Quinn from *Cicero and Virgil: Studies in Honor of Harold Hunt* edited by John R. C. Montagu, copyright © 1972 by A. M. Hakkert, Amsterdam. Reprinted by permission.

"The Idea of Art in Virgil's *Georgics*" by Adam Parry from *Arethusa* 1, vol. 5 (1972), copyright © 1972 by *Arethusa*. Reprinted by permission.

"Aeneas the Politician" by Douglas J. Stewart from *The Antioch Review* 4, vol. 32, copyright © 1973 by *The Antioch Review*. Reprinted by permission.

"Labyrinthine Ways" by J. William Hunt from *Forms of Glory: Structure and Sense in Virgil's "Aeneid"* by J. William Hunt, copyright © 1973 by Southern Illinois University Press. Reprinted by permission.

"The Worlds Virgil Lived In" by W. R. Johnson from *Darkness Visible: A Study of Vergil's "Aeneid"* by W. R. Johnson, copyright © 1976 by The Regents of the University of California. Reprinted by permission.

"Aeneas and the Metamorphosis of Lausus" by Michael C. J. Putnam from *Arethusa* 1, vol. 14 (1981), copyright © 1981 by Department of Classics, State University of New York at Buffalo. Reprinted by permission.

Index